The Bofors Gun

The Bofors Gun

Terry Gander

Pen & Sword
MILITARY

First published in Great Britain by
PEN AND SWORD MILITARY
an imprint of
Pen and Sword Books Ltd
47 Church Street
Barnsley
South Yorkshire S70 2AS

Copyright © Terry Gander, 2013

ISBN 978 1 78346 202 5

The right of Terry Gander to be identified
as the author of this work has been asserted by him
in accordance with the Copyright, Designs and Patents Act 1988.

A CIP record for this book is available from the British Library.

Printed and bound in Malta by
Gutenberg Press Ltd

Typeset in Times by CHIC GRAPHICS

Pen & Sword Books Ltd incorporates the imprints of
Pen & Sword Books Ltd incorporates the imprints of Pen & Sword
Archaeology, Atlas, Aviation, Battleground, Discovery,
Family History, History, Maritime, Military, Naval, Politics,
Railways, Select, Social History, Transport, True Crime, and
Claymore Press, Frontline Books, Leo Cooper, Praetorian Press,
Remember When, Seaforth Publishing and Wharncliffe.

For a complete list of Pen and Sword titles please contact
Pen and Sword Books Limited
47 Church Street, Barnsley, South Yorkshire, S70 2AS, England
E-mail: enquiries@pen-and-sword.co.uk
Website: www.pen-and-sword.co.uk

Contents

Preface

The first edition of *The 40mm Bofors Gun* was published back in 1986. It was published to mark the fiftieth anniversary of the Model 1936 Bofors Gun which became one of the most famous and widely used artillery pieces of all time. As the contents of this book will show, the Bofors Gun shows no sign of fading from the defence scene, for in the second decade of the twenty-first century the Bofors Gun continues to perform many roles, some of which would have not have been thought possible by the AB Bofors designers of the early 1930s and which were not even contemplated back in 1986. The 40mm Bofors Gun is now allied to electronic and other technological marvels that were mere pipe dreams only a few years ago.

The 40mm Bofors Gun entered the international defence market during an era when its primary quarry, the military aircraft, was still a slow and fragile machine that could be terminally damaged by a single hit from a 40mm projectile. Despite all the recent increases in target speed and other performance parameters, the Bofors Gun can still inflict a one-hit kill on almost any aircraft, helicopter or guided missile it might engage, but these days the Bofors Gun is almost always deployed as part of a weapon system. Within that system the various target sensors, numerous black boxes and even the ammunition are now every bit as important as the gun, to the extent that the basic gun is reduced to being just a component. However, being the weapon delivery part of the system it continues to maintain its importance. What is really remarkable is that under all the black boxes and other adjuncts of any modern weapon system, the fundamentals of today's Bofors Guns remain virtually unchanged from the very first examples that came off the Karlskoga production line.

New roles have been found for the basic gun. In recent years it has found a new lease of life as the main weapon for a series of armoured vehicles. Other guns continue to find viable roles as air defence weapons for naval and land platforms and the basic gun's versatility has even found air-to-ground applications, completely reversing its original function as a ground-to-air weapon. In all its forms the 40mm Bofors Gun continues to be a sound, reliable, sturdy and lethal piece of military hardware that has given good service to gunners all over the world. The Bofors Gun has become a familiar piece of kit to numerous generations of military personnel and has become so familiar that the 40mm Bofors Gun is known to all and sundry simply as the Bofors Gun, despite the design being but one of very many artillery products that have carried the AB Bofors label. There has even been a play, later expanded into a motion picture, bearing the title of 'The Bofors Gun'.

There continues to be something remarkable about a gun that entered service so long ago and yet continues to extend its service life into the foreseeable future. Considering the importance of the Bofors Gun to the artillery world at large, the 1986 edition of this book was something of a lone voice regarding the remarkable history of the Bofors Gun yet since then much more has come to light regarding the many different owners and forms of the gun. That first edition was restricted in size and scope by various considerations, not the least of them being page space, so much that might have been included then had to be omitted. This latest production is not a mere rehash of the earlier editions' contents but is a complete re-write that enables us to expand an extraordinary story still further and re-emphasise the achievements of those AB Bofors designers that gave rise to one of the most significant artillery products of the twentieth (and twenty-first) century.

Acknowledgements

The author of this book is more than aware that this edition is the work of numerous individuals. Numerous inputs have been made by many people, not the least of them being the many members of the AB Bofors organisation (now BAE Systems Bofors AB) who gave freely of their knowledge and experience accumulated over many years. Sadly, their numbers are now dwindling but their considerable assistance and support must be marked by my continued appreciation of all their past efforts

Special thanks for much of the content of this book, both pictorial and written, are due to Svein Wiiger Olsen. His input to this work has been prodigious and freely given, as has long distance access to his extensive library. Thanks are also due to Chris Foss, the late Peter Chamberlain and Michel van Best for their considerable assistance. Many others will recognise their contributions.

Terry Gander
Alderney. July 2013

Chapter 1

Beginnings

The name Bofors originally related to a small, unremarkable community located on what was known as the Boo estate not far from the then small mining town of Karlskoga, itself located in the province of Värmland to the west of the Swedish capital, Stockholm. Bofors was of little concern to anyone other than the inhabitants and their close neighbours until 1646. During November of that year a local artisan, Paul Hossman, was granted a royal charter to construct a forge and foundry in Bofors. From these modest beginnings grew the mighty industrial monolith of AB Bofors, a concern that, although the name has changed, still looms large on the international defence industry scene, although it no longer concentrates its activities on artillery products.

Little of note outside the immediate locality happened at Bofors until the nineteenth century. Yet by the middle of that century the concern had gradually expanded until it was the largest producer of steel roll bar stock in Sweden. By gradually taking other Swedish steel makers (and other metallurgical concerns) under its wing, in 1873 the position was reached when the business became a joint stock company with the title of *Aktiebolaget Bofors-Gullspång*, generally known as AB Bofors. Since then the corporate name has undergone several changes, at one time assuming the banner of Swedish Ordnance, but the name Bofors was considered so valuable as an identification and marketing device that it still survives in the current name (at the time of writing) of BAE Systems Bofors AB.

Following their 1878 acquisition of the French Martin cast steel process, during 1883 AB Bofors made the momentous decision to enter the armaments business with the manufacture of ten coast defence guns for the Swedish Admiralty. Those guns, the *8cm fästningskanon M/1883* (actual calibre 84mm), were a Krupp design, and were the first of many to bear the AB Bofors trademark (a blue capital B pierced left to right by an arrow) although AB Bofors made only the barrels and breech mechanisms. Their first export order arrived from Switzerland in 1888, this time for twenty-eight 12cm guns. By the time of the 1914–1918 War the company had expanded in size and expertise to the point where the name Bofors could be uttered in the same breath as such European defence giants as Krupp, Vickers, Škoda and Schneider. Much of this expansion was due to the 1894 acquisition of AB Bofors by Doctor Alfred Nobel, the well-known originator of various explosives and the instigator of the Peace Prizes that are awarded annually to this day. Although Nobel died in 1896 his dynamism and forward planning meant that the company expanded into the development and manufacture of explosives and propellants and, by about 1900, into the highly specialised art of designing and manufacturing artillery fuzes.

The company underwent another period of expansion during the Great War years when, despite the Swedish nation's strict policy of neutrality, it was able to sell its products to a wide and voracious export market. The years after 1918 were marked by another corporate change when the German Krupp AG steel and armaments concern arranged an association with AB Bofors that further extended the numerous licence manufacturing arrangements between the two concerns that dated back to the *8cm fästningskanon M/1883*.

This new and closer association, brought about by the acquisition of a significant proportion of AB Bofors shares (some references mention as much as 33 per cent), had several influences upon the subsequent histories of both AB Bofors and Krupp AG. One of the immediate measures introduced soon after the Bofors/Krupp arrangement was that a contingent of Krupp technicians and designers moved from Essen to Sweden to utilise AB Bofors facilities and work closely with Bofors personnel on state-of-the-art artillery projects.

This was important to Krupp for the terms of the 1919 Treaty of Versailles specifically excluded Krupp AG from indulging in artillery (and other weapons) development and from the manufacture of heavy artillery, fields in which they had formerly been world leaders. During the early 1920s the Treaty terms were strictly enforced and monitored so the move to Sweden and away from the scrutiny of Treaty observers enabled the Germans to continue their former activities to ensure they could be ready for whatever the future might bring

The Krupp/Bofors association extended to an exchange of existing patents and was fruitful for both sides with AB Bofors gaining access to Krupp designs, expertise and know-how, especially regarding the latest manufacturing and production techniques. On the other side was the continuing ability of the Krupp design bureaux personnel to remain abreast of the latest technological and design developments without attracting unwanted attention. Numerous joint projects, many of them confined to paper studies, were undertaken, one of the most important being the design and development of a 75mm anti-aircraft gun, also produced in 80mm and 76.2mm calibre, the latter for Finland. The intention was to produce a heavy anti-aircraft gun for both the Swedish Army and for potential export sales, with the prospect of its adoption by the future German armed forces. In time the 75mm version was adopted by the Swedish Army as the *7.5cm luftvärnskanon m/36* (static) and *7.5cm luftvärnskanon m/37* (on a mobile field carriage). However, the Germans wanted something heavier so from the 75/80mm design evolved the famous 88mm FlaK series used to such effect on all Fronts between 1939 and 1945 – but that is another story.

Such results gave rise to the suggestion that the 40mm Bofors Gun was developed from Krupp expertise and was greatly influenced by Krupp experience with various automatic cannon designs introduced during the Great War years (none of which entered service under the Krupp AG banner). While a high degree of technical cross-fertilisation no doubt took place at purely personal levels between Swedish and German personnel, it was a corporate policy that some AB Bofors projects were kept concealed from their Krupp associates, presumably primarily for commercial reasons or (perhaps) at the behest of the Swedish Government.

Among these projects was the 40mm automatic gun project, a strictly guarded Swedish programme. Another factor that mitigated against any significant Krupp influence regarding the 40mm gun was that during 1931 the association between Krupp AG and AB Bofors was terminated by the introduction of a law passed by the Swedish parliament that severely restricted the degree to which foreign concerns could invest in Swedish industry. The Krupp technicians and designers therefore returned to Essen at a time when the 40mm Bofors Gun was barely past the preliminary drawings stage and with much of the highly involved development work and transition to production standards still outstanding. Perhaps the best indication of the lack of German influence on the 40mm Bofors Gun was that while the German 3.7cm FlaK series of air defence guns bore a passing visual resemblance to the ultimate appearance of the Bofors Gun, such impressions were highly misleading. The German 3.7cm FlaK series utilised entirely different operating and loading mechanisms, owing virtually nothing to their AB Bofors counterparts. In addition, the guns in the German 3.7cm FlaK series were not Krupp products but were designed and manufactured by Rheinmetall-Borsig AG.

Although, as mentioned above, some Krupp ideas were no doubt bandied about during the early development days the 40mm Bofors Gun was very much a Swedish product. Yet the Krupp influence myth persists. Exactly how the 40mm Bofors Gun came about follows.

Early Days

During the early 1920s the minds of many naval staff planners were becoming increasingly focussed on the defence of warships against aircraft. The Great War years had witnessed the first attempts to employ aircraft to attack naval vessels with bombs and torpedoes while by the early 1920s the first tentative experiments with what were to become dive bomber tactics had begun. Measures had to be introduced to deter such attacks but the exact means were still undetermined.

Two main streams of thought emerged. One was the emergence of the heavy calibre anti-aircraft gun, even though such guns were large, heavy, slow-firing and expensive. Yet such guns could ensure that one hit would neutralise any airborne target at whatever altitude they might be flying, other than at the lower altitude band below about 3,000m which, for fire control and other reasons, was considered their lowest effective range. Low-flying aircraft were deemed suitable for engagement by rifle-calibre machine guns but the maximum ceiling potential of such weapons was at the extreme about 750m. That left a considerable altitude gap between the target engagement potential of the machine gun and that for the heavy anti-aircraft gun.

The Royal Swedish Navy were well to the fore in exploring the means to fill this altitude gap and initially investigated the potential of 20mm cannon, then still in their infancy but with some combat experience gleaned from before the end of 1918. At one stage AB Bofors were requested to produce a 20mm cannon but before any hardware emerged it was realised that the high explosive payload of any 20mm projectile was insufficient to ensure that one hit on an aircraft meant one kill. The immediate response was to double the calibre specification to 40mm, a measure that would result in the required destructive performance without enlarging the resultant gun and mounting beyond the realms of practicality.

Swedish sailors had already acquired some experience of the 40mm calibre for in 1922 the Royal Swedish Navy had adopted the Vickers 2-pounder 'Pom-Pom' as their *40mm automatkanon* (*akan*) *M/22*. At around the same time AB Bofors obtained a licence to manufacture the gun and its ammunition. The Vickers guns turned out to be large, heavy and prone to jamming in the choppy sea conditions that could arise in the Baltic, the Swedish Navy's main operational theatre. In addition the fabric ammunition feed belts soaked up spray in rough weather and broke or caused further jams. Overall, the gun performance was rated as poor and the 40 x 158mm ammunition proved to be underpowered. AB Bofors were asked to investigate the problems but soon came to the conclusion that as the gun was a scaled-up Maxim dating from the early days of machine-gun development there was little that could be achieved to enhance their overall performance. AB Bofors therefore never did manufacture any Vickers guns although they had started to manufacture 2-pounder ammunition and had managed to introduce a few improvements of their own to the design of the basic round, even if the muzzle velocity was still considered too low.

By the late 1920s the Swedish Navy Board had reached the point where they approached AB Bofors with the notion of their designing and developing a state-of-the-art 40mm gun for naval applications. The Navy considered that to ensure a reasonable degree of reliability a semi-automatic gun coupled with some form of loading mechanism would be preferable, rather than a fully automatic gun.

AB Bofors executives were not enthusiastic for commercial reasons. The size of any resultant Swedish Navy order was seen as likely to be small so the considerable development involved in producing a gun of the required type

The starting point, the Vickers 2-pounder Pom-Pom, known to the Royal Swedish Navy as the 40mm automatkanon M/22 *but which turned out to be unsatisfactory in Swedish service.*

would be, for them, uneconomic. At that stage they also foresaw little sales potential elsewhere. But the Royal Swedish Navy was persistent and eventually, on 25 November 1928, delivered a letter that offered funds to finance the development of a prototype 40mm gun. That letter altered the commercial climate somewhat and AB Bofors agreed to go ahead as requested. A contract between AB Bofors and the Royal Swedish Materiel Administration (*FMV*) was duly signed on 28 November 1929, the contract calling for a gun capable of firing 250 rounds in five minutes with the barrel at an elevation angle of +80°. A fee of 10,000 Swedish Kroner was to be paid for a test gun.

Test firing with what would now be described as a technology demonstrator began during 1929 using a *37mm Kanon M/98 B* naval gun re-bored and re-chambered to accept a new design of 40mm ammunition. The semi-automatic test gun employed a vertical sliding breech block coupled to a loading mechanism that resulted in a rate of fire of from 200 to 250 rounds in five minutes. It was soon discovered that the loading mechanism was to prove more problematic than the gun for early on it had been decided that to provide the muzzle velocity deemed necessary to ensure the guns would be effective against aircraft targets of the future (about 850m/s) would require a propellant case almost twice as long as the 40mm Vickers case. The Bofors Gun case length eventually emerged as 310.8mm, resulting in an overall round length of 447mm. The problems involved in mechanically handling such a lengthy round (the projectile was fixed to the case) enforced a compromise between making the mechanism light and handy enough to render the gun manoeuvrable while ensuring that the associated components were strong enough to endure the necessary accelerations and actions.

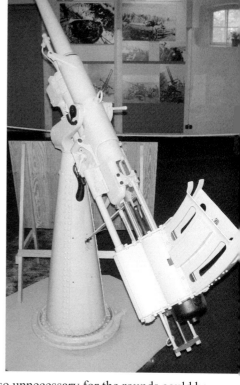

The technology test bed for the loading system of the 40mm L/60 gun now held in the Bofors Museum at Karlskoga.
(S. Wiiger Olsen)

As early as 11 July 1929 it was decided that the first test gun could be ready in fourteen months. By then, experiments and experience had demonstrated that the loading sequence could be reduced to a straightforward sequence of ramming and spent case ejection to the extent that the entire operation could be fully automatic rather than semi-automatic. The Swedish Navy Board was therefore informed that their rate of fire specifications could be considerably enhanced, as they rapidly were. Further tests in mid-1930 further showed that the conventional ramming action was also unnecessary for the rounds could be simply propelled ('flicked') into the breech, thereby taking less time between firings and thus increasing the cyclic rate of fire. By 17 October 1930 the first three rounds had been fired with an automatic loader mounted on the test bed gun.

By June 1930 the preliminary drawing stage for the new gun had been reached and design work proper could then get under way. The first gun was ready for firing trials that commenced with single-shot firings on 10 November 1931. A week later the first two-round sequence was fired, followed by a three-round burst the following day. On 25 November 1931 a gun with an automatic loader demonstrated that it could fire eight rounds in 7.58 seconds. These tentative beginnings demonstrated that the loading mechanism could work but further detail changes still had to be made to the mechanisms to produce expectations of a cyclic rate of fire of approximately 130rpm. This development work, typical for its time, was largely empirical. If something worked it was adopted. If it did not work it was altered until it did. Experiment followed experiment until the required results were obtained. The design team for the gun was led by Victor Hammar, ably assisted by Emanuel Jansson who was responsible for the automatic loading system, or autoloader, and a group of

The prototype of the 40mm L/60 Bofors Gun photographed in 1932 and showing the loading mechanism later to become very familiar to generations of gunners.

colleagues for whom technical challenges were there to be overcome.

The prototype gun was demonstrated to the Navy Board on 21 March 1932. The gun they saw bore only a slight visual resemblance to the guns that would follow for the barrel was shrouded by a tubular collar culminating in a slotted muzzle brake, the shroud concealing a recuperator spring reaching almost to the muzzle. It was at the breech end of the gun that the main Bofors Gun recognition feature was to be observed in the form of the loading mechanism housing and its ammunition feed guides, items that were to become very familiar to future generations of gunners. Unfamiliar to many of the Navy Board observers was the principle that depressing the firing pedal did not actually fire the gun. It merely initiated the loading sequence, after which all firing operations proceeded automatically, another Bofors Gun feature that survives to this day. Another unusual but welcome feature was the two-man laying system that involved two crew members operating manually cranked handles, one for elevation and the other for traverse, both capable of pointing the barrel at high acceleration rates to meet the challenge of any airborne target.

Navy Guns

The prototype gun required a further two years of detail development before it was considered ready for handing over to the Navy Board. Firing trials against towed air targets were conducted at a range near Karlsborg during the summer of 1933. By October 1933 the detail design work was all but complete following some 30,000 hours of drawing board activity to produce 1,800 working drawings, plus a further 1,600 drawings for the necessary machine tooling.

Yet the initial result of all this work was a 1934 Navy order for a gun intended to be mounted on submarines. This was the *40mm ubätsautomatkanon M/32*, a gun unlike anything else in the Bofors Gun saga for it was a short-barrelled (43-calibre) model designed to be stowed in a waterproof tubular

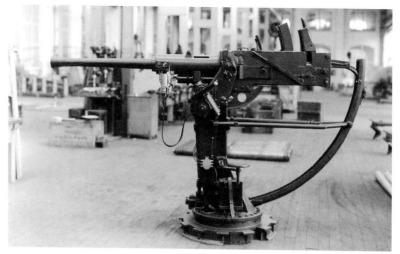

A Bofors workshop photograph of the 40mm ubätsautomatkanon M/32, a 43-calibre gun intended for mounting on submarines.

A 40mm ubätsautomatkanon M/32 folded up and ready to be stowed.

Five non-folding versions of the 40mm ubätsautomatkanon M/32 awaiting delivery (almost certainly to the Polish Navy).

compartment under the carrier submarine's conning tower or decking. To stow the gun the barrel was elevated to +90°, the fire-control handles were folded against the barrel and loading mechanism housings and the gun and its mounting were then lowered into its recess. The M/32 gun fired the same ammunition as the full length L/60 model but with a reduced propellant charge (220 grams as opposed to the usual 285 to 300 grams). This reduced charge combined with the shorter barrel resulted in a nominal muzzle velocity of 700m/s.

A twin-barrel version of the M/32 was produced, although with no apparent fold-away facility, and at least four were sold to the Polish Navy (see Chapter 6). A non-folding single-barrel mounting was also produced, apparently again for the Polish Navy. Stabilisation gear was available but was not installed on any of the guns delivered to the Royal Swedish Navy or Poland. The twin-barrel guns and mountings weighed 2,800kg.

The nine Swedish *Sjölejonet* class submarines each had two single-barrel L/43 guns, the last of them being decommissioned in 1964. Each of the three *Neptun* class submarines had a single L/43 gun located on the rear of the conning tower. The last of those vessels was decommissioned in 1966. (See also Chapter 6.)

DATA FOR 40MM M/32	
Length of barrel	approx. 1.72m
Number of grooves	16
Weight in action	approx. 900kg
Weight of barrel	110kg
Elevation	-10° to +90°
Traverse	360°
Height in firing position	1.46m
Rate of fire (cyclic)	120–140rpm
Rate of fire (practical)	80–90rpm
Muzzle velocity	700m/s
Max range, horizontal*	approx. 4,370m
Max range, vertical*	approx. 4,460m
Max possible horizontal range	approx. 9,980m
Weight of complete round	approx. 2kg
Weight of projectile	0.9–1kg
Weight of explosive filling	300g
Number of rounds in autoloader	8

* with projectile self-destruct function

Apart from that odd digression the fortunes of the Swedish Navy Bofors Guns proceeded at a slow pace. It was 1936 before the first L/60 guns were

The rival, the 25mm naval air defence gun ordered by the Royal Swedish Navy from AB Bofors as a possible alternative to the 40mm Bofors Gun. In the event both the 40mm and 25mm guns were ordered. (T. J. Gander)

Ready for production, a naval version of the 40mm L/60 Bofors Gun being demonstrated on the Karlskoga ranges.

delivered to the Royal Swedish Navy, of which more later (see Chapter 3), by which time the Swedish Navy had been pre-empted by Poland and The Netherlands, the former ordering two twin-barrel mountings during May 1934 and the latter ordering five twin-barrel naval mountings during 1935.

The Swedish Navy Board had to take some of the responsibility for the delay for they had introduced a change of priorities. Despite their initial insistence for a 40mm air defence gun, interest persisted in the need for a lighter-calibre weapon of from 20mm to 25mm. During 1931 firing tests were conducted with a number of imported weapons having calibres of from 13mm to 25mm but none completely met the exacting requirements of the Navy Board. During 1931 AB Bofors were again asked to see what they could do, the result being a 25mm automatic gun with an L/64 barrel, using the operating and loading principles of the 40mm gun, something that considerably accelerated development. As a result both the 25mm and 40mm guns were able to undergo live firing tests against airborne targets at Karlsborg during the summer of 1933.

At one stage it seemed that the Navy Board favoured the 25mm gun more than the 40mm gun but by 1935 they had resolved to acquire both, the 25mm gun eventually becoming the *25mm akan M/32* which served on as many as five different mountings, some twin-barrelled. The 40mm naval guns involved from that stage onwards are dealt with elsewhere (see Chapter 3) for by 1936 a land service model of what had hitherto been a naval programme had arrived on the scene.

Land Service Guns

While the Royal Swedish Navy might have initiated the development of the 40mm Bofors Gun, AB Bofors sales and marketing personnel gradually came to appreciate the commercial potential of their emerging product. The new gun arrived on the market at exactly the right time. All over Europe the aircraft was emerging as a significant and growing threat to armed forces on land and sea. Aircraft were becoming more powerful, faster, less vulnerable to damage and were provided with ever-increasing weapon lift capacities. While aircraft flying above about 3,000m could be readily tackled by existing or soon to enter service heavy anti-aircraft guns, those aircraft flying at lower altitudes were becoming an increasing menace to land forces and had to be countered somehow.

The air defence lower-altitude gap problem existed for land-based forces as well as for those at sea. For many nations the need to provide their ground forces with some form of defence against what were then futuristic threats such as dive bombers and strike aircraft took precedence over their need to defend their seaborne assets. As matters were to turn out the land-based defence needs were to exceed naval requirements to the extent that during the early Second World War years the numbers of land-based Bofors Guns manufactured far exceeded the numbers of their naval equivalents. By 1945 that situation had been reversed, with demands for naval guns exceeding those for land-based guns.

AB Bofors planners came to appreciate that their new 40mm gun had considerable potential as a means to plug the air defence altitude gap. The early 40mm Bofors Guns had a maximum vertical range of 5,000m and a muzzle velocity of about 850m/s. Increasing aircraft speeds could be readily countered by what was then a relatively high rate of automatic fire. After all, the new gun could put two projectiles into the sky every second. If just one of those projectiles, each weighing from 0.9kg to 1kg, could score a hit the result would be the destruction of even the most modern aircraft.

Of their own volition AB Bofors went ahead with the development of a land service carriage for their 40mm gun. Whereas the navy gun models were mounted on a variety of low pedestal or platform mountings, the solution for the land version emerged as a highly mobile cruciform mounting with a folding outrigger each side.

For its time the land service mounting was considered quite advanced for it had several very progressive features. Detailed descriptions of this carriage are provided in Chapter 2 but suffice to say that the entire carriage could be lowered from its travelling wheels by using the barrel clamp assembly and the draw bar as lowering and lifting levers. Once off the wheels and with the outrigger arms

Ready to travel, a very early example of the 40mm L/60 Bofors Gun off to the ranges for yet another demonstration.

extended the entire carriage could be rapidly levelled using jacks at the end of each cruciform arm. The entire preparation for firing routines could be completed by a trained crew in less than two minutes after arriving at a firing position. Fire control was greatly aided by optical reflex sights under the control of a manually-operated mechanical analogue computer that off-set the optical sights to allow for target range and speed. The gun remained basically the same as the original Navy model, apart from the fact that the barrel was air-cooled rather than water-cooled, and could be rapidly changed by the crew when necessary.

The first land service gun was ready for demonstration during 1934 and to differentiate it from what was to follow this model was given the general designation of Model 1934. It was to form the prototype for all the land service guns that were to follow and while many of the later variants would come to have their own, sometimes quite drastic, modifications for one reason or another, the Model 1934 could be detected in all of them.

Representatives of armed forces from all over Europe and elsewhere started to beat a path to the Karlskoga and Karlsborg ranges from 1934 onwards, while AB Bofors salesmen spread word of the new gun far and wide. They were to receive a somewhat overwhelming response.

In November 1934 a firing demonstration was put on at the Karlsborg range for representatives from Argentina, Belgium, Brazil, Hungary and Switzerland. From that demonstration came three orders and two licence manufacturing agreements. However, sales were only just beginning. By mid-1935 a gun sent to Belgium for demonstrations resulted in an order to equip army units based in the Belgian Congo (*La Force Publique*). The demonstration gun then moved on to Felixdorf and Neusiedlersee in Austria, resulting in the first export order for guns on field carriages. From Austria the demonstrator travelled to Hungary, making a 400km overnight road journey to a range at Haimatskör to catch the sales moment. In this the sales team were once again successful for a licence manufacturing agreement followed, as did orders from neighbouring Yugoslavia.

The journey of the demonstration gun was still not over for it travelled on to Warsaw in Poland over a period of two days. On arrival the gun fired 700 rounds and hit no less than nine targets, results that produced the largest order to that date, this time for sixty land service guns plus, eventually, the confirmation of a licence manufacturing agreement.

During 1936 negotiations with Switzerland were well under way but, for once, they were not destined to be successful. The Swiss wanted guns in a hurry but the growing AB Bofors order backlog meant that delivery delays were inevitable so the Swiss eventually ordered locally-manufactured Oerlikon guns. This disappointment was offset by the breakthrough of an order from France, a nation notoriously dependent on indigenous resources regarding weapon

A firing demonstration in progress, this time before a Swiss delegation.

supplies. Iran also displayed an interest in the Bofors Gun but delayed as they were already involved in procuring Bofors mountain guns. In the event Iran did not place an order.

Perhaps the furthest-flung demonstrations were held in Bangkok in Siam, now Thailand. That was during 1937, resulting in an order for naval guns for vessels then under construction in Italy. Further demonstrations were also held in the Dutch East Indies, some of them observed by Chinese authorities who expressed a keen desire to purchase as many guns as could be delivered within a short time scale. However, the Chinese approach came to very little for by the time they came forward the order backlog at Karlskoga was such that further orders, no matter how important and lucrative, could not be met without indeterminate and unacceptable delays for any customer. Looking back, it seems that AB Bofors could have sold as many guns as they could manufacture but their production facilities were limited and already fully occupied to a degree that their marketing executives could not have foreseen.

Bofors Order Book

The market response to the Bofors Gun is best summarised in a table that covers those guns scheduled to be manufactured by AB Bofors themselves. Further pre-1939 production was carried out (or planned) by licensees in Austria, Belgium, Hungary, Poland and the United Kingdom. Details of these licensees and their activities are provided in Chapters 5 and 7.

Year	Month	Nation	Land	Navy Single	Navy Twin	Static
1932	March	Sweden		1		
1933	July	Netherlands			5	
1934	May	Poland			2	
	October	Sweden		2		
	December	Poland			4	
1935	July	Austria	8			
	August	Belgium	8			
	December	Poland	60			
1936	January	Yugoslavia		8	6	
	February	Belgium	20			
	April	Norway		3		
	October	Estonia		2		
	November	Sweden				58
	December	Netherlands*	72			32
	December	Sweden				12
1937	May	UK	100			
	August	Argentina	60			
	September	Sweden**				8
	September	France	34			
	November	Finland	1			
1938	March	UK	50			
	March	Egypt	32			
	April	Netherlands	52			
	April	Norway	8			
	May	Latvia	48			
	July	Sweden	68			
	November	UK	80			
	December	UK	100			
	December	Finland	30	4	2	
	December	Greece			22	
1939		Sweden			16	53
		Belgium	106			
		Denmark				2
		UK	179			
		Netherlands			24	
		Netherlands*	21			
		Norway	25			
		Portugal	54			

* For Netherlands colonies (Dutch East Indies)
** Paid for by civilian funding to defend important industrial sites

Chapter 2

The Land Service Model 1934 L/60 Described

The heart of the 40mm L/60 Bofors Gun was the gun itself but what at first appeared to be just the gun was in fact two entirely different items. What looked like the gun body at the breech end was actually a breech casing supporting and containing the loading mechanism, or autoloader. The gun itself consisted of three main components: the barrel, the breech ring and the breech casing.

The vertical sliding breech block system was based on an action originally designed for a naval gun dating from the 1880s, namely the *57mm Snabbskjutande Kanone M/89 B* (*57mm Ssk M/89 B*), a Finspong product (Finspong was once the only ordnance manufacturer in Sweden). In its turn the Finspong gun was a derivative of a quick-firing Nordenfeldt anti-torpedo-boat gun.

The barrel on the land service Model 1934 was air-cooled while naval models were water-cooled, with the water-cooling arrangements contained within a thin metal jacket extending the full length of the barrel. Air cooling was considered adequate for land mountings as it was considered that most engagements would be of short duration so the vulnerable complexities of a water-cooled system would not be needed. If barrel over-heating or excessive wear conditions arose, each land service Model 34 was provided with two barrels so that four members of the gun crew could exchange a barrel within one to two minutes, probably between lulls in firing. Two gunners supported the barrel weight on a support bar while the other two operated a barrel wrench to unlock or lock the barrel from the breech ring. Barrel length was a nominal 56 calibres (actual length 56.25 calibres) but AB Bofors personnel and literature always referred to the gun as a 60-calibre gun and for most practical purposes the Model 1934 was called the 40mm L/60 or 40/60.

In its original form as manufactured by AB Bofors the barrel was made from forged chrome nickel steel and was of monobloc construction. Inside the barrel the rifling had 16 grooves with a non-uniform twist increasing from one complete turn in 45 calibres at the breech end to one turn in 30 calibres at the muzzle. At the muzzle the barrel culminated in a removable conical flash hider (also referred to as a flame guard), the muzzle brake employed on the prototype

A very early example, possibly the prototype, of the full production standard Model 1934 Bofors Gun, seen here in the ready to fire configuration.

having been dispensed with as unnecessary. A recuperator spring was positioned around the breech end of the barrel and was originally of Keystone (rectangular) cross-section, later changed to a circular cross-section. The weight of a barrel complete with its recuperator spring was 129.7kg. Recoil forces were accommodated using an oil-filled hydraulic buffer. Barrel life before the barrel had to be replaced due to excessive wear (rather than changing for cooling between periods of firing) was between 9,500 and 10,000 rounds.

Interrupted screw threads secured the barrel into the breech ring which also had grooves to accommodate the vertical block breech mechanism. It also contained the locating grooves and catches used when changing barrels.

The breech casing was a box of rectangular section enclosing the breech mechanism and part of the loading mechanism, while under the casing was the elevating gear arc; the casing also supported the trunnions. A cylindrical extension at the front of the casing surrounded the recuperator spring, apart from some slots left to assist barrel cooling. Several hinged covers were placed around the breech casing to provide access to the various internal mechanisms, while the fire selection and operating levers were located along the left-hand

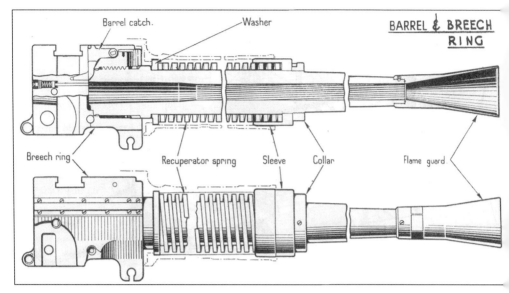

Although taken from a British Army service manual dated 1946, this cross-section drawing of the Bofors Gun barrel assembly is much the same as on a Model 1934 gun.

Another illustration from the service manual, this time of the breech assembly.

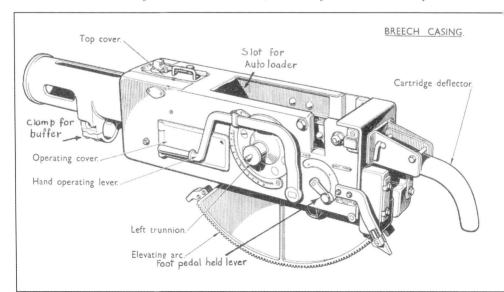

A Model 1934 40mm Bofors Gun ready to be towed but still minus its usual protective canvas covers.

side. The breech mechanism could be operated by hand but, once cocked (charged), was normally operated by the gun recoil. There were three fire selector positions: single shot (forward), automatic (centre) and safe (rear).

Operation

The opening and closing of the vertical sliding breech block was assisted by a clock-type spring that was not actuated until the rims at the rear of the propellant case being loaded actuated the extractors as it was propelled into the breech by the loading system at the point where the barrel moved forward following the ejection action.

The first round was always loaded into the breech manually under the control of a lever to the left of the breech casing. Recoil after firing forced back the mechanisms until the recoil forces were arrested by the hydraulic buffer, after which the barrel returned to its original position by the action of the recuperator spring around the barrel. Recoil length could vary from 195mm to 200mm with the barrel horizontal to as much as 225mm at the maximum elevation angle of +90°.

The loading mechanism, often referred to as the autoloader, was located over the breech casing although some components were inside it. On top of the casing were the guides that accepted the rounds being loaded in four-round chargers, although it was possible to load rounds one at a time by hand. On the Model 1934 the feed guides could hold one four-round charger, although another could be inserted as soon as firing commenced. Later autoloader guides could accommodate two chargers. When the autoloader was not in use or during travelling, the mechanisms and guides were protected against the elements by a thin steel cover.

Adding a second four-round charger to rounds already located in the autoloader.

In brief, the loading mechanism used a set of star wheels, indexing levers and stops to move each round downwards onto a loading tray with the empty chargers being removed automatically. Once on the loading tray a spring-driven rammer automatically propelled the round into the breech, tripping the extractors with the case rim to allow the breech block to rise and close with spring assistance to commence the firing sequence which ended when the firing pin contacted the primer cap in the base of the propellant case. On recoil the breech block opened downwards again with considerable force to enable the extractor arms to propel the spent case back along the loading tray and down an open semi-circular chute that guided the case under the gun for forward travel and ejection from under the gun barrel. If automatic fire was selected and the foot pedal was kept depressed the whole loading and firing process then continued.

It bears repetition that pressing the firing foot pedal did not actually fire the gun. Pressing the pedal initiated the loading cycle and once initiated the entire firing and loading operation was completely automatic. Details of every stage of the loading and firing operations will not be given here as they were complicated by the large number of levers, guides and pawls involved. All these arms and levers moved in their respective guides and grooves in an interdependent sequence of operations, some happening all at the same time and others sequentially. These operations depended on a large number of highly-skilled machining operations using high-quality materials during manufacture, coupled with careful maintenance and care once in service, but the Model 1934 mechanism was no more involved and demanding to maintain than numerous other contemporary weapons then deployed with many armed forces. What was to cause some future headaches as far as war economy production planners were concerned was that the painstaking workmanship standards employed on the production lines meant that many components were hand-finished to a high degree, to the extent that even slight variations from specifications that technicians thought could be introduced to simplify or hasten manufacture often led to functional or reliability problems. But in 1934 such problems lay in the future.

The maximum theoretical (cyclic) rate of fire for the Model 1934 was 120–140rpm, but in practical terms to allow for reloading, etc, this was reduced to about 80–90rpm. With the barrel horizontal and with reduced gravitational forces acting on the loading mechanisms the cyclic rate could be as high as 150rpm. Prolonged non-stop firing was possible if the loader could keep up with the gun but too much fully automatic fire without intervals could shorten the life of an air-cooled barrel.

A Model 1934 ready to fire in a wintry setting.

Carriage

On the Model 1934 field carriage the whole of the top carriage, including the gun and its associated components, rested on a bottom plate which also supported the platform frame assembly that carried most of the working area for the gunners who served the gun in action. In turn the bottom plate was carried on the field carriage. Construction utilised rivets throughout.

On the Model 1934 the carriage was transported on a twin cranked axle, four-wheeled arrangement from which the carriage was lowered before the gun went into action. It was possible to fire the gun from its wheels although with some reduction in stability when firing. All four wheels had independent suspension. The carriage itself was cross-shaped (cruciform) with one arm of the cross being formed from two riveted, box-section girders aligned fore and aft of the central turntable that carried the bottom plate and traversing rack for the top carriage. The two side arms of the cross were folding outriggers that folded inwards for transport and outwards when emplaced. At the extremes of the four sections of the carriage were levelling screw jacks that could be adjusted to place the carriage on a level when in action. Further carriage stability could be achieved by hammering pickets down through brackets located on one side of each of the carriage arms once they had been levelled.

The cruciform carriage was not just a device to keep the gun level and stable when firing. It also contained or carried several carriage components including the front and rear axle balancing gear units that were designed to assist in raising or lowering the carriage onto or from the front and rear axles. These units were composed of springs and their associated chain links located inside the fore and aft carriage legs. The entire carriage could be raised and lowered using the barrel clamp frame and draw bar as actuating levers. Once off the axles, spirit-level bubbles were provided at the end of each carriage leg for the convenience of the members of the crew operating the levelling screw jacks. This facility allowed the crew to level the gun as rapidly as possible.

The front axle was steerable, using an Ackermann steering system, and was operated via the draw bar that connected the front axle unit, and thus the entire carriage, to the towing vehicle. The rear axle assembly was not steerable but supported the barrel clamp frame that held the rearwards-facing barrel secure when the gun was on tow. Lockheed-type hydraulic brakes were provided on all four wheels.

The mounting with all its associated systems and components rested on a base ring with the traversing gear rack around its periphery. The main component of the mounting was the body, basically two side walls connected by a cross tube, with the cradle trunnions resting on the top. From this body assembly were slung or secured all the systems used to control the gun in action, including the platform frame assembly for the loader who fed the ammunition chargers into the autoloader.

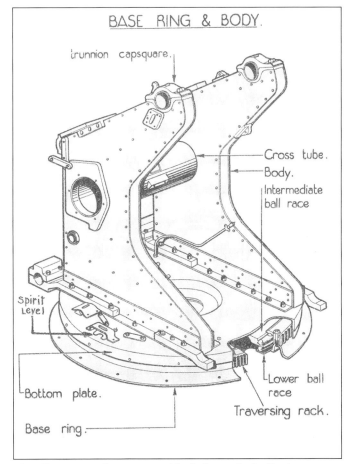

BASE RING & BODY.

trunnion capsquare.

Cross tube.

Body.

Intermediate
ball race

Spirit
Level

Bottom plate.

Lower ball
race

Traversing rack.

Base ring.

The all-important base ring and body from which all other
components were hung or supported.

If the gun was destined to be mounted in a static position the field carriage
was not necessary. With static installations the top carriage was so arranged that
it could be bolted onto a holdfast, usually some form of concrete or timber
anchor platform or low pedestal. Special transport carriage frames were
developed to carry the top carriage to its operational position.

On each side of the body assembly sat the two gun layers, with the layer
operating the traversing mechanism on the right of the gun and the elevating
mechanism layer on the left. The elevation layer also fired the gun by pressing
a foot pedal, although some customers insisted on the opposite or some other
form of pedal arrangement. Both layers operated cranked handles that were
turned using both hands in a motion that enabled smooth and rapid changes of

Close-up of the Bofors Course and Speed Sight, also known as the Bofors Corrector Sight.

The Bofors Course and Speed Sight showing the sight units.

traverse and elevation to be introduced. The hand cranks drove toothed gears against their respective arcs via oil-filled gearboxes. There was also provision for powered drives to be incorporated. Traverse over an unlimited number of 360° arcs was possible while the elevating limits were –5° to +90°.

Fire Control

On the Model 1934 the sights were optical reflex units mechanically coupled to a form of mechanical analogue computer known as the Bofors Course and Speed Sight or Bofors Corrector Sight. This computer, originally developed for the Bofors 25mm automatic gun and adapted for the 40mm Model 1934, used a control unit secured to the right-hand side of the mounting body so that the operator, usually the gun commander, entered target data such as estimated speed, range and angle of dive. Using a system of gears, rods and links the control unit then off-set the reflex sight so that all the layers had to do was keep the target in the centre of the sight graticule and the various aiming deflections were automatically introduced. Firing accuracy could be monitored by observing the tracer elements in the base of the projectiles in flight.

Each of the layers had their own sight unit mounted on a cross shaft and it was possible to illuminate the sight graticules. Illumination was also provided on the control unit for the various knobs and dials, power coming from a 6-volt battery. The system was able to introduce corrections for targets flying at up to 563km/h (350mph) but it was a complicated system making much use of screws and gears. It took time to get used to and required careful calibration to obtain optimum accuracy. Only time, careful training and experience enabled many users to become fully familiar with the system.

The number of gun crew members on the carriage when in action could be three or four. Apart from the two layers and the loader, there was a seat provided for the gun commander close to the Bofors Corrector Sight control unit. However, many gun commanders elected to either stand by the loader when in action or even stand off the gun altogether and locate themselves in a position where they could observe targets and transmit fire-control orders by voice, rendering the Corrector Sight somewhat redundant. The total crew for a Model 1934 was usually six or sometimes seven. Crew members not actually on the gun acted as ammunition handling and supply numbers.

The Model 1934 was not provided with a gun shield.

Ammunition

The 40mm ammunition for the Bofors Gun was designed by a team led by T. Wennerström. The first round introduced for use on the Model 1934 was HE-T, or High Explosive-Tracer. Over the years many more ammunition natures were introduced and some of them are still available from various sources. As a general rule the same forms of ammunition were fired from both land and naval service guns.

All AB Bofors 40mm ammunition for L/60 guns was of the fixed type, i.e. the projectile and propellant case were crimped together for handling and loading in one piece. Rounds were usually loaded in aluminium chargers holding four rounds, the chargers being automatically removed from the gun during the loading sequence.

On the HE-T round the hollow projectile casing was high-fragmentation steel and could be filled with various forms of high explosive. With early rounds a typical explosive payload weighed about 300 grams. A copper drive band on the projectile engaged with the rifling in the bore to impart stabilising rotation while a sensitive percussion fuze designed by AB Bofors was threaded into the nose of the projectile. The base of the projectile contained a tracer element which burned for between seven and ten seconds and on most HE-T projectiles the end of the tracer burn initiated a self-destruct relay train that detonated the explosive filling about 12 seconds after firing. Projectile weights could vary between 0.9kg and 1kg according to the type of filling and the manufacturer.

Propellant for the round was contained within a rimmed (strictly speaking semi-rimmed) brass case 310.8mm long. Propellant types varied considerably according to the manufacturer and to the passage of time. As time progressed improved propellants were developed so the initial muzzle velocity of about 850m/s increased to around 890m/s, creating a nominal muzzle energy of about 345,000 joules. Firing was via a percussion igniter in the centre of the base of the propellant case.

Also available for the Model 1934 was a high explosive (HE) round without a tracer element, while in peacetime the most common rounds encountered had inert training projectiles (TP) with or without a tracer element and devoid of any explosive payload. Following developments elsewhere (such as in Poland and the United Kingdom), during 1942 AB Bofors introduced an armour-piercing (AP) round with a solid hardened steel projectile. Inert rounds for drill purposes and ammunition handling training were also available, as were Blank rounds consisting of just the propellant case and contents, the mouth of the case being crimped closed. Other natures of 40mm L/60 ammunition were to follow as time progressed.

Also as time progressed many nations negotiated licences to manufacture 40mm L/60 ammunition – some nations still retain the ability to manufacture all manner of rounds for the L/60 gun. At the beginning of the twenty-first century the following nations were still marketing their ability to supply 40mm L/60 ammunition although some of them now manufacture only to special order or on an as-needed basis: Argentina, Belgium, Brazil, Egypt, Finland, France, Germany, Greece, Italy, South Korea, Pakistan, South Africa, Spain and some states of the former Yugoslavia.

DATA FOR LAND SERVICE 40MM MODEL 1934	
Length of barrel	2.25m
Length of rifling	1.9325m
Number of grooves	16
Weight in action	1,920kg
Weight of complete barrel	129.7kg
Elevation	-5° to +90°
Traverse	360°
Length travelling	6.248m
Length in firing position	5.18m
Width travelling	1.93m
Width in firing position	4.036m
Height travelling	2.1m
Height in firing position	1.689m
Height of axis of bore	1.15m
Turning diameter of muzzle	5.715m
Wheelbase	3.2m
Wheel track	1.5m
Ground clearance	451mm
Rate of fire (cyclic)	120–140rpm
Rate of fire (practical)	80–90rpm
Muzzle velocity	850m/s
Max range, horizontal*	approx. 4,950m
Max range, vertical*	approx. 4,930m
Max possible horizontal range	approx. 11,200m
Weight of complete round	approx. 2.1kg–2.15kg
Weight of projectile	0.9kg–1kg
Weight of explosive filling	285g–300g
Number of rounds in autoloader	>8

* with projectile self-destruct function

Chapter 3

The Swedish L/60 Guns

Despite all the apparent anxiety expressed by the Royal Swedish Navy to get AB Bofors to develop the 40mm L/60 gun it was 1934 before they placed any firm order (other than for the *M/32* submarine gun variant – see Chapter 1) and that for just two twin-barrel, water-cooled guns (see below). By 1936 several more significant orders had been placed by The Netherlands, Belgium and Poland and negotiations were well advanced with various other countries. Much of this early sales activity concerned land service guns for, although naval gun orders were forthcoming, the need for land service guns was considered by many as more urgent at that time.

The first Swedish Army land service model was the *40mm luftvärnautomatkanon m/36* (*40mm lvakan m/36*), a fixed-installation gun ordered in November 1936. It was virtually the same gun as the Model 1934 (see previous chapter) and was also ordered for the Royal Swedish Navy during 1936, on a static mounting (*40mm automatpjäs* (*apjäs*) *M/36*). Note that the method of denoting the model (*modell*) number differed between the Swedish Army and Navy. For the Army the word *modell* was written and abbreviated with a lower case *m*. The Navy employed a capital *M*.

Thereafter the orders for home employment guns gradually grew in number but by the end of 1938 the total for the Swedish armed forces was still only forty. Yet by the end of 1940 the number of Bofors Guns in service in Sweden was 154. Exactly how this expansion came about is rather involved but it was a direct result of Sweden's neutral stance during and even before the start of the Second World War.

Not long after the first orders started to arrive the production lines at Karlskoga were soon overwhelmed. Although AB Bofors had grown into a major European defence manufacturer by the end of the 1930s the production facilities at Karlskoga were still relatively modest compared to those of giants such as Krupp or Vickers, and the 40mm gun was not the only item being manufactured by them. AB Bofors therefore requested Poland and Hungary to manufacture 40mm land service Bofors Guns on their behalf. Both nations had obtained manufacturing licences (see Chapter 6) and had established their own production lines so were able (and willing) to comply with the Swedish request. Polish and Hungarian facilities manufactured the required guns and carriages

During 1939 Argentina ordered a batch of forty-two guns that were virtually identical to the Swedish Model 1936 but by 1940 the prospects of delivery were so remote that the batch was taken over for Swedish service as the 40mm lvakan m/36A, *an example of which is seen here.*

and delivered them to Sweden. Some final inspection and finishing touches would then be carried out at Karlskoga before deliveries to the intended recipient could be made. But even before what became known as the Second World War commenced on 1 September 1939 Sweden's strict neutrality laws had been imposed, in practice from January 1939 onwards. No further deliveries could then be made so stockpiles of completed guns were stranded in Sweden. Guns destined for Argentina, The Netherlands and the United Kingdom were all affected.

Those guns were therefore taken over by the Swedish armed forces for their own purposes. Although Sweden was neutral during the Second World War the Swedish armed forces were mobilised to ensure that national neutrality would not be violated in any way by any nation and for that purpose light air defence guns were in as much demand as many other forms of military materiel. So pressing was the need for 40mm guns that Sweden even purchased batches from Germany.

The first such purchase was made during 1939 and involved guns licence-manufactured in Austria by the *Österreichischen Staatsfabrik* in Vienna and the *Gebrüder Böhler* steelworks at Kapfenberg (see Chapter 6). When Germany

This example is one of the very first on the sub-contracted guns ordered from Hungary when the AB Bofors production lines became overwhelmed with orders. It was photographed soon after it had arrived for final checks and finishes at Karlskoga. As many of these Hungarian-produced guns could not be delivered to their intended end-users from 1939 onwards they were taken into Swedish service as the 40mm lvakan m/38.

took over Austria following the 1938 *Anschluss* the entire holdings of the Austrian armed forces were subsumed into the German armoury but a batch of fifty-two Bofors Guns did not quite fit into any particular slot in the German inventory. At the same time Germany was anxious to obtain all manner of products from Sweden, ranging from timber, nickel and iron ore to finished steel products (especially ball bearings) so the guns were offered to the Swedes as part payment.

The same happened in the aftermath of the 1939 Polish campaign when large numbers of Polish-manufactured Bofors Guns fell into German hands. Sixty guns were sold to Sweden in part exchange for various items important to the German war economy. Sweden already held stocks of Polish guns stranded in the country *en route* to the United Kingdom when the start of the war prevented their delivery. The same thing happened to another batch of United Kingdom guns manufactured in Hungary. They all ended up in Swedish service, a service which lasted until the war ended and for many years after.

By 1945 the number of 40mm Bofors Guns in service with the Swedish armed forces stood at 924.

Land Models

While the Swedish Army and the Coast Defence arm were no doubt glad enough to receive their Bofors Guns, it was almost inevitable that there were small differences between them due to the various sources from which they stemmed. In fact the Swedish armed forces employed no less than eight different variants of 40mm land service guns on both static and field mountings. Static mountings varied from simple timber- or concrete-lined pits to large and complicated towers with the guns perched on top to obtain the maximum possible field of fire.

The base model was the *40mm lvakan m/36*, the model manufactured by AB Bofors specifically for Swedish service. It remained in production at Karlskoga throughout the war years, as follows:

1938	8
1939	32
1940	60
1941	108
1942	198
1943	92
1944	178
1945	2

Troops of the Swedish Home Guard militia manning a Bofors Gun while still wearing their distinctive headgear. Known as Charles XII hats from their origins in the seventeenth century, these hats had been adopted by the militia in the early nineteenth century but were still being worn in the 1940s.

A 40mm Bofors Gun on a static Fast uppställning *mounting carried on a* transportvagn m/38 *carriage.* (T. J. Gander)

Swedish Army gunners emplacing a 40mm Bofors Gun.

The other models of Swedish gun were essentially similar to the twin-barrelled *40mm lvakan m/40 järnvägs dubbel* but each with some small differentiating variation. Some of the totals given below include guns issued to the Coast Artillery. As elsewhere, the models are best tabulated.

40mm lvakan m/36A. Originally a batch of forty-two guns was ordered by Argentina during 1939 but by 1940 the delivery prospects were so poor that the first twelve manufactured were taken over by Sweden. Another thirty were completed and issued for local service the following year. The main differences from other models were the sight units which were delivered from either Zeiss or AGA-Baltic. Number of guns in service in 1945 – forty-two.

40mm lvakan m/36H. The Netherlands had ordered 145 land service guns by 1939, ninety-three of them for the Dutch East Indies of which thirty-two were

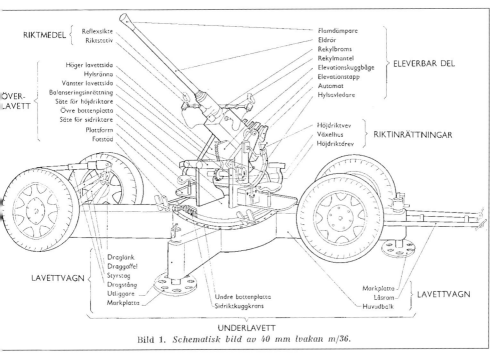

RIKTMEDEL { Reflexsikte
Riktstativ

ÖVER-
LAVETT {
Höger lavettsida
Hylsränna
Vänster lavettsida
Balanseringsinrättning
Säte för höjdriktare
Övre bottenplatta
Säte för sidriktare
Plattform
Fotstöd

Flamdämpare
Eldrör
Rekylbroms
Rekylmantel
Elevationskuggbåge
Elevationstapp
Automat
Hylsavledare
} ELEVERBAR DEL

Höjdriktvev
Växelhus
Höjdriktdrev
} RIKTINRÄTTNINGAR

LAVETTVAGN {
Draglänk
Draggaffel
Styrstag
Dragstång
Utliggare
Markplatta

Undre bottenplatta
Sidriktkuggkrans

Markplatta
Låsram
Huvudbalk
} LAVETTVAGN

UNDERLAVETT

Bild 1. *Schematisk bild av 40 mm lvakan m/36.*

A page from a Swedish Bofors Gun manual identifying the main parts of the gun in Swedish.

to be placed on static mountings. The war interrupted most of these deliveries so thirty-six were pressed into Swedish service in 1940, to be joined by another twenty-four the following year. These guns had the odd feature that the left-hand layer had a firing pedal while the right-hand layer had a foot pedal that disconnected the firing linkage. Zeiss reflex sight units were fitted. Number of guns in service in 1945 – sixty.

40mm lvakan m/36P. These guns came from the batch of sixty Polish-manufactured guns sold by Germany to Sweden. They entered service in 1940 and were fitted with Zeiss sight units. Number of guns in service in 1945 – sixty.

40mm lvakan m/36P(E). These guns were manufactured in Poland for eventual delivery to the United Kingdom but which remained in Sweden after the neutrality laws were imposed. Simple ring sights were involved. Some of these guns were 'loaned' to Finland in late 1939 after clearance had been given by the appropriate United Kingdom authorities.

40mm lvakan m/38. Manufactured in Hungary by MAVAG to try and clear part of the order backlog created by the sheer weight of orders taken from 1935 onwards. Number of guns in service in 1945 – fifty-two.

40mm lvakan m/39. Austria ordered a batch of eight guns in 1935 and also

One of the twin-barrelled Bofors Gun naval mountings first produced during 1935 and later taken over by the Swedish forces as the 40mm lvakan m/40 järnvägs dubbel, *usually with the manual stabilisation system still operational.*

A 40mm lvakan m/40 järnvägs dubbel *mounted on a railway flatcar to provide protection against air attack for important railway deliveries.*

Two 40mm lvakan m/40 järnvägs dubbel *Bofors Guns guarding a railway shipment.*

negotiated a manufacturing licence. In 1939 fifty-two of these Austrian guns were sold to Sweden by Germany and entered Swedish service the same year to become the *40mm lvakan m/39*. However, by the end of 1939 thirty of them had been 'loaned' to Finland to serve in the Winter War. Another twelve followed in 1942. These guns had reflex sight units provided by Goerz. Number of guns in service in 1945 – twenty.

40mm lvakan m/40 järnvägs dubbel (jvg dbl). The number of these equipments in Swedish service is uncertain although it may have been twelve. They were twin-barrel naval guns originally part of a Netherlands order for twenty-four such guns placed in 1939 but only a few could have been manufactured. The manual stabilisation facility was retained. At least three of these twin-barrel mountings were placed on railway flatcars that were employed by army units to defend rail deliveries of iron ore, guard important industrial areas and patrol sectors of the Swedish coastline. These guns served on after 1945 until at least the mid-1950s.

40mm lvakan m/36-43 i luftvärnskanonvagn. Twin-barrel mounting for installation on Lvkv 43 air defence vehicles. See Chapter 10.

Platforms
Several types of platform were used with land service guns, the base model used with the *40mm lvakan m/36A* being the *Fältlavett m/38*. It was essentially the same platform designed for the Model 1936 gun. By contrast, the *Fältlavett m/39* was not an AB Bofors product but a much simpler AB Landsverk design supposedly manufactured for the armed forces of what would now be termed the Third World; Ethiopia is frequently mentioned in connection with this platform. Whatever the provenance, the platform was taken into Swedish service.

Two further platforms were intended for static use. One could be termed as semi-mobile since it was a cruciform platform, the *Korslavett m/38*, which could be carried on the back of a truck or railway flatcar but was for transport only, not for firing. By contrast the *Fast uppställning* was a purely fixed mounting on either a mounting plate or some form of timber or concrete holdfast. The guns and upper mountings were carried to their intended positions as a single unit on a towed, twin-axle carrier frame known as a *transportvagn m/38*. On this frame were rails that carried a wheeled trolley onto which the gun and mounting could be lifted and secured for transport.

One further platform remains to be mentioned even though it did not arrive in Sweden until 1948. This was the *Fältlavett m/48E* obtained as war surplus from the United Kingdom and featuring the British-manufactured 40mm gun mounted on the Platform Mark 3, the model introduced to speed war production (see the following chapter).

A 40mm Bofors Gun on a static Fast uppställning *mounting carried on a* transportvagn m/38 *carriage.* (T. J. Gander)

Close-up of the mobile trolley carried on a transportvagn m/38. (T. J. Gander)

Navy Guns

Even without the 42-calibre *40mm ubätsautomatkanon M/32* mentioned in Chapter 1 the list of types of 40mm Bofors Gun operated by the Royal Swedish Navy and its close cousin, the Coast Artillery, was a long one. (The Coast Artillery eventually had 100 guns, sixty of them static and forty mobile, all delivered between 1955 and 1959.) Once again the best method of covering all known types is to present them in tabular form:

40mm apjäs M/36. These air-cooled guns were exactly the same as the Army's *40mm lvakan m/36* and were produced on both field carriages and for fixed installations.

40mm apjäs M/36-36A. This time these guns were exactly the same as the Army's Netherlands-sourced *40mm lvakan m/36H*, but on static mountings only.

40mm apjäs M/36 hs. An air-cooled naval mounting with manual stabilisation and the usual barrel equilibrator springs replaced by counterweights.

40mm fältpjäs M/36. Destined for the Coast Artillery this gun was exactly the same as the Army's *40mm lvakan m/36* and employed a fully-mobile field carriage.

40mm fältpjäs M/36-36B. These guns were the same as the Army's *40mm lvakan m/36A*, the guns originally destined for Argentina.

40mm fältpjäs M/36-39. Guns from the batch of former Austrian guns sold to Sweden by Germany and identical to the Army's *40mm lvakan m/39*.

40mm dblapjäs M/36. Twin air-cooled barrels on a converted *M/36* submarine mounting.

40mm dblapjäs M/36-40 hs. Twin-barrel, manually-stabilised naval mounting on which the manual crank handles could be disconnected when power drive was selected. A fire-inhibition foot pedal was provided.

40mm dblapjäs M/36-41 hs. These guns were the same as the *40mm lvakan m/40 jvg dbl* guns mounted on railway flatcars (see above) but for shipboard or submarine installation. Originally ordered by The Netherlands.

40mm dblapjäs M/36-41 A hs. Twin-barrel, manually-stabilised guns on *M/41 A* mounting.

40mm apjäs M/36-36 B. Single barrel on *M/36 B* naval mounting with folding platform.

40mm dblapjäs M/36 F-36 gs. Twin water-cooled barrels on *M/36* gyro-stabilised twin mounting with an integral 1.25m-base Hazemeyer rangefinder.

40mm dblapjäs M/36 F-36 A gs. Twin, water-cooled barrels on *M/36 A* gyro-stabilised twin mounting with an integral 2m-base Hazemeyer rangefinder.

40mm dblapjäs M/36 F-36 B gs. The only difference between this model and the previous one was that the layers had operating wheels in place of crank handles.

Swedish Coast Artillery personnel undergoing training post-war on a 40mm lvakan m/40 järnvägs dubbel.

40mm dblapjäs M/36 F-36 C gs. Twin-barrel, water-cooled *M/36 C* guns supposedly manufactured in Austria, although this seems most unlikely. They were placed on twin, gyro-stabilised mounting with an integral 2m-base Hazemeyer rangefinder.

Totals

AB Bofors 40mm L/60 production totals over the first ten years of manufacture, both for export and home use, were as follows, although it should be noted that the totals were for the number of guns that could be for installation on either single- or twin-barrel mountings and no differentiation is made between naval and land service guns:

Year	Mobile	Static
1933		1
1936	12	24
1937	48	16
1938	62	48
1939	118	92
1940	84	173
1941	18	240
1942	86	234
1943	18	105

Swedish Coast Artillery personnel manning a 40mm lvakan m/40 järnvägs dubbel.

By the time the Second World War started 40mm land service gun production by AB Bofors had reached 182 for the Swedish Army and a further 295 were exported. The pre-war figures for naval guns were eleven guns for Sweden and sixty-one exports.

During the war years 178 single-barrel and twenty-two twin-barrel guns were manufactured for the Swedish armed forces and some exports were able to continue. For instance, a 1939 order for fifty-four guns for Portugal, a neutral nation during the Second World War, was delivered in full during 1943, deliveries being made by rail through German-controlled territory and neutral Spain. (These guns became the *4cm M/940.*) Also delivered was a further order for twenty-two guns from Finland, so the war year exports total came to seventy-six. Naval guns produced for the Royal Swedish Navy during the war years amounted to no less than 320.

One of the export guns sent to Portugal during 1943 and seen here gracing an outdoor museum display just outside Lisbon, still sporting its Bofors Course and Speed Sight. (T. J. Gander)

In addition to all the above activities, during the years 1939–1945 AB Bofors alone manufactured approximately 4,000,000 rounds of 40mm ammunition.

When the Second World War ended in 1945 Sweden was once again able to rejoin the international defence market although, with the land service gun market in a state of over-supply, nearly all 40mm gun production by AB Bofors was centred on naval guns. From 1945 until 1954, when L/60 production ceased, AB Bofors manufactured thirty-eight guns for the Royal Swedish Navy and 460 guns for export.

Chapter 4

British and Commonwealth L/60 Guns

The British War Office first had their attention drawn to the 40mm Bofors Gun in 1933 when their defence attaché in Sweden began to send back reports regarding the new AB Bofors product. Those early reports aroused little interest for the General Staff planners then considered that any future low-level air defence requirements could be met by machine guns, and if anything heavier was needed there was always the Vickers 40mm (2-pounder) naval Pom-Pom. Three hundred Vickers 40mm Mark VIII guns on Mark II static land mountings were ordered for distribution around various locations throughout the United Kingdom, although that order was not placed until late 1936. Once in service the Pom-Pom proved to be unsatisfactory for land use so only sixty were delivered.

That choice left the field army with no viable defence against low-level aircraft attack other than machine guns, so to accelerate the selection of suitable guns for the British Army without the time delays attendant on developing a new design, a series of demonstrations for British observers was provided in Sweden by AB Bofors while various mobility and firing trials were conducted in the United Kingdom by military personnel, all with favourable reactions. The main result was that, following negotiations that started in December 1936, on 23 April 1937 an initial order was placed with AB Bofors for 100 40mm guns and 50,000 rounds of ammunition. During the following year a manufacturing licence was negotiated for British industry to manufacture guns and ammunition for both the United Kingdom and Commonwealth armed forces. Orders for another 409 guns were also placed. By that stage AB Bofors were overwhelmed by orders and there was no way their limited production facilities could immediately meet such a large requirement, no matter how important to the company, so part of the order was sub-contracted by AB Bofors to Poland where Bofors Guns were already being manufactured under licence. Such was the strain on all production lines that some of the first 100 were supplied by Hungary as well as Poland (see Chapter 6).

Deliveries of the first two batches purchased were prolonged beyond the required schedules but by the time the Second World War began in September

A very early (1938?) publicity shot purporting to demonstrate that the 40mm Bofors Gun was already in British Army service, but note that there are no sights installed.

1939 a cadre of Royal Artillery gunners had at least been granted a short period in which to master their new equipments, the very first deliveries apparently arriving from Poland (via Sweden) during late 1937. By late March 1938 the first fourteen guns were ready to participate in one of the emergency deployments around London in response to ominous events in Czechoslovakia, namely the imminent German takeover of the Sudetenland.

The start of United Kingdom production was slower than planned because existing artillery production facilities were already fully occupied. The intention was for the Bofors Guns to be manufactured in new plants scattered as 'Shadow Factories' all over the United Kingdom wherever suitable pools of labour could be utilised. Some of the new factories would make complete guns and carriages, others barrels only, while others manufactured just the carriage or other components.

What became one of the main centres of British Bofors Gun production was the factory complex that formed Nuffield Mechanisation at Coventry, part of the Nuffield Organisation which normally made motor cars. It was Nuffield personnel who went to the AB Bofors plant at Karlskoga to collect production drawings and almost as soon as they returned to Coventry moves were made to introduce mass production techniques to manufacture guns and their carriages.

Somewhere in Southern England during 1940/41 – a 40mm Bofors Gun in a British Army emergency emplacement.

An early British Army 40mm Bofors Gun originally delivered direct from AB Bofors but later updated by the addition of a shield and a Stiffkey Sight. (T. J. Gander)

An alternative view of a 40mm Bofors Gun *as originally delivered direct from AB Bofors but updated by the addition of a shield and a Stiffkey Sight.* (T. J. Gander)

However, not only did the new shadow factories take time to establish and equip but it also took time for the necessary training to be imparted to workers (many of them women) who in many cases had never operated any form of machine tool before. It was therefore late 1939 before the first 'British' Bofors Guns began to appear and by then demands for them were growing in leaps and bounds.

Production continued to lag well behind what were increasingly seen as over-optimistic expectations. The first 'British' Bofors Gun, as opposed to those ordered from Sweden, was not delivered to the British Army until 15 June 1939. By early 1940 the monthly production totals were only about thirty equipments a month. This was far too low to meet an initial requirement of 3,744 guns and carriages, to the extent that by the end of 1940 only 1,233 had been manufactured. It was 1942 before production totals began to approach the levels where they came anywhere near satisfying demands, demands that grew with the establishment of airfield defence units of the Royal Air Force Regiment from 1 February 1942 onwards, along with growing calls from the Royal Navy and Defensively Equipped Merchant Ships (DEMS), to mention but a few.

When the war began on 3 September 1939 Anti-Aircraft Command, responsible for the defence of the United Kingdom, had just eighty Bofors Guns ready for operational deployment. At the height of the Battle of Britain in September 1940 there were 474 guns in service, not all of them serviceable. By February 1941 that total had risen to 631 and by 1943 the total was 1,414, all these totals being well below forecast requirements.

An indication of the growth of British production totals during 1940 and 1941 can be seen from the following table:

1940	
May	81
June	119
July	128
August	124
September	116
October	138
November	104
December	119
1941	
January	155
February	144
March	213
April	176
May	190
June	250
July	225
August	233
September	270
October	301
November	260
December	295

A static British 40mm Bofors Gun on a purpose-built Flak tower.

Set against these totals were too many losses. During the Northern Norway campaign of early 1940 many of the seventy-two Bofors Guns sent there were left behind when the British withdrew. While some guns were evacuated on board Royal Navy warships an undetermined number fell into German hands. In June 1940 101 precious guns had to be left in France when the British Expeditionary Force (BEF) was evacuated, while more became German war trophies in Greece and Crete. During late 1941 and early 1942 yet more guns (about 100) and their crews were lost to the Japanese in Malaya and Singapore. The few Bofors Guns that could be spared to defend Hong Kong were also lost.

Production Changes

The growth in Bofors Gun production totals by the end of 1941 was greatly assisted by a major redesign of the carriage. The first Model 1936 guns delivered to the United Kingdom were all virtually identical to the Model 1934 (see Chapter 2) and were substantially the same as the guns delivered to the Swedish Army. British production planners soon came to appreciate that the Model 1936 was difficult and time-consuming to manufacture, as well as being demanding in raw materials, so they began to look for short cuts. They found them. An

An Anti-Aircraft Command 40mm Bofors Gun statically emplaced on a purpose-built Flak tower.

France 1940 and a BEF 40mm Bofors Gun awaits a target.

indication of how well they succeeded was each of the first British guns took 2,420 hours to complete. After redesign this was lowered to about 1,500 hours, a time saving of 38 per cent.

The basic mechanism of the gun was left virtually untouched apart from a few details. A simplified Type B autoloader mechanism appeared but, while it worked, it later had to be modified to Type M standard to improve reliability.

To reduce costs the steel employed for the barrel was changed. The original Mark 1 barrel used high-quality forged chrome nickel steel. For the Mark 2 barrel a less refined grade of nickel steel was substituted with no noticeable loss in barrel life, accuracy or any other gun-related criteria.

The main changes to speed production were introduced to the lower platform. The spirit levels at the end of each of the cruciform platform arms were among the first things to go and the side arms went as well. They were replaced by tubular steel legs that, instead of folding on hinges, were inserted into holes in the central frame. For travelling they were removed and stowed alongside the central carriage arms. Not only were the tubular legs simpler and less expensive to manufacture, they were also lighter. To simplify matters further, the balancing gear for the transport axles was removed so the main carriage fore and aft legs could be much reduced in cross-section and weight. The travelling axle assemblies were also much simplified. Out went the independent suspension, the steering axle became a trolley steer unit and the axles themselves, originally cranked, became simple tubes. In place of the earlier cranked lifting and lowering arrangements the axle units were simply removed from the main carriage legs before action. The end result became the Platform Mark 2 or 3, the Mark 3 being the more numerous. The Mark 2 retained the Swedish hydraulic brakes while the Mark 3 had mechanical over-run brakes.

The only disadvantage of these carriage modifications, apart from the fact that emplacing the gun for action or preparing it for travelling involved more labour on the part of the gun crews, was that the ground clearance when travelling was reduced. In practice this was no major disadvantage other than when traversing the roughest terrain. In addition the minimum turning circle was increased from 11.33m to 13.5m. What mattered more than these bearable drawbacks was that the supply of completed guns to where they were needed could be considerably accelerated.

Other detail changes were introduced to assist manufacture while yet more changes were enforced by the type of carriage involved, some of them devised to cater for novel forms of transport such as transport aircraft or gliders. These changes are outlined later in this chapter but perhaps the most drastic modification was to the Platform Mark 4 where all four carriage legs could be removed from the central carriage assembly to allow the gun to be stowed inside Hamilcar gliders as well as transport aircraft. The entire gun and carriage could also be dismantled into ten units for pack transport.

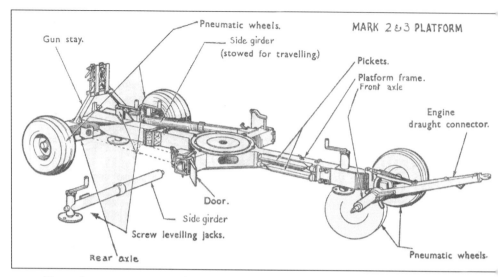

Pneumatic wheels.

Side girder
(stowed for travelling.)

MARK 2 & 3 PLATFORM

Gun stay.

Pickets.

Platform frame.
Front axle

Engine
draught connector.

Door.

Side girder

Screw levelling jacks.

Rear axle

Pneumatic wheels.

The main component parts of a Mark 2 or 3 carriage taken from a service manual dated 1946.

One notable addition to the British Bofors Guns was the installation of a gun shield during the latter war years. Not every gun acquired a shield but for those that did, usually (but not always) guns accompanying field formations, the shield was a flat, two-piece, spaced double-layer assembly.

Another add-on modification common by 1944 was a rack next to the autoloader holding four-round chargers ready to load when engagements became prolonged and hectic. It was widely known as the 'toast rack'.

Fire Control

Some of the first guns to arrive in the United Kingdom were manufactured in Poland so they were equipped with a variant of the Bofors Corrector Sight that was soon dubbed the Polish Course and Speed Sight. This sigh did not prove popular with British gunners for the usual reasons of being complex, difficult to master and expensive and demanding to manufacture and maintain. By the end of 1940 most of these Corrector Sights had been removed and replaced by open 'Forward Area Sights' that were much easier to install and look after. All aiming off for target speeds was made on the sights themselves. They consisted of a wheel pattern foresight and a crosswire rear sight. In 1943 this form of sight began to be replaced by a simple cartwheel foresight with three aim-off rings to cater for targets with speeds of 100mph, 200mph and 400mph (161km/h, 322km/h and 644km/h).

One of the reasons that the British first became interested in the Bofors Gun was that the gearboxes engaging with the elevation and traversing arcs had provision for the optional addition of power drives. Various defence research establishments in the United Kingdom had for some years been involved in the basic studies involved in removing human error from anti-aircraft gun-laying by combining power controls on a gun mounting with some form of central predictor, a procedure already well established on warships. The intention was that the predictor would be used to track an aircraft target, determine the range, and process the resultant data to calculate where the target would be after the time interval during which the delivered projectile travelled from the gun to the target. This involved barrel aim-offs for elevation (range) and traverse (target speed) and combining these with such niceties as angles of target approach, dive or departure. If the system worked properly the predictor, basically an electro-mechanical analogue computer, could calculate such aiming data and transmit the results directly to the gun to operate the power drives that pointed the gun barrel. This meant the gun crew had no part in laying the gun, thereby removing any possible human error on their part, always a major cause of inaccuracy, to a significant degree. However, most users of the remotely-controlled systems were able to introduce fine fire corrections by observing tracer paths or, in the case of the heavy anti-aircraft guns, projectile bursts under the control of their time fuzes.

By the late 1930s a system devised by Colonel A. V. Kerrison was introduced to heavy anti-aircraft (HAA) batteries and a similar system was proposed for Bofors Guns. For the latter application Colonel Kerrison developed the Predictor, LAA No 3, soon known as the Kerrison Predictor, in conjunction with the Admiralty Research Laboratory at Teddington. It was a heavy (227kg) and bulky electro-mechanical instrument that required three operators so it was too large to be placed on a gun mounting. It was therefore located close to a troop of guns with cables transmitting the predicted target data direct to the power drive units on the gun carriages. The No 3 Predictor could also be mounted on naval vessels.

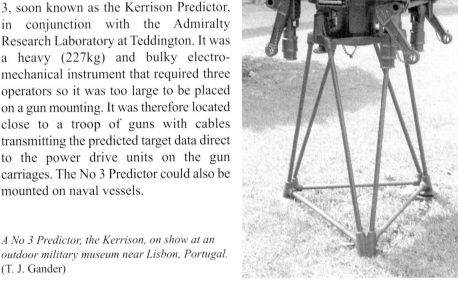

A No 3 Predictor, the Kerrison, on show at an outdoor military museum near Lisbon, Portugal.
(T. J. Gander)

The main trouble with the Kerrison Predictor was that in many ways its concept was ahead of the available technology of the period. Using the predictor to best effect took time and time was not always on the side of the gunners. When tested in action many targets proved to be too fleeting for accurate range and track estimations to be made to initiate the calculation processes and by the time corrections had been introduced the target was gone. Attempts to increase the maximum traversing speed of the predictor unit from 20°/s to 40°/s made little practical difference. This was particularly true with close-range or low-level targets where utilising open sights on the gun could often prove far more effective. Only well trained and experienced operators could get the best out of the No 3 Predictor and it remained a delicate and complicated instrument to maintain and operate. Few gunners mourned its passing when it came but its principles were to be resurrected when electronic-based predictor systems later came into being.

As time went on the Kerrison Predictor was used less and less until by late 1943 it, and its associated power drives, had been withdrawn altogether (except in a few special cases) and by then simple cartwheel sights were in use. 1943 also saw the introduction of the Stiffkey Sight, or Stiffkey Stick. The word Stiffkey was pronounced 'Stookey' by those in the know for it was named after the gunnery training range on the North Norfolk coast where its outline principles were developed as early as 1941. Officially known as the Mark 4 Correctional Sight the device was a return to the original Bofors Course and Speed Sight principles but this time in a purely mechanical form. An extra sight operator was located on the gun platform, actuating a ratchet bar and a train of levers and rods to mechanically offset the layers' cartwheel sights according to the target speed. All the layers then had to do was keep the target in the centre of their cartwheel sights. The sight could also be used against ground targets. The Mark 5 and Mark 5/1 Correctional Sights were improved and more robust versions of the original Mark 4. Stiffkey Sights were gradually retrofitted to all existing guns and remained in use for many years after 1945.

By 1944 radar had been added to low level air defence both for target acquisition and tracking, but initially only on an experimental basis. The Bofors Gun entered the electronic age as the guns came under the control of radars such as the British No 3 Mark 2 or American SCR 584 (No 3 Mark 5), with the target information obtained being passed through a Predictor No 10 (still basically an analogue computer complete with numerous electrical/mechanical interfaces and all the other inherent shortcomings) from where data was produced to power the gun controls and point the gun with the necessary degrees of aim-off, including at night or under poor visibility conditions. There were numerous other such radar/predictor/gun arrangements, some of which were successfully tested in action to counter the 'Diver' raids against South-East England by German V-1 cruise missiles during the summer and autumn of 1944. Although

Pick-up sight.   Toast rack in raised position   Check sight.

Training on a Bofors Gun with the various parts of the Stiffkey Sight helpfully annotated.

Taken at an August 1945 demonstration in Hyde Park, London, this Bofors Gun is under the control of a radar-enhanced director of an experimental type.

Fire control the hard way. By 1944 it was a standard practice for Bofors Gun crews to travel on the roof of their towing vehicle and with two gunners seated on the carriage and ready to bring the gun into immediate action from off its wheels, measures taken to guard against surprise air attack.

sometimes very successful, those early experiments with what was to become known as weapon system technology were, in the short term, destined to remain as experiments. It was to be the late 1950s before any more formal radar control of low level air defence was introduced to the British Army.

Ammunition

The most numerous rounds fired in action from wartime Bofors Guns were HE-T but in the rush to mass production the numbers of marks of round grew to be prodigious, especially during the early years. A British Army service manual dated 1941 listed no fewer than forty-one marks of HE and HE-T, nine marks of semi-armour-piercing (SAP), five marks of armour-piercing (AP), no less than twenty-four marks of practice (TP and TP-T), six marks of proof ammunition, four marks of barrel-cleaning ammunition, five marks of break-up ammunition for training and gun checking, and a solitary mark of paper shot ammunition, again for training and functional checking in confined areas. This profusion was further compounded when inert drill and handling rounds were added.

All these marks were far too many for logistical comfort so after 1941 a drastic rationalisation programme was implemented so that by 1945 the number of marks of HE and HE-T had been reduced to three. That same programme was also directed to making 40mm ammunition cheaper and easier to produce. One example of this was the introduction of low cost gilding metal for the driving bands in place of the more expensive and scarce copper. Rounds with gilding metal driving bands were denoted by the use of the letter T after the mark number, e.g. HE Mark 6T.

Following early supply difficulties, armour-piercing (AP) 40mm ammunition was introduced to the British Army during the late summer of 1940 after it had been decided to deploy the Bofors Gun in an anti-tank capacity in addition to the usual anti-aircraft role, a measure first implemented by the Poles during their September 1939 campaign. This was supposed to be an expedient measure to

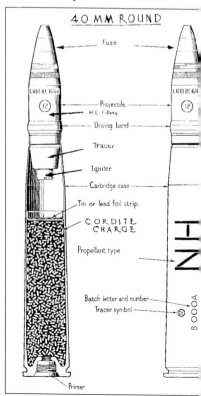

The main component parts and typical markings for a 40mm L/60 Bofors Gun rounds, taken from a 1946 British Army service manual.

Changing a Bofors Gun barrel under the august gaze of a group of visiting dignitaries – note the on-carriage clips of ready-use ammunition.

increase the number of potential anti-armour weapons should the United Kingdom be invaded. Although this never happened, AP ammunition remained available throughout the war years and after. A rough guide was that the AP projectile could penetrate 40mm of armour plate set at an angle of 60° at a distance of from 100 to 150m while the maximum effective range was a nominal 400 yards (365m). An immediate burn tracer element could be involved and was usually installed.

One ammunition-related innovation for the Bofors Gun was as a directional aid for other arms during night operations. First employed during the Second Battle of El Alamein in late 1942, this procedure involved firing HE-T or TP-T along fixed lines of traverse at a low angle of barrel elevation so that the tracer arcs outlined the direction and limits of an advance through cleared minefields or towards a required objective. Once established this practice became widespread until the war ended.

Right rear detail view of a 40mm L/60 Bofors Gun on Mark 2 or 3 carriage with Stiffkey Sight, gun shield, on-carriage ammunition clips (toast rack) to assist the loader, and with the autoloader cover in place.

Detail view of the equilibrators for a 40mm L/60 Bofors Gun.

Direct rear view of an L/60 Bofors Gun on a Mark 2 or 3 carriage with the side legs in the firing position but without the pickets emplaced as if for firing.

Left rear view of an L/60 Bofors Gun on a Mark 2 or 3 carriage – note that the left-hand cartwheel sight is not fitted for some reason.

Whatever its nature all British and Canadian-produced ammunition weighed 2.438kg or thereabouts for a complete round, and 0.9kg to 1kg for the projectile. A HE or HE-T round was 448.3mm long with the projectile painted a buff colour. When first rounds were issued (the Mark 1T) the early production nose-mounted, point-detonating (PD) fuze was based on an AB Bofors design known as the No 250. A simplified version to speed production became the No 251. The projectile's explosive payload was usually TNT or the more effective RDX/BWX (a mixture of RDX and Beeswax). AP and SAP (semi-armour-piercing) rounds were 446.5mm long with their projectiles painted black. The SAP projectile had a white tip to the nose and a red ring was added if the projectile contained a tracer element. AP shot had a white tip and an extra white ring; again a red ring was added if the projectile contained a tracer element.

British-made propellant cases usually contained about 248 grams of Cordite W from numerous manufacturers, although by 1945 nitrocellulose-based propellants that considerably enhanced barrel life had been introduced into service. British and Commonwealth Bofors Gun propellant cases were brass, despite attempts to develop steel or aluminium cases.

Rounds were issued packed in boxes or hampers. The two most common types of steel box were the C.216 and the C.219. Both had the same dimensions of 523mm x 450mm x 265mm but the C.216 contained twenty-four rounds in six chargers (weight 70.3kg) while the C.219 contained twenty-four rounds individually packed in paper tubes (weight 74.8kg). The C.297 was a wooden equivalent of the C.219 weighing 80.3kg while the C.280 was a wicker hamper holding twenty-four rounds in six chargers (weight 63kg).

Commonwealth

Bofors Guns were also manufactured in Canada and Australia for the British and Commonwealth armies. Canadian production began during the autumn of 1940 (the first Canadian barrel was finished during October 1940). One production centre was operated by the Dominion Bridge Company at Vancouver, British Columbia, while another was the Otis-Fensom Elevator Company at Hamilton, Ontario. On behalf of the Canadian Department of Munitions and Supply Otis-Fensom constructed a factory in Hamilton specifically to manufacture Bofors Guns. Chrysler Canada was a major supplier of components while other sub-contractors were spread across the country. Naval versions of Bofors Guns, including the Boffin (see below in this chapter), and self-propelled carriages (see Chapter 10) were also produced in Canada.

By October 1942 Canadian Bofors Gun production was running at a rate of around 200 guns a month but by then a lack of shipping allocations had reached

Emplaced and ready for action, a Bofors Gun on a Mark 2 or 3 carriage.

The Canadian Bantam mounting for airborne applications, seen here complete with optional shield.

A Boffin deployed in a land application for defending the two Royal Canadian Air Force air bases in what was then West Germany (see page 71).

the point where the Canadian Army Overseas was below its required establishment of Bofors Guns. As a result many Canadian Army formations stationed in the United Kingdom (and elsewhere) were provided with guns from British stocks, while a proportion of the Canadian-produced guns were either passed to the United States or issued to Allied Defensively Equipped Merchant Ships (DEMS) calling at Canadian ports. The naval Boffin is mentioned under Navy Models.

One important all-Canadian achievement was the so-called Bantam two-wheeled carriage. This was devised to make the Bofors Gun suitable for carrying inside transport aircraft such as the C-47 Dakota. The design used a three-legged girder carriage carried on a single axle towed by a Jeep. When on tow two of the girder legs were joined to form a tow bar while the third girder leg was telescoped into the central assembly. A gun shield was an optional accessory. The Bantam was not designed to be para-dropped.

Another Canadian Bofors Gun project involved two custom-built railway cars, each carrying two Bofors Guns (plus 400 rounds for each gun), as part of the armament of No 1 Armoured Train, Canada's only such train, assembled to defend a stretch of British Columbian coastline once frequented by Japanese fishing boats. The train patrolled a length of railway line between the important supply port of Prince Rupert and the inland town of Terrace from July 1942 until August 1943. It never fired a shot in anger.

Prior to the end of 1936 no artillery piece of any kind had ever been produced within Australia but with few opportunities to obtain modern equipment from anywhere else that situation changed. Using drawings obtained from the United Kingdom, Australian production commenced at the Government Ordnance Factory at Maribyrnong, Victoria, soon after the Australian Army placed an order for forty-three Bofors Guns in January 1941. In October 1941 that order was increased to 500 Mark 1* guns, an order that enforced a drastic revision of the production line and some sub-contracting. Eventually the order total stood at 1,200. Special machine tools were designed at Maribyrnong to save floor space and speed production. Sub-contractors engaged to meet the second order included the local Ford Motor Company, H.V. McKay, Massey Harris and the Paton Brake Company. Some components such as the autoloader and elevation and traverse drive units had to be imported from the United States. Australian Glass Manufacturers Pty Ltd of Sydney was about to commence autoloader production just as Australian Bofors Gun production ceased.

In July 1942 the production rate at Maribyrnong was one gun a month but by August 1943 this had increased to twenty-five a month. Orders were greatly reduced during 1943 for by then the dangers of war had moved away from the Australian mainland and guns became easily obtainable from elsewhere. For a while production ran at ten guns a month until 290 complete guns and 700 spare barrels had been manufactured. Australian Bofors Gun production then ceased.

Land Service Models

Between 1939 and 1945 British and Commonwealth Bofors Gun production centres between them managed to develop a surprising array of guns, mountings and other items, although some differentiated marks differed from others only in detail. The only way to make any sense for useful reference is to list all these items under separate headings. Thus the list covers the guns under the heading of ordnance, autoloaders, mountings and the platforms or carriages.

The Mark numbers are here given as straightforward numerals. Many war year references used roman numbers, e.g. Mark 4 was often written as Mark IV.

Naval mountings have their own summary list later in this Chapter.

Ordnance

The official designation for the Bofors Gun ordnance was Ordnance, Quick Firing 40mm Mark (whatever). Ordnance, Quick Firing was frequently abbreviated to OQF.

OQF 40mm Mark 1. The version delivered direct from AB Bofors equipped with the Type A autoloader. It was later declared obsolescent and modified to Mark 1* standard.

OQF 40mm Mark 1*. A Mark 1 capable of accommodating any type of autoloader. Also manufactured in Australia.

OQF C Mark 1. The Canadian-produced version of the Mark 1.

OQF C Mark 1*. The Canadian-produced version of the Mark 1*.

OQF 40mm Mark 1/2. Developed for use with the various two-wheeled single-axle airborne mountings, this was a conversion of the Mark 1* to accommodate a double-baffle muzzle brake in place of the usual conical flash hider.

OQF 40mm Mark 2. Originally a naval version, this designation was not used in order to avoid confusion with the American Carriage M2.

OQF 40mm Mark 3. The main production model of the war years developed to speed production. Could use only the B, C, M and M* types of autoloader.

OQF 40mm Mark 4. Naval version. See later in this chapter.

OQF 40mm Mark 6. For use on Crusader AA tanks. Used Type A* autoloader. Spent cases were ejected upwards.

OQF 40mm Marks 7 to 11. Naval versions. See later in this chapter.

OQF 40mm Mark 12. For use on remote power-controlled mountings. Basically a Mark 1 with provision for cut-out switches on the elevating arc.

OQF 40mm Mark 12/1. A C Mark 1 modified to Mark 12 standard.

Autoloaders

Type A. The original Swedish design capable of accommodating two four-round chargers. Used only on Mark 1 and Mark 1* guns. Empty chargers ejected to the left.

Type A*. A Type A with an adjustable peep-sight in the rear guide. Used only with Mark 6 guns on Crusader AA tanks.

Type B. A simplified design that could take three four-round chargers. Used only with Mark 1* and Mark 3 guns. Empty chargers ejected to the right.

Type C. A non-standard Type B manufactured by the Chambon Company. Used only with Mark 1* and Mark 3 guns.

Type D. Intended for naval applications. Project abandoned.

Type E. Intended for naval applications. Project abandoned.

Type F. Would have been used on naval Mark 8 left-hand guns. Project abandoned.

Type G. Would have been used on naval Mark 8 right-hand guns. Project abandoned.

Type M. A Type B modified to improve reliability. Used only with Mark 1* and Mark 3 guns.

Type M*. A Type C modified to Type M standards. Used only with Mark 1* and Mark 3 guns.

Mountings

It will be noted that some types of mounting had two designations, those given within brackets being the designations employed during the war years. The order for the change of nomenclature was not issued until late 1946.

The terms IS and HS will also be found with some marks of mounting. The original traversing rate in degrees (°) and minutes (') was 6°10' for every turn of the traversing crank handle. On some later mountings this was increased to an intermediate speed (IS) of 13°8' for every turn, while for high speed (HS) mountings the traversing rate was increased to 17°9'. On all mountings the barrel elevating rate was 4°1' for every turn of the elevating crank.

Mounting Mark 1. The original AB Bofors mounting with provision for data-receiving dials but not fitted with them.

Mounting Mark 1A. The Polish version of the AB Bofors mounting with no provision for data-receiving dials.

Mounting Mark 1B. Modified Mark 1 mountings that could be converted for power control if required. Only two were made.

Mounting Mark 2. Designation not used. The original intention was that it would have been a Mark 1 modified for power control but none were made.

Mounting Mark 3. A British design for remote power control.

Mounting C Mark 3. The Canadian version of the British Mark 3.

Mounting Mark 3/1 (Mark 3A). This was a Mark 3 on which the elevating and traversing handles could be disengaged when power control was selected.

Mounting Mark 3/2 (Mark 3B). This was a Mark 3/1 with revised firing arrangements.

Mounting Mark 3/3 (Mark 3HS). A Mark 3 with high speed (HS) hand traversing.

Mounting Mark 3/4 (Mark 3A/HS). A Mark 3/1 with high speed (HS) hand traversing.

Mounting Mark 3/5 (Mark 3B/HS). A Mark 3/2 with high speed (HS) hand traversing.

Mounting Mark 3/6 (Mark 3/IS). A version of the basic Mark 3 with intermediate speed (IS) hand traversing.

Mounting Mark 3/7 (Mark 3A/IS). A Mark 3/1 with intermediate speed (IS) hand traversing.

Mounting Mark 3/8 (Mark 3B/IS). A Mark 3/2 with intermediate speed (IS) hand traversing.

Mounting Mark 4. A version of the Mark 3/2 fitted with an emergency cease-fire stop device operated by a lanyard.

Mounting Mark 4/1 (Mark 4/HS). Also known as the Mark 4A, this was a Mark 4 with higher speed elevating and traversing gears manufactured by the Linotype Company.

Mounting Mark 4/2 (Mark 4/IS). A Mark 4 with an intermediate speed (IS) hand traversing gear that was slightly slower than the Mark 4/1.

Mounting Mark 5. A version of the Mark 4 modified for installation on the Morris self-propelled carrier (see Chapter 10). This version had provision for one-man power control.

Mounting C Mark 5. The Canadian version of the Mark 5.

Mounting Mark 5/1. A Mark 5 with no provision for power control.

Mounting Mark 5/2. Not produced.

Mounting Mark 5/3 (Mark 5/IS). A Mark 5 with the same intermediate speed (IS) traversing control as the Mark 4/2.

Mounting Mark 5/4 (Mark 5/1/IS). A Mark 5/1 with the same intermediate speed (IS) traversing control as the Mark 4/2.

Mounting Mark 6. A Mark 4 modified for use on the Crusader AA tank (see Chapter 10).

Mounting Mark 7. A Mark 3 converted for use on a two-wheeled, Jeep-towed carriage intended for use by the Indian Army.

Mounting Mark 8. A Mark 4 converted for use on a two-wheeled, Jeep-towed carriage intended for use by the Indian Army.

Mounting Mark 9. A C Mark 3 converted for use with the Canadian Bantam two-wheel carriage for airborne operations.

Mounting Mark 10. A Mark 4/2 converted for use with the Canadian Bantam two-wheel carriage for airborne operations.

Mounting Mark 12. This was for the Bristol Bofors. See below in this chapter for details.

The special mounting for this Bofors Gun is the Mounting Mark 7 intended for use by the Indian Army.

Platforms (Carriages)

Platform Mark 1. The original AB Bofors design with riveted construction and all original features such as cranked axles, Ackermann steering, hydraulic brakes, etc.

Platform Mark 1A. The Polish version of the original AB Bofors design. The main change was that the wheels were secured by five bolts instead of six.

Platform Mark 2. Simplified British design to speed production by using tubular side arms, trolley steering and other changes. Equipped with hydraulic brakes. Could accommodate Mountings Marks 1 to 4 and their sub-marks.

Platform C Mark 2. The Canadian production version of the Mark 2.

Platform Mark 3. Version of the Mark 2 with mechanical over-run brakes on the front axle only.

Platform Mark 4. A much-modified version of the Mark 3 on which all four arms could be removed from the central frame for stowage inside gliders or similar transports. It could be broken down into ten pack transport loads. When off the arms the frame rested on castor wheels. It could accommodate Mountings Marks 1 to 4.

Platform 2-wheeled C Mark 1. A Canadian single-axle platform for air transport.

Carriage Transporting Mark 1/India. Single axle, two-wheeled light carriage suitable for air transport and Jeep towing. Intended for Indian Army use.

Carriage Transporting Mark 2/India. As for Mark 1/India but with a shorter axle and no brakes.

Holdfast Mark 1. Four steel beams with eight hold-down bolts set into concrete.

Platform Firing Mark 1. A wooden base for emergency use when no holdfast or field carriage was available.

Platform Firing No 16. A steel platform for use with the Mounting Mark 3 on the Maunsell sea forts in the Thames Estuary.

Demonstrating the mobility of the Bofors Gun on the Mark 2 or 3 carriage.

DATA FOR OQF MARK 3 ON PLATFORM MARK 2	
Length of barrel	2.25m
Length of rifling	1.9325m
Weight in action	2,457kg
Weight in action (static)	1,181kg
Elevation	-5° to +90°
Traverse	360°
Length travelling	6.5m
Length in firing position	5.18m
Width travelling	1.93m
Width in firing position	4.038m
Height travelling	2.1m
Height in firing position	1.689m
Turning circle diameter	13.5m
Turning diameter of muzzle	5.715m
Wheelbase	4.407m
Ground clearance	210mm
Rate of fire (cyclic)	120–140rpm
Rate of fire (practical)	80–90rpm
Muzzle velocity (HE)	853m/s
Max range, horizontal	approx. 9,000m
Max range, vertical	approx. 5,000m
Weight of complete round	approx. 2.15kg
Weight of projectile	0.9–1kg
Weight of explosive filling	300g

Post-war Postscript – the Bristol Bofors

One wartime development of the L/60 Bofors Gun that was not introduced into service until after the war years was the Bristol Bofors. Originally developed by the Nuffield Organisation using experience gained manufacturing Bofors Guns, this variant was originally an attempt to allow only one crew member to lay the gun instead of the usual two. The Nuffield designers introduced a system whereby a pair of motorcycle control grips were so arranged that they controlled both elevation and traverse via a series of mechanical links and hydraulic drives.

Once the concept had been demonstrated the project was passed to the Admiralty Research Laboratory who replaced the mechanical/hydraulic drives by an electrical system. On board ships this involved only the normal on-board power circuits but for land service the new control system meant the introduction of electric generators. This involved the installation of a petrol-driven generator on the carriage, the engine and generator being located inside

A Bristol Bofors preserved at the Heugh Battery museum, Hartlepool. (T. J. Gander)

a housing to the right of the barrel. An off-carriage generator could also be used.

The United Kingdom's post-1945 economic situation meant that early plans to upgrade existing manually-controlled L/60 guns to powered control standard had to be continually postponed until 1949 and even then it was 1951 before a firm order to provide upgrade kits for 2,100 guns was placed, the conversions to be completed by 1954. Around the same time it was decided to order a new target acquisition and fire-control radar (code name 'Red Indian') to go with the upgraded gun. As things were to turn out, the radar never did receive the necessary funding, while the conversion programme was phased over a couple of extra years, all in response to declining budgetary allocations.

The conversion kits for the one-man control system were produced by the Bristol Aircraft Company so the modified carriage was known as the Bristol Bofors (officially the Mounting Mark 12). The electric power system imparted very high traverse rates to the carriage, so high that the loader on the carriage had to be supported in position within a padded rail waist support structure. The early motorcycle control grips were replaced by an aircraft-like control handle fitted with triggers and side-mounted control latches to switch the system on and off. Even a slight movement of the controls produced smooth and rapid responses. The layer was provided with a gyro-stabilised reflex sight with an integral computing facility to provide a potentially high level of accuracy.

The Bristol Bofors replaced many of the wartime versions of the Bofors Gun in the British Army and they were not phased out of service until after the new Bofors 40mm L/70 guns were introduced during the late 1950s. Even then a number remained in reserve service with Territorial Army light anti-aircraft (LAA) batteries for many years. Others saw service with the Australian Army as late as 1963.

Navy Models

British and Commonwealth navy service Bofors Guns varied from being almost identical to their land service counterparts to large and complex mountings weighing tons. Only a few of the guns produced specifically for naval service were air-cooled, with the water-cooled guns, complete with water jackets and pumping systems, being manufactured at the Royal Ordnance Factory at Nottingham or Vickers-Armstrong at various locations. As far as the Mark 3 and 7 series air-cooled guns were concerned there was little to choose between them and their land-based counterparts as the only differences were slight to allow them to be installed on naval mountings. The guns themselves, both water- and air-cooled, operated in exactly the same manner as the land service guns.

It has been estimated that the production total for British-manufactured Bofors naval pattern guns of all types came to about 4,000. More naval pattern guns were produced in Australia and Canada.

A British Army Bofors Gun in an improvised emplacement defending the port of Harstadt during the short-lived Norwegian campaign of 1940.

The British naval mountings of the Second World War were mainly simple arrangements that were virtually the mountings from the land-based Bofors Guns adapted for ship-board use. On smaller vessels the elevating and traversing hand cranks were usually retained unchanged but on larger ships power controls and remote laying from the ship's central fire-control systems could be introduced.

The Mountings Marks 1 and 2 involved American standard naval guns supplied under Lend-Lease. The Mark 1 mountings carried two barrels and the Mark 2 four (see Chapter 5).

As mentioned above, when it came to the Mark 3 air-cooled single-barrel mountings many Navy mountings were little more than land service weapons adapted to some degree or another for ship-borne installations, usually on the lighter and smaller vessels ranging from heavy landing craft to destroyers and other escort vessels. The first such naval employment of land service weapons on board British warships was during the 1940 evacuation of the Norwegian ports following a foray against invading German forces, but that was only a temporary and emergency measure involving 'rescued' Army guns. By 1941 some land service guns had been more formally placed on board warships such as the single example present on board HMS *Prince of Wales* when she was sunk by the Japanese on 10 December 1941. About that time some 136 guns and mountings were handed over for use on board Defensively Equipped Merchant Ships (DEMS). By the end of the war the Royal Navy had received 1,392 land service Bofors Guns, about 568 of which ended up on DEMS. These totals should be taken as a guide only for more seagoing land service Lend-Lease guns came from the United States and Canada.

These gun and mountings were denoted as LS Mark 3. There was also a RPLS Mark 3 (RPLS – Remote Power Land Service) mounting with remote powered laying under the control of a No 3 Kerrison Predictor. The Mark 3 CN even had a land service shield and retained manually-operated fire controls. With the Mark 3* manual operation continued but the mounting was modified by the installation of a Type 6 gyro-stabilised sight unit. The guns involved with all these sub-marks were known to the Navy as the N/1. Land service guns modified for the power-operated Mark 7, 8 and 9 mountings (see below) were known as the N1/1, N1/2 and N1/3 respectively.

One wartime mounting that was rather ahead of its time was the Twin Bofors Mark 4 mounting, usually known as the Hazemeyer mounting, manufactured at the Royal Ordnance Factory, Nottingham. This had all its fire-control equipment, including radar, actually on the mounting and it also featured a 'cross roll' device on the cradle that moved at right angles to the normal fore-and-aft line of the mounting for better stabilisation.

The Mounting Mark 4 Hazemeyer was originally developed in The Netherlands, Hazemeyer being a Dutch subsidiary of Siemens Halske. When the Germans invaded The Netherlands in 1940 the working drawings were whisked away out of German hands and taken to the United Kingdom. Also in 1940, an actual example was delivered into British hands on board the Dutch minelayer *Willem van der Zaan*. After further development this mounting was installed on many Royal Navy vessels as its tri-axial movements made it a very stable weapon platform. Target ranging was obtained from a Type 282 radar (another equipment with Dutch origins) located on the mounting although there was a secondary optical system and an on-carriage predictor system as well. Open sights were another option. In many ways the Hazemeyer was a better concept than the technology of the time allowed and it was a frequent source of trouble for the fitters. The usual Royal Navy nickname for this mounting was the Haslemere. The guns involved were the Mark 4 or 4/1 and the mountings were the Marks 4, 4* or 4**. Two hundred and forty-two pairs of guns were produced.

The follow-on twin Bofors mounting to the Hazemeyer was the Mark 5, a much simpler mounting first placed on board a ship in February 1945. This mounting, an adaptation of the US Navy's Mark 1 twin mounting but using all-British components including some taken from Vickers 2-pounder Pom-Pom and 4in Mark 5 mountings, was nicknamed the 'Utility'. The mounting could use remote RP 50 metadyne or local fire control and it lacked many of the on-board fire controls used previously so the Mark 5 lacked any blind fire capability. The first order was for 304 twin-barrel mountings (carrying the Mark

The naval Mark 4 Hazemeyer mounting developed from a Dutch design with two barrels and triaxial mounting.

11 gun) and more were manufactured in Canada as the Mark VC. It proved to be a reliable weapon and at 5.5 tons was much lighter than the Mark 4 Hazemeyer.

The Mark 6 mounting was somewhat more complicated as it carried no less than six Mark 9 guns. It did not enter service until after the war had ended and was combined with the RP 50 metadyne remote-control system. Three hundred and twenty-four were manufactured. The mountings were primarily intended for mounting on battleships and the largest aircraft carriers then in service. The first battleship to receive a Mark 6 mounting was HMS *Vanguard* which eventually mounted ten. Aircraft carriers such as HMS *Eagle* and HMS *Ark Royal* had eight. These Mark 6 mountings had automatic feed ammunition trays operated by gun recoil. Each tray provided thirty-six rounds per gun after which it was necessary to reload the trays manually. The lack of operating space for these large mountings on some ships meant that the ammunition trays could only be reloaded when the mountings were facing a fixed bearing while on other ships the reloading process had to be carried out while the guns traversed at an automatically reduced rate. In both cases the gun barrels were maintained at an elevation angle of +25° during reloading. The last Mark 6 mounting was fitted to HMS *Victorious*.

The Mark 6 was followed by the Twin 40mm Bofors STAAG Mark 2 produced by the Royal Ordnance Factory at Nottingham. The STAAG would probably take the prize for being the largest, heaviest and most complex of all the operational Bofors mountings of the period.

The initials STAAG stood for Stabilised Tachymetric Anti-Aircraft Gun but it was more usually known as the 'Antlered Beast' or other, less printable, names. It had a notorious reputation for unreliability, due in no small measure to numerous black boxes filled with thermionic devices and electrical/mechanical interfaces being located directly on the gun mounting and thus prone to movement and vibration stresses. By any name the STAAG was a complex mounting that carried a Type 262 radar, automatic target acquisition, a predictor, a target tracking radar, a stabilisation system, a secondary rangefinder and even an on-board generator for emergency use. The mounting had its own large shield and all controls and drives were hydraulic.

As on the Hazemeyer, the mounting moved tri-axially but the barrels on the STAAG used a lateral deflection movement to allow them to aim ahead of the target position relative to the fire-control equipment. A STAAG weighed no less than 17 tonnes and for all its complexity it was only marginally more efficient than other contemporary mountings. On many ships the early Hazemeyer mountings were replaced by STAAGs and in its turn the STAAG was often replaced by the Mark 5 mounting which was considered as far more reliable.

The prototype STAAG, the Mark 1, was a single-barrel mounting. The twin

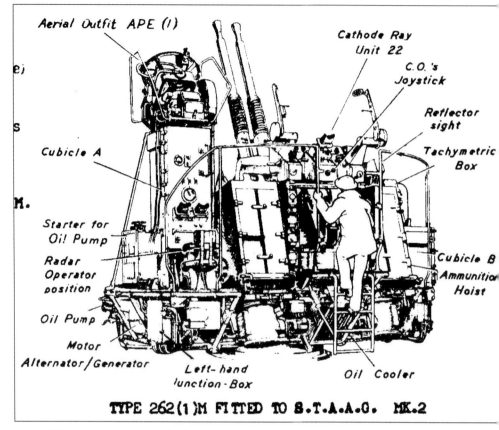

Aerial Outfit APE (1)

Cathode Ray
Unit 22

C.O.'s
Joystick

Reflector
sight

Cubicle A

Tachymetric
Box

Starter for
Oil Pump

Radar
Operator
position

Cubicle B
Ammunition
Hoist

Oil Pump

Motor

Alternator/Generator

Left-hand
Junction-Box

Oil Cooler

TYPE 262(1)M FITTED TO S.T.A.A.G. MK.2

Although only a sketch, this illustration does give an impression of the bulk and complexity of the Mark 2 STAAG naval mounting.

barrel Mark 2 was the prototype for the Mark 2* with DC electrical drives while the Mark 3 used AC drives. The Mark 2** had no radar on the mounting and was used for training.

A STAAG had a brief moment of success during the 1956 Suez campaign when it managed to shoot down an aircraft. Unfortunately it was a Royal Air Force Hunter.

The post-war Buster mounting was another tri-axial mounting carrying twin barrels but it turned out to be even more complex and heavier (at well over 20 tonnes) than the STAAG. Only eight of the Mark 8 guns intended to be used with Buster were actually produced (in right- and left-hand form), all well after 1945, before the programme was terminated.

Ordered for production at the end of May 1945, the Mark 7 was a much simpler mounting than those mentioned above and was adapted from a twin-barrel 20mm Oerlikon Mark 5 powered mounting much modified for the heavier gun. It was an air-cooled, single-barrel mounting suitable for a wide variety of naval applications ranging from fast patrol boats upwards. Hydraulically-powered, the Mark 7 used one-man laying with a single loader on the carriage and was replaced during the 1950s by the Mark 9 which was virtually an all-electric Mark 7, the interim Mark 8 being a re-engineered Mark 7 that was supposed to operate on battery power; it was not adopted. The Mark 9 was deployed operationally during the 1982 Falklands Islands campaign.

Some upgraded mountings involving modified Mark 7 mountings powered by a low-pressure, oil/hydraulic system, entered service with the Royal Australian Navy during 1980. About thirty were produced. Known as the 40/60 AN, this Australian variant was produced at the Maribynong Ordnance Factory. A small number of these mountings were reported as being sold to Thailand.

One wartime mounting destined to have a long post-war career was the Canadian Boffin, originally a conversion of the powered Oerlikon twin 20mm Mark 5 or 5C mounting to accommodate a single air-cooled Bofors 40mm gun and a gyro-stabilised sight unit. Most of these conversions, similar in approach to the Royal Navy's Mark 7, were employed by the Royal Canadian Navy during the latter war years and for many years afterwards, some being installed on Royal Navy vessels, especially on destroyers. Numbers were still in service after the Canadian Navy dragged them out of storage (and military museums) for operations in the Persian Gulf during the First Gulf War of 1991. The Boffin had hydraulically-powered controls and a crew of three on the mounting; the commander, layer and loader. During the Cold War years Boffins were also deployed for land service to provide low level air defence around the Royal Canadian Air Force air bases at Baden and Lahr in what was then West Germany.

In addition to the Canadian Boffin output, a further 100 or so Boffin mountings were converted from existing twin 20mm Oerlikon mountings in Australia. These mountings were for Royal Australian Navy (RAN) applications, as were a further 280 Australian land service Bofors Guns from various sources that were converted for naval mountings for RAN vessels, although some were also issued to Royal Navy Pacific Fleet vessels, all the installations being completed in Australian shipyards.

Toadstool was a post-war attempt to convert a land service pattern gun to naval power operation with control introduced by a joystick. Although Toadstool underwent considerable testing it was not adopted for service.

Soon after 1945 the Royal Navy began to place into reserve a significant proportion of the warships accumulated during the war years, prior to their disposal. Gradually, and along with their carrier vessels, many of the L/60 naval guns and mountings mentioned above became dispersed to navies as far apart as Denmark, Egypt, Mexico and Bangladesh.

Although strictly speaking not coming into the naval gun category, mention must be made of the Bofors Guns, mounted on what had once been pleasure steamers, that defended the Thames Estuary during 1940 and for a few years afterwards. This provided some measure of defence against German aircraft and raiding and minelaying vessels that used the Estuary as a pointer towards London. Placing guns on readily-available paddle steamers provided a means of extending the local defences some way out to sea. Three steamers mounted a single land service Bofors Gun (minus its lower carriage), two searchlights and a number of Lewis Guns. They were known as the *Queen* class, formed into the Nore Flotilla. Involved were the *The Queen of Kent*, *The Queen of Thanet* and *The Thames Queen*. The guns were manned by Army personnel but the vessels were crewed by the Royal Navy. In time the *Queens* were replaced by the larger *Eagle* class. The Nore Flotilla was kept in being until the first of the Maunsell sea forts was constructed, after which the vessels involved were gradually withdrawn from their air defence role to be converted for other purposes.

Naval Mounting Models
The following is only a brief summary for rapid reference purposes. More information is provided in the text provided above.

Ordnance
Mark 4 and 4/1. Water-cooled. For use on the twin-gun Hazemeyer mountings. The Type D was for the left-hand gun and Type E for the right-hand gun. Many later converted to Mark 11 standard for Mark 5 mountings. 442 in service by 1945. Total gun production was 484.

Mark 5. Project abandoned.

Mark 7. Air-cooled. 400 ordered from Vickers-Armstrong for use on an early version of the STAAG with no trunnions installed. The project was cancelled.

Mark 8. Water-cooled. Eight produced for the Buster mounting. No provision for single-shot firing. Left- and right-hand versions produced.

Mark 9. Air-cooled. Used on six-gun Mark 6 mounting. No provision for single-shot firing. Left- and right-hand versions produced.

Mark 10. Water-cooled. Used with Mark 2 STAAG and fitted with trunnions. No provision for single-shot firing.

Mark 11. Water-cooled. Many converted from Mark 4 and 4/1 for use on Mark 5 mounting. 342 in service by 1945.

Mountings
Mark 1. American Lend-Lease twin-gun mounting. Equipped for remote fire control.

Mark 2. American Lend-Lease quadruple mounting. Equipped for remote fire control.

LS Mark 3. Land service mounting. Manually-operated.

RPLS Mark 3. Land service mounting with power drives controlled by No 3 (Kerrison) Predictor.

Mark 3 CN. Manually-operated with gun shield. Some small modifications for naval service.

Mark 3*. Manually-operated with Type 5 gyro-stabilised sight.

Mark 4 Hazemeyer. Developed from a Dutch design with two barrels and triaxial mounting. See text.

Mark 5. Twin mounting derived from US Navy Mark 1 mounting using British components. See text.

Mark 5C (or VC). Canadian-manufactured version of Mark 5 twin mounting.

STAAG. Complex and unreliable twin-gun mounting with on-carriage radar. See text.

Mark 6. Six-gun mounting used only on large warships. Employed 36-round loading trays operated by gun recoil. See text.

Buster. Twin-gun multi-sensor mounting that proved to be too large, complex and heavy for service. See text.

Mark 7. Single-gun mounting adapted from a twin Oerlikon 20mm naval service mounting but extensively modified for a wide range of naval roles. Hydraulically powered. See text.

Mark 8. A Mark 7 meant to operate from batteries. Not produced.

Mark 9. An all-electric Mark 7. See text.

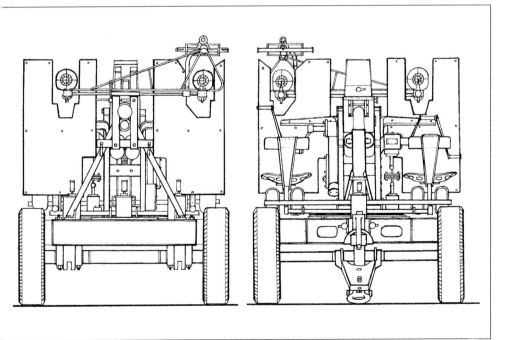

Toadstool. Basically a land service mounting altered for one-man joystick control. Not proceeded with.

Boffin. A Canadian development produced by placing a Bofors Gun on an Oerlikon twin-gun Mark 5 or 5C mounting. See text.

Royal Navy Postscript

When outlining British naval Bofors Gun mountings it is worth a mention that what was probably the last aircraft to be shot down by the L/60 Bofors Gun was credited to the Royal Navy. On 27 May 1982 the Mark 9 mounting guns of HMS *Fearless* and HMS *Intrepid* between them shot down an Argentinian A-4B Skyhawk over Ajax Bay in the Falkland Islands, emphasising the Bofors Gun's naval origins 50 years after the first gun appeared.

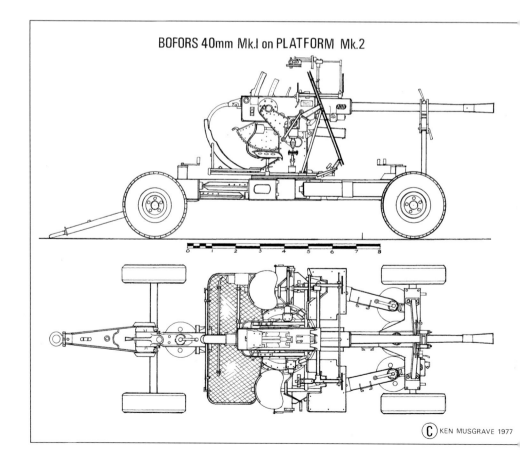

BOFORS 40mm Mk.I on PLATFORM Mk.2

Ⓒ KEN MUSGRAVE 1977

Chapter 5

The American Guns

The Royal Swedish Navy was not the only military organisation with concerns regarding air attack against their combat assets during the 1920s. On the other side of the Atlantic the US Army and Navy were both developing measures to counter what was regarded as a growing airborne threat. An opportunity for both services to co-operate in equipment procurement therefore arose but, as usual, since their foreseen requirements appeared to differ, both went their separate ways.

During the mid-1930s, when AB Bofors representatives started making visits to various defence agencies in Washington DC and elsewhere to broadcast the merits of the new Bofors Gun, they therefore met with a blank response. The representatives were told that the US Army and Navy were both involved in their own low-level air defence development programmes and were not interested in any alternative product.

The US Army's involvement with light anti-aircraft guns dated back to the early 1920s when the development of a 37mm automatic gun had been initiated by the US Ordnance Department, assisted by the small arms designer John Moses Browning and the Colt's Patent Fire Arms Company of Hartford, Connecticut. During the 1920s development funding for such projects was in short supply so although the gun was deemed fully developed by 1926, it was not until 1935 that further funding was found to complete the final development of the necessary field carriage. Between 1926 and 1935 the entire 37mm project was simply kept on hold.

Superficially the Colt/Browning 37mm gun and carriage emerged as resembling the Bofors Gun but, as with the German Rheinmetall 3.7cm FlaK series, appearances were misleading. As with the Rheinmetall design, the Colt/Browning gun employed an entirely different operating mechanism and ammunition feed system and, as was to be demonstrated, the overall performance of the American gun was nowhere near as good as that of the Swedish product, mainly due to the underpowered 37mm ammunition. In addition, the American gun and carriage combination was heavier than the Bofors Gun and carriage.

At one point during the 1930s it was suggested that the US Navy could also adopt the same 37mm gun but that approach soon ended in favour of a series of trials involving lighter automatic weapons, the philosophy then being that the latter could produce a more effective barrage of fire against dive bombers. At the bottom end of this light automatic weapon range were the 0.50/12.7mm M2 water-cooled machine guns and, it was to emerge, 20mm Oerlikon cannon, although the latter were not finally approved for adoption until late 1940. As combat experience was to painfully demonstrate, neither type of gun could deliver a projectile heavy enough to definitely bring down an aircraft target at the low and close ranges really determined attackers were to adopt.

Further up the calibre scale came a US Ordnance Board water-cooled cannon with a calibre of 1.1in (27.94mm) that fired a relatively heavy projectile (415 grams). Developed for the US Navy from March 1929 onwards, the first production example of the 1.1in cannon, the Mark 1/1, was ready during 1935 on an over-complicated side-by-side quadruple, tri-axial mounting. It was not long before the guns began to display all manner of feed troubles together with mounting cracks and excessive vibrations. It soon became apparent that the 1.1in cannon was in need of further development.

A view of the troublesome 1.1in quadruple mounting that was at one time regarded as the US Navy's main close-in air defence weapon – until the Bofors Gun arrived on the scene. This example is on display as the Navy Yard, Washington DC. (T. J. Gander)

Thus by the late 1930s both the US Army and Navy were busy following their own paths towards guns with overall defensive concepts very similar to that of the Bofors Gun. This did not preclude either service from keeping an active eye on developments taking place elsewhere. During 1938 the US Army decided to allocate funds for the purchase of a single Bofors Gun for technical test purposes. In response, AB Bofors offered to send to the United States a single gun and a technician who would be on hand during any trials the Americans might like to conduct. In addition, 2,600 rounds of various ammunition natures were offered at a cost of from US$6.00 to US$12.00 a round. The total cost of this package would come to US$20,200.00.

There followed what turned into a rather unfortunate episode for all concerned. All the above communications were transmitted via cable messages, the fastest commercial communications medium of the period. During the transmission of the cables some unfortunate errors occurred either in the writing of the texts or in their reading. The form in which the cables were sent was such that 10,000 was received as 10 1000 and the term dollars appeared only towards the end of a message. When the Americans read all the figures and totted them up their results worked out at US$243,000.00. In short, the mix-up meant that the US Army ignored the AB Bofors offer and, to compound matters further, before any confirmation letters could arrive or consultations with attachés could be made, the Army equipment selection board decided to go ahead and fully type classify the Colt/Browning 37mm gun and its carriage. Production was scheduled to commence during 1939.

The Bofors Gun was therefore denied an early opportunity to demonstrate its capabilities to the Americans. It was to be mid-1939 before another chance arose via an unorthodox path. This time an association between an American businessman Henry Howard, from Newport, Rhode Island, and a Swedish financier, one Mr Wenner-Gren (owner of a controlling interest in AB Bofors stock), resulted in Mr Howard attending a trade convention in Stockholm. During his visit Mr Howard was persuaded to attend a Bofors Gun demonstration at a nearby range where he was so impressed with what he witnessed that on his return to the United States he visited Admiral Furlong, Chief of the US Navy Bureau of Ordnance, and enthusiastically expressed his opinions regarding what he had seen. Exactly what Mr Howard's qualifications were for expressing any opinions on air defence weapons are not known but after a second visit from Mr Howard, the Bureau Chief decided to provide funds to purchase a twin-barrelled, water-cooled Bofors Gun direct from AB Bofors, along with 3,000 rounds of ammunition. The cost of the gun was US$40,000.00 and each round was priced at US$10.00. The gun was duly shipped to New York and arrived at the end of August 1940, having been sent via Petsamo in what was then neutral Finland. The gun was immediately transported to the Dahlgren Proving Grounds in Virginia.

Things were beginning to happen. Around that same time a Mr J. A. Cunningham, a senior executive of the York Lock & Safe Company of York, Pennsylvania, also witnessed a Bofors Gun demonstration. Sensing an opportunity to enter the defence hardware market as the Second World War carried on its bloody way, and having been made aware of the US Navy's approval of such a course of action, the York company decided to try and negotiate a licence to manufacture the Bofors Gun in the United States. Before a team from York could sail to Sweden to start negotiations on a possible deal the April 1940 German invasion of Norway forced them to abandon their journey. The US naval attaché in Stockholm was therefore called upon to bring about the purchase of a Bofors Gun but for some reason his purchase consisted of a single air-cooled gun rather than the desired water-cooled twin. The transaction involved gun spares, sights and 3,000 rounds of ammunition but nothing appears to have been actually sent.

Bofors Gun demonstrations were being made thick and fast about that period, namely August 1940. During that month the Dutch naval attaché in Washington arranged a demonstration of the four Bofors Guns (two twin-barrelled mountings) then on board the Dutch destroyer HNMS *Van Kinsbergen* (U93). The fact that the Dutch vessel was conducting the demonstration off Trinidad in the Caribbean no doubt ensured a good turn-out of observers, and they approved of what they saw. The Bofors Guns on the *Van Kinsbergen* were controlled by a Dutch-German fire-control system which failed to stir the Americans but they were highly impressed by the guns. Thus when the firing trials of the twin-barrelled mounting purchased from Sweden took place at Dahlgren shortly afterwards there was a small nucleus of observers who were already enthusiastic.

The Dahlgren trials involved some other weapons, including the Army's 37mm gun, for it was by then apparent that the US Navy's 1.1in cannon, was still not up to the required standard of performance and it was proving very difficult to eradicate all the many seemingly inherent technical problems. However, the Colt/Browning gun was soon eliminated from consideration as the Navy considered that the 37mm ammunition imparted an unsatisfactory performance.

Another gun under test at Dahlgren was the British Vickers 2-pounder, the same naval gun procured by Sweden in 1922 and later selected by the British Army for static installations at strategic points around the United Kingdom. The 2-pounder was again destined to be unsuccessful, despite hopes that international standardisation would ease an already overstretched supply chain, especially for the Royal Navy. The Bofors Gun out-performed the 2-pounder on all counts but this could have been offset by the Vickers product giving a good account of itself when on Royal Navy ships. The main point against the 2-pounder was that it used Cordite as the propellant. There was no Cordite manufacturing facility in the United States, and the rounds could not be adapted to utilise American nitrocellulose-based powders. Once that point had been accepted the only difficulty was that of actually manufacturing the Bofors Gun in the United States.

In what was then a rare case of inter-service co-operation some US Army observers also witnessed the Dahlgren trials. What they saw impressed them so much that they reported back to their superiors that the Bofors Gun should be procured instead of the 37mm Colt/Browning gun, by then in series production as the 37mm Antiaircraft Gun M1. There was an understandable reluctance to follow this course of action for the Army had made a considerable investment in their 37mm gun and did not wish to drop it in favour of a new weapon that had yet to be placed in production in the United States.

Adoption

However, the Bofors Gun demonstrations had been so impressive that it was obvious to the Army that the Swedish product was much better than their own in all respects. They therefore decided to adopt the Bofors Gun and initiated moves to obtain an example from the United Kingdom. It arrived during December 1940. Army authorities also agreed that the Navy, already in the process of making contact with AB Bofors towards the same end, should handle the manufacturing licence negotiations with the Swedes on their behalf and agreed to pay their share of the costs. In the meantime the 37mm gun would have to remain in production until Bofors Gun production was fully under way. As time would tell, that would not happen until late 1943, so 37mm guns were to soldier on in front-line service until the war ended. This dual production approach had to be tolerated for by early 1941 the demands for low-level air defence guns from all fronts were numerous and strident. That situation was partially the result of American military observers witnessing the impact of ground attack aircraft and dive bombers as part of the German *Blitzkrieg* in France and elsewhere during 1940. Apart from the 37mm Colt/Browning gun (of which only 170 had been completed by the end of 1940) the only defence the Army and Navy then had against any such forms of attack was the relatively short range 0.50/12.7mm M2 machine gun. The Navy was particularly anxious to obtain the Bofors Gun following the problems experienced with their 1.1in cannon, so the more powerful Bofors Gun was urgently needed by both services.

The acceptance of these unfortunate facts coloured what was about to happen. Even before the Army's formal type classification of the gun and carriage on 29 May 1941, the rush to get the Bofors Gun into series production was such that various agencies were taking measures to obtain drawings and production facilities before a formal licence agreement had been finalised with AB Bofors. For the Navy, moves to obtain working drawings had commenced

One of the very first Bofors Guns to be manufactured in the USA undergoing mobility trials during July 1941.

The very first American Bofors Gun on display at the Aberdeen Proving Ground, Maryland. (T. J. Gander)

soon after the Trinidad demonstrations. The Navy efforts were directed via the Dutch for although The Netherlands were by then occupied by the Germans an almost complete set of drawings was available in the Dutch East Indies. These were microfilmed and sent to the United States for conversion into working drawings that conformed to American working and manufacturing practices. That task was passed to the York Lock & Safe Company who started work immediately. More drawings were obtained from the Canadian Otis-Fensom Elevator Company plant already manufacturing Bofors Guns at Hamilton, Ontario.

In addition to the Canadian drawings, more drawings appear to have been provided along with the land service gun sent over from the United Kingdom and these were passed to the Chrysler Corporation to convert them for American production methods. Unfortunately, this dual approach by York and Chrysler meant the initial American production of Bofors Guns resulted in an almost complete lack of component inter-changeability between early production land and naval service guns. The two concerns were using drawings based on different measuring systems, both derived from what were originally European metric measurements, then little used in the United States. The Navy drawings produced by York were converted into American terms using decimals while the Chrysler drawings were prepared using imperial fractions. Such a situation could not be allowed to continue so a complete upheaval of production for both Navy and Army guns resulted.

The Chrysler Corporation, based at Detroit, Michigan, became the prime contractor and produced a standard set of working drawings that reduced the number of disparities between Army and Navy guns from over 200 to ten, and nearly all of those related to differences between air- and water-cooling. The York concern was eventually relieved of their responsibility for converting and updating production drawings, the work being passed to the Naval Gun Factory at Washington, DC.

Chrysler became the prime contractor for Army and Navy guns while York concentrated on Navy orders. Such was the rush towards production that Chrysler were able to deliver the first two pilot guns to Firestone Tire & Rubber on 27 June 1941 (using barrels supplied from Canada to be rifled and finished at Watervliet Arsenal) and full series production began on 4 February 1942. The initial order given to Chrysler was for 300 guns a month but by 2 July 1942 the Army alone was asking for 1,500 guns a month, each with a spare barrel. It remains a lasting memorial to the industrial power of the United States that those totals were being achieved by November 1942. In December 1942 monthly production totals of 1,600 Army guns and 135 Navy twin-barrelled guns were reached.

June 1941 plans for Navy guns production mentioned 500 twin mountings and 500 quadruple mountings. These numbers were soon increased by the addition of a further 500 twin and 300 quad mountings for Lend-Lease. By 1945 those totals had been left far behind.

Legalities

The American rush to Bofors Gun production completely overlooked the fact that during the early preparation period no legal agreement had yet been signed to allow the Americans to forge ahead as they did. On their part the Americans were so anxious to obtain Bofors Guns that legalities were simply overlooked. The situation was compounded by delays introduced into what turned out to be prolonged negotiations between the American authorities and AB Bofors by the need to obtain the agreement of the Swedish Government who, in their turn, tried to use the negotiations to obtain aircraft export and manufacturing licences. To this the US Government could not agree. There were also difficulties in the wording of the agreement for at first the Swedes, as they were dealing with US Navy representatives, insisted on providing their consent to manufacture naval service guns only, which would have precluded the manufacture of guns for the US Army.

Eventually the Swedes gave way and the wording was altered to 'for the United States' use' to allow guns to be manufactured for both services. It was 21 June 1941 before the contract was signed in Stockholm, and by then American Bofors Gun production planning was well under way. The total price agreed was US$600,000, the Army paying half, of which US$100,000 was to pay for the services of two Bofors production engineers to smooth the path to series production in the United States. In the event the two engineers were not sent due to the prevailing war conditions so that US$100,000 was never paid. The signing of the agreement also resulted in AB Bofors handing over a complete set of metric production drawings to add to those already in American hands.

It was not long before the licence agreement wording gave rise to misgivings on the part of AB Bofors. The Americans were soon manufacturing guns not just for themselves but for others as well, including the United Kingdom. Bofors soon realised that this could seriously affect their own commercial prospects and initiated legal moves in the United States to clarify the situation.

At the end of 1941, by which time the United States had become a belligerent in what had become a true World War, the American legal representative of AB Bofors wrote to the Lend-Lease administrator of the United States, Harry L. Hopkins, to draw attention to the terms of the contract signed between the United States and AB Bofors. Without going into legal technicalities, the written answer to AB Bofors' legal adviser is worthy of inclusion here since it provides an indication of the importance of the Bofors Gun to the American war effort at that time. The letter is quoted in full.

THE WHITE HOUSE
WASHINGTON

January 21, 1942

Sir:

I have your letter of December 30 telling me to tell the Army and Navy to stop manufacturing Bofors guns for use of the United Nations in the defeat of Germany and Japan.

I can only say that if I had a client who asked me to do what you are asking your [*sic*] Government to do I should tell him to jump in the Lake. Very truly yours,

Signed, Harry L Hopkins

Thus, quite apart from the good gentleman's indignation, it would appear from the letter that the American authorities were so determined to supply themselves and their Allies with as many Bofors Guns as they might require that they were quite prepared to overlook the terms of their contract with AB Bofors. Faced with such obduracy and well aware that there was little they could do to alter the situation, AB Bofors had to be content to waive their objections to the actions of the United States Government for as long as the war lasted. However, they did register a legal objection to the American actions.

An M2 Bofors Gun ready for action somewhere in the Pacific theatre, 1944.

A post-war (May 1954) M2 Bofors Gun team undergoing training at the Yakima Firing Center, Washington State.

There the matter rested until after the war ended and the Americans started to dispose of their accumulated wartime stocks by selling them at what were, in effect, knock-down prices or even giving them away. It was then that AB Bofors brought up their objections again for the American disposal activities were on such a scale that AB Bofors could not possibly compete in world markets for what was then still one of their major products. The case was taken to the United States' Court of Claims and the verdict was decided in favour of AB Bofors on 12 July 1957. All the legal details were completed during the following year.

Production

Back in 1941 Chrysler concentrated on production of the ordnance while production of the land service field carriage was passed to the Firestone Tire & Rubber Company of Akron, Ohio. The first Chrysler guns were clones of a British-supplied Mark 1* gun which were test fired at the Aberdeen Proving Ground in Maryland without manifesting any troubles whatsoever. Those

'British' guns, basically the Bofors Model 1936 with most of the original features retained, were used as the basis for all future American production for Army and Navy air-cooled guns.

The Bofors Gun became one of the main American war production programmes. Chrysler production was distributed around twelve main production facilities and more than 2,000 sub-contractors became involved. The York Lock & Safe Company also used sub-contractors so that by 1943 some 481 concerns were involved in manufacturing sub-assemblies for naval mountings.

Chrysler's main facilities in the Detroit area were Plymouth, Chrysler Jefferson-Kercheval, Dodge Forge, Lynch Road, Highland Park, the Amplex Division and Dodge Main. Other plants involved were at New Castle, Indiana, Airtemp-Dayton, Ohio, De Soto, Wyoming, and Kokomo, Indiana. The three main production centres of all these facilities were Plymouth, Jefferson-Kercheval and Highland Park. Other company names associated with gun and carriage production included the Ford Instrument Company, Webster Electric, Vickers Inc, General Electric and the Northern Pump Company.

Concerns involved with Navy guns, for which the York Lock & Safe Company acted as prime contractor, included Blaw-Knox, based at Pittsburgh, who manufactured mountings at Martins Ferry, Ohio. Firestone also manufactured Navy mountings at Akron, Ohio. In January 1944 the York

A US Army M2 Bofors Gun coming ashore during one of the amphibious landings carried out in the Mediterranean theatre during the Second World War.

concern was relieved of part of its manufacturing responsibilities when the Government-constructed Special Ordnance Plant at York became the Naval Ordnance Plant, with the Blaw-Knox Company taking over as contractor and operator.

Chrysler design engineers marvelled at the ingenuity and mechanical refinements of the Bofors Gun mechanisms but production engineers were less enthusiastic. One of them is supposed to have remarked that the Bofors Gun had been designed by a man trying to solve the American unemployment problems of the early 1930s. The production challenge was certainly demanding at first sight for the Army and Navy were demanding guns in huge numbers and they wanted them <u>NOW</u>! Yet some gun components seemed to defy mass production using American methods.

One early source of trouble was the gun breech block. This began life as an oblong steel billet weighing 15.65kg yet 110 machining operations later it emerged as a sculptured component weighing only 4kg. The breech ring was even more demanding as it took 140 machining operations to reduce a 120.2kg steel billet to the 47.63kg finished product, involving along the way no less than 625 inspection gauges. These operations and a high degree of accuracy had to be accepted for the gun mechanisms had been refined to a very high degree during the development stages to the extent that any deviations from the close dimensions and tolerances resulted in malfunctions and a short operational life for some critical components. But if the fine tolerances had to be accepted it was possible to manufacture some parts in ways that allowed some increase in production speeds.

The production rates achieved by the Chrysler, Firestone and York facilities demonstrate how well they managed to overcome the many problems they encountered. Just as important as speeding production was a gradual reduction in overall production costs, both in materials and labour. For instance, the cost of a twin-barrel naval gun and mounting was reduced from US$62,300 to US$43,640. The cost of a naval quadruple gun and mounting fell from US$86,000 to US$67,520.

The output rate was such that by the end of 1944 the production of Army guns could be wound down to almost nothing (other than spare parts) as the numbers produced were far in excess of what the Army could actually absorb. Yet at that time the Navy were asking for more and more guns. The production totals for Army guns alone were as follows:

1941	0
1942	8,912
1943	13,485
1944	1,500
1945	0

To these totals can be added single-barrel guns produced for the US Navy and
Coast Guard, as follows:

1941	0
1942	60
1943	2,519
1944	6,644
1945	796 (January to March only)

To these totals can be added a further 8,979 land service guns manufactured for
Lend-Lease. Although the annual production rates for these guns cannot be
determined they were distributed as follows:

United Kingdom and Commonwealth	2,834
China	80
French Forces	448
USSR	5,511
American Republics	4
Others	2

Production figures for US Navy and Coast Guard mountings can only be given
in approximate numbers, as follows:

	Twin	Quad
1942	510	230
1943	1,700	510
1944	3,650	750
1945	3,020	800

In addition to these totals, by 1945 the numbers of single-barrel guns and
mountings issued to the Navy (see below in this chapter) had reached over
10,000, many of them having been taken over from Army stocks.

A proportion of the Navy mountings were allocated for Lend-Lease. The
UK alone received 393 Mark 1 twin-barrel guns, 400 Mark 2 four-barrel guns
and about 380 of the single-barrel Mark 3.

Throughout its Army service life there was only one version of the Bofors
Gun, the 40mm Automatic Gun M1, although a few minor mounting
attachment changes were introduced to allow the guns to be placed on self-
propelled carriages (see Chapter 10). At first the towed carriage was the
40mm Antiaircraft Gun Carriage M2. While there was an M1 carriage, the
original riveted construction carriage as designed by AB Bofors, it was not
accepted for service other than as 'Substitute Standard'. Apart from

introducing all-welded construction to the M2 field carriage, Firestone also introduced tubular axles, simpler and cheaper oilite bushings (in place of manganese-bronze), and electric brakes powered by the towing vehicle. Firestone went on to manufacture 20,231 land service carriages plus a further 10,434 mountings for the Navy.

That was not the limit of Firestone's contribution to the American Bofors Gun programme, for they also manufactured power drive units and ran a training school for gun fitters and instructors. The need for the latter became painfully obvious soon after the first completed guns had been issued to front line units. Technical training on the guns was at first perfunctory to the point that routine stripping and maintenance were ignored. In typical American fashion this omission was partially rectified by the making and showing of short instruction movies which sufficed until properly-trained instructors became available.

There was also a M2A1 carriage with higher gear ratios for traversing, the rate being increased from 6° for one turn of the crank handle on the M2 to 17.1° on the M2A1. On both types of carriage the rate of barrel elevation for one turn of the crank remained at 4°. An attempt to introduce a T2E1 carriage with spring-air suspension was not proceeded with, although a test carriage was manufactured.

There was one further American carriage originally known as the T8E1, later type classified as the M5 (Airborne). It was the American equivalent of the

Close-up of some of the drive gear boxes on the first American Bofors Gun. (T. J. Gander)

generally similar British and Canadian single-axle carriages intended for air transport. This carried a standard M1 gun on a four-armed carriage that could be folded to carry the gun and mounting on a single unsprung axle. For transport by C-46 cargo aircraft the side outrigger arms were removed and so was the gun barrel. When the gun had to be loaded into a C-47 Dakota or C-54 the autoloader and sights had to be removed as well. Once at a firing position a team of three gunners could prepare the gun and mounting for action in about five minutes. Only 200 M5s were produced, all of them during 1943, and they appear to have been very little used operationally other than during the latter stages of the Pacific campaigns. A T13 carriage appeared in prototype form in August 1945 as a possible replacement for the M5 but the end of the war terminated the project.

For fire control the US Army adopted the Sight, Computing, M7 or M7A1, both of which could be used in conjunction with the Telescope M7 (for traverse) or M74 (for elevation). Devised by the Frankford Arsenal, this sight system involved the usual twin cartwheel foresights for both layers while a sight operator fed target speed and range data into a mechanical computer control unit mounted to one side of the sight bar, from where the sights were off-set the appropriate amount. Not all US Army guns had this sight for it suffered the usual fate of other such systems in that it was an expensive and complex device. Many gunners relied on the cartwheel sights alone without any other aid.

An unusual photograph of a M5 predictor being used in conjunction with a US Army M2 Bofors Gun.

The same fate was to befall the device adopted for fully predicted fire control, namely the British No 3 Kerrison Predictor modified to incorporate a stereoscopic rangefinder. Other American modifications to suit local manufacturing methods included redesigned oil bearings and some revised mechanisms. Known to the US Army as the Director, AA, M5A2 (there was also a M5 and M5A1), it was originally adopted for the 37mm M1 Colt/Browning gun but was also produced for the 40mm gun by the Singer Manufacturing Company of Elizabethport, New Jersey. Getting the M5A2 into production proved to be a major industrial undertaking yet Singer eventually manufactured 30,950 units, many for Lend-Lease as well as for 37mm guns, before production was terminated during 1944. When the Director was in operation power for the equipment and to power the on-carriage drives came from a Unit, Generating, M5.

DATA FOR 40MM AUTOMATIC GUN M1 ON 40MM ANTIAIRCRAFT GUN CARRIAGE M2		
Length of gun	2.25m	
Weight of gun and carriage	2,517kg	
Length travelling	5.727m	
Width travelling	1.823m	
Height travelling	2.019m	
Wheelbase	3.2m	
Ground clearance	368mm	
Elevation, gun level	-6° to +90°	
Elevation on jacks	-11° to +90°	
Traverse	360°	
Range:		
Vertical	6,858m	
Effective	2,743m	
Tracer burn-out	3,840m	
Rate of fire (cyclic)	120rpm	
Ammunition		
Type	HE	AP
Weight:		
Complete round	2.186kg	2.0775kg
Projectile	930g	889g
Propellant	0.3266kg	0.2948kg
Muzzle velocity	875m/s	879m/s

Data for 40mm Gun Carriage M5 (Airborne)		
Configuration	Travelling	Stripped in aircraft
Weight	2,034kg	1,578.5kg
Length	4.94m	2.99m
Width	1.746m	1.422m
Height	1.924m	1.924m
Elevation	-5° to + 90°	
Traverse	360°	

Navy Mountings

Production of Bofors Guns for the US Navy was primarily concentrated on twin-barrelled, water-cooled mountings. These were based on an American-modified AB Bofors design and were mounted on just about every type of American warship, the first mounting being placed on the destroyer *Coghlan* (DD-606) on 1 July 1942. In time the US Navy came to prefer the 40mm Bofors Gun by far as opposed to their other close-in air defence weapon, the 20mm Oerlikon. Once production was under way the Navy initiated a programme to re-equip their existing light air defence weapon installations, mainly 0.50/12.7mm Browning machine guns and the troublesome 1.1in cannon, with twin-barrel Bofors guns. It was 1944 before the programme was completed as the conversion from 1.1in to Bofors Guns was a time-consuming process carried out in a shipyard due to the fire-control rewiring involved. New warships were provided with twin-barrel Bofors mountings as a matter of course. In addition to the guns destined for the Navy, 1,252 twin-barrel mountings were earmarked for Lend-Lease for the Royal Navy but of these only 393 were ever delivered, some of them fitted aboard vessels undergoing repair or refit in American shipyards.

The usual Navy mounting was the 40mm Twin Mount Mark 1. It had two barrels arranged side-by-side (the left-hand guns were Mark 1s, the right-hand Mark 2s and the gun centres were 243mm apart), with the loaders standing on a spacious platform to the rear of the guns. Early production mountings involved friction-coupled drives which proved to be prone to salt corrosion and thus gave troubles. Once the drives had been replaced by hydraulic equivalents there were no further problems.

Mountings were power-controlled with fire control coming via a combination of the Sight Mark 14 and the Director Mark 51. The Mark 14 sight had originally been developed by the Massachusetts Institute of Technology for the 20mm Oerlikon but was easily adapted for the Bofors Gun. It could be located on or close to the gun, as required, but by placing the sight on a 'dummy' gun platform more accurate fire for a larger number of mountings (up to six)

In its element, a US Navy 40mm Twin Mount Mark 1.

could be achieved under the control of a single operator. This arrangement formed the basis of the Director Mark 51 which proved to be so successful that about 14,000 directors were produced by the Sperry Gyroscope Company along with about 85,000 Mark 14 sights. There was also a Director Mark 63 which operated with an on-mounting ranging radar but it did not appear until 1945.

The first of many quadruple gun mounts for the Navy was completed during April 1942 and installed on the gunnery training ship *Wyoming* (AG-17) on 22 June 1942. It was originally intended that the quadruple mountings would be the direct replacement for the existing 1.1in quadruple mountings but it was not long before the 40mm quadruple mounting was replacing the 40mm Twin Mount Mark 1 mountings on the larger American warships from cruisers upwards.

The quadruple mounting was the 40mm Quadruple Mount Mark 2. This American-produced mounting was devised at the suggestion of a Mr P. W. Burk, a US Navy Bureau of Ordnance engineer. It was basically two twin-barrel mountings placed side-by-side and 1.524m apart on a single power-driven turntable, parts of the drive system being adapted from components developed for the US Army's 90mm Antiaircraft Gun M1. They were controlled in exactly the same way as the lighter twin mountings and they proved to be formidable air defence weapons. By 1945 the Mark 2 quadruple mounting had been joined by the Mark 4 of which about 100 had been manufactured before the war ended. The Mount Mark 4 was generally lighter than the Mark 2 and employed more powerful drives to impart a faster rate of gun movement.

The demand for multiple naval mountings rose continuously until 1945 when it began to be appreciated that not even the quadruple mounting could neutralise the really determined suicidal attacker at a safe distance. Plans were therefore made to replace them with the 3in 50-calibre (3in/50) gun that could fire proximity-fuzed ammunition. The war ended before any such measures could be introduced and the planned post-war programme was never fully implemented due to a lack of funding.

There was also a single-barrel mounting known as the Mark 3 that was mainly confined to submarines, light patrol vessels and other small craft. It was virtually the same as the land-based gun, complete with air-cooled barrel. By late 1943 surface targets for the US Navy were becoming fewer and further between while at the same time that the threat from attack aircraft was becoming greater. This was especially true in the Pacific where the first

The main component parts of the 40mm Quadruple Mount Mark 2, taken from a 1945 service manual.

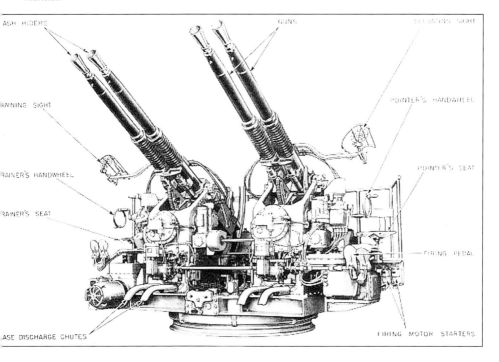

At the ready – the crew of a US Navy 40mm Quadruple Mount Mark 2 await a target.

indications of *Kamikaze* suicide tactics were becoming apparent. Yet the programme to install twin and quadruple Bofors Guns on Navy warships was still not complete. The aircraft threat was deemed so dangerous that it was decided to place Bofors Guns on small warships such as destroyers and other escort vessels. As many such vessels lacked the necessary space or weight capacity for even twin-barrel mountings, many destroyers had their torpedo tube arrays removed and replaced by Mark 3 Mod 0 Army pattern single-barrel guns and upper carriages bolted to the deck. Since these equipments could not utilise any on-board fire-control methods they were used as 'free fire' weapons that were prevented from firing on their own on-board installations by the provision of guard rails beyond which the barrels could not move.

Manually-powered guns and mountings using the usual Army-pattern cranked handles were known as the Mark 3 Mod 0 intended for light craft and supply vessels; there was no provision for power drives. When powered controls operated by a single gun layer were incorporated the guns and mountings became the Mark 3 Mod 4, this model also having provision for manual control in an emergency. The Mark 3 Mod 5 and Mark 3 Mod 6 were both manually-powered guns with waterproofing measures incorporated to allow them to be installed on submarines. The Mark 3 Mod 7 was a post-war, power-driven variant with the single operator housed in an on-carriage cabin. The ammunition feed featured a 48-round drum.

As late as 1977 the US Navy still had twenty-four Mark 3 Mod 0 Army-pattern guns and carriages on the active fleet list.

Mark 3 Bofors Guns were brought back into service during the Vietnam conflict when they were used as deck guns on riverine and coastal patrol craft.

A service manual illustration of a US Navy Mark 3 Mod 4 40mm Bofors Gun showing the main components.

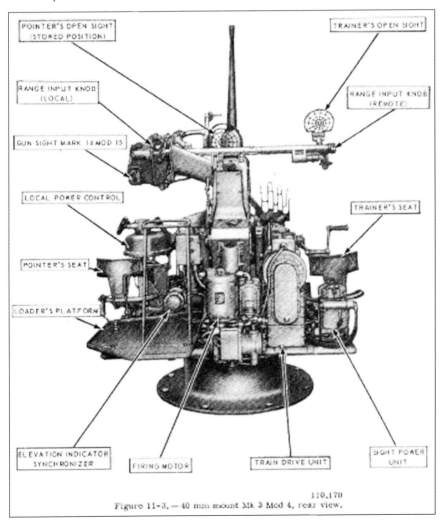

POINTER'S OPEN SIGHT
(STOWED POSITION)

TRAINER'S OPEN SIGHT

RANGE INPUT KNOB
(LOCAL)

RANGE INPUT KNOB
(REMOTE)

GUN SIGHT MARK 14 MOD 15

LOCAL POWER CONTROL

TRAINER'S SEAT

POINTER'S SEAT

LOADER'S PLATFORM

ELEVATION INDICATOR
SYNCHRONIZER

FIRING MOTOR

TRAIN DRIVE UNIT

SIGHT POWER
UNIT

110,170

Figure 11-3. — 40 mm mount Mk 3 Mod 4, rear view.

For this role they were placed under the control of a single crew member on a powered mounting, the Mark 52, complete with a ranging 0.50/12.7mm M2 machine gun. The ammunition supply was provided by a 48-round drum magazine (the same as that fitted to the Mark 3 Mod 7) that proved to be unpopular due to its unreliability and difficulty in handling to the extent that manual loading was often employed instead. These guns saw service in the Persian Gulf during the 1980s.

Back in 1945 most of the larger US Navy warships were liberally festooned with Bofors Guns. Most *Iowa* class battleships had as many as twenty quadruple mountings, the record apparently being held by the aircraft carrier *Saratoga* (CV-3) which carried no less than twenty-three quadruple mountings plus two twin-barrel mountings, making ninety-six barrels in all. The numerous *Essex* class aircraft carriers each had seventeen or eighteen quadruple mountings.

During the latter stages of the war in the Pacific nearly half of all Japanese aircraft shot down were attributed to Bofors Guns. In a bout of post-war book-keeping, the number of rounds fired against aircraft targets were itemised and analysed, differentiating between *Kamikaze* and non-*Kamikaze* targets. The time period was from 1 October 1944 to 31 January 1945. Over that period the Pacific

A hard-working gun crew manning a 40mm Quadruple Mount Mark 2 in the heat of battle.

A 40mm Quadruple Mount Mark 2 on display in the US Navy Museum at the Navy Yard, Washington DC. (T. J. Gander)

Fleet fired 259,057 40mm rounds against *Kamikaze* targets, bringing down 114 of them, an average expenditure of 2,272 rounds per kill. Against non-*Kamikaze* targets, 154,627 rounds were expended, bringing down forty-six aircraft at an average expenditure of 3,361 rounds per kill. This meant that during the period under examination 40mm guns brought down 160 aircraft of all types. Between them all the other types of Navy air defence weapons brought down 227 aircraft.

The first Royal Navy vessel to mount the quadruple Mark 3 40mm mounting was the light cruiser HMS *Phoebe*, provided with three during June 1943. Most of the American guns destined for the Royal Navy were handed over on Lend-Lease ships such as escort carriers. Even the *Queen Mary*, the famous Cunard liner used as a troopship during the war years, was equipped with American-supplied Bofors Guns.

Some of the American guns issued to the Royal Navy remained in service during the 1950s. None of the wartime production gun models are retained by the US Navy today but examples remain with numerous other navies provided with American military aid in the form of warships and guns over a period of decades. A list of navies known to be still employing American-built guns at the end of 2012 is as follows, although it should be noted that within some navies the vessels involved have provision for the guns rather than actually mounting them: Argentina, Bangladesh, Brazil, Chile, Colombia, Croatia, Ecuador, Greece, Iceland, India, Indonesia, Iran, Japan, South Korea, Mexico, Myanmar, Paraguay, Peru, Philippines, Portugal, Taiwan, Thailand, Turkey and Vietnam.

Ammunition

When the Americans decided to adopt the Bofors Gun they managed to overlook one detail. According to the strict guidelines laid down by the US Board of Ordnance the ammunition fired by the Bofors Gun was considered unsafe. The main problem lay with the British-sourced HE round that carried a Bofors-designed point-detonating (PD) nose fuze which the American authorities considered as too sensitive for service aboard ships to the point where it might function before the projectile left the barrel. Since the ammunition was employed by British and other armed forces without apparent cause for concern this point might have been overlooked, as it had to be to get the ammunition into service, but the Ordnance Board insisted on a redesign of the fuze which was considered to be too complicated for mass production anyway.

The problem was soon solved by one R. L. Graumann of the Naval Ordnance Laboratory in Washington, DC. He devised a fuze on which not only was the unwanted sensitivity hazard removed but the fuze could be readily mass produced at low cost while needing a minimum of critical raw materials. This fuze was designated the Mark 27 (Navy) and was so successful that it was adopted by the Army until the even cheaper M71 PD fuze became available. It also went into production on British fuze assembly lines.

As American-produced 40mm ammunition was based on UK-sourced samples, American and British rounds could be freely interchanged between British and American guns, greatly simplifying the ammunition supply situation in many theatres of war. By 1945 the supply situation was also greatly aided by the number of operational ammunition natures being whittled down from numerous marks to just two main types. For the Americans they were the HEI-T Mark 2 and the AP-T M81 or M81A1, the two AP-T types differing only in the method of securing the windshield over the nose of the projectile. The usual training round used for live firing training was the TP-T M91, while the M17 was an inert drill and handling-training round that could not be fired.

For land service the usual propellant case was the M25 manufactured from drawn brass. There was also a M25B1 which was manufactured using steel in place of brass, and another brass case known as the M22 which had a primer thread suitable for British-produced primers. Navy rounds were almost always brass as they were considered less prone to corrosion. All American manufactured cases were filled with 266 grams of a nitrocellulose-based powder propellant of a standard known as FNH (flashless non-hygroscopic). Another American propellant was a powder known as NC 025.

Until December 1942 the main ammunition contractor for 40mm ammunition was the Triumph Explosives Company Inc of Elkton, Maryland. By the end of 1941 a new 40mm loading plant was under construction at Charlotte, New Carolina, and was opened at the end of 1942 with the United States Rubber Company as facility manager. In addition to these sources further 40mm lines were added to facilities already under construction at the Naval Ammunition Depots at Hastings, Nebraska, and McAlester, Oklahoma. During 1943 the National Fireworks Company also became involved in 40mm ammunition production activities at some of its numerous facilities.

The production of 40mm ammunition in the United States was prodigious. Between 1941 and the end of August 1945 no less than 60,474,000 operational 40mm rounds of all types were procured by the US armed forces at a cost later estimated at over US$700,000,000. More rounds than that were actually manufactured and stockpiled. At one stage during late 1943 12,000,000 40mm rounds a month were coming off the production lines.

Gunships

By the late 1950s American-owned Bofors Guns were being gradually phased out of service, apart from some retained for a few small patrol craft, although many were still mounted on inactive Reserve Fleet vessels as late as 1977 (thirty-two twin-barrel mountings and thirty-nine quadruples). Most of the guns withdrawn from service were stockpiled against some future requirement, a requirement that arose when the United States became involved in another war during the late 1960s, this time in Vietnam. During that war the US Air Force pioneered the employment of gunships, transport aircraft converted to carry a multiple machine-gun armament for firing at ground targets, usually at night.

The first gunship was the AC-47D ('Puff the Magic Dragon'), a conversion of a C-47D Dakota to carry a number of 7.62mm M134 Minigun Gatling-type machine guns firing out from one side of the aircraft. The success of this conversion prompted the modification of other aircraft types including the C-130 Hercules transport which became the AC-130. By the time the AC-130 arrived on the scene with its four 20mm M61A1 Vulcan cannon (another Gatling-type weapon) and four 7.62mm Miniguns, the Vietcong were bringing anti-aircraft guns into use to retaliate against the nocturnal gunships and the large and slow AC-130s became vulnerable to their fire. A call was made to equip the AC-130s with more powerful, longer-range weapons that would enable them to stand off from defended targets and away from the defending fire.

By July 1969 a special study group had reported that one possible way to provide this heavier armament was to install two Bofors Guns, with 256 rounds for each gun, in place of two of the Miniguns. This project, known as 'Surprise Package', also provided target illumination systems, a low-light television

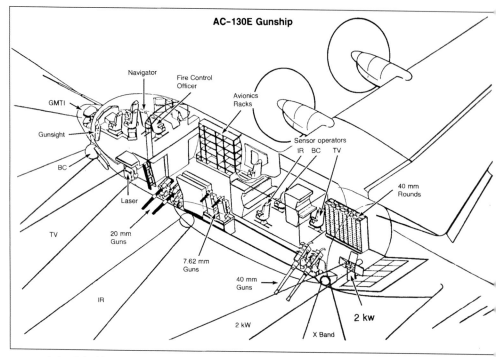

A simplified layout drawing of the weapon installations for an AC-130E Gunship.

system for target acquisition and observation, and infra-red sensors. Approval was given in September 1969 and a C-130A was converted using air-cooled Bofors Guns from US Navy stocks. The first of these gunships was ready for trials at Eglin Air Force Base by the end of October 1969 and by the end of the following month the test aircraft was ready to be flown to South-East Asia for highly successful operational trials.

During the operational trials the main targets were Vietcong supply trucks that operated under cover of darkness through Laos and South Vietnam to supply Vietcong units operating within South Vietnam. Other targets included supply bases and fuel depots and/or pipelines. For the latter a special 40mm projectile lined with a substance known as Misch metal was developed. Misch metal involved the use of a highly pyrophoric metal resembling a cigarette lighter flint that produced a shower of incendiary sparks on impact to enhance the projectile's own incendiary effects, thus enabling fires to start more readily in fuel-related targets.

The success of the early AC-130 trials led to the modification of a number of existing AC-130 gunships to the new AC-130A Bofors Gun configuration. The full armament of an AC-130A, also known as a Gunship 2 or 'Coronet Surprise', was two Bofors Guns, two 20mm M61A1 Vulcan cannon, and two 7.62mm M134 Miniguns.

It was also decided to convert a number of C-130A transports to a new AC-130E Spectre standard which would have the same armament as the AC-130A but with a revised and improved package of sensors, sights and other equipment to enhance target observation. AC-130E Spectres were in service in South-East Asia by early 1971. Once there they, and the AC-130As, maintained constant nocturnal attacks on Vietcong supply lines with a high degree of success.

The 40mm installations on the AC-130A and AC-130E Spectre consisted of two guns side-by-side and close together on fixed mountings, firing through housings in what would normally have been the port side rear of the aircraft cargo compartment, with the barrels pointing at a slight angle downwards. The guns were aimed using a sight located close to the pilot's position. Four-round chargers were carried in racks on the compartment wall opposite the guns and ready for hand-loading into the guns in the usual manner.

One special round developed for the gunships was developed by the AAI Corporation of Hunt Valley, Maryland. Known as the Model 68462, this APFSDS (Armour Penetrating, Fin Stabilised, Discarding Sabot) round had a special armour-penetrating projectile with an arrow-like profile that travelled at a muzzle velocity of approximately 1,335m/s to employ its velocity, mass (the sub-calibre, fin-stabilised penetrator rod weighed 230g) and density to penetrate armoured targets. The tungsten penetrator rod diameter was 11mm

Head-on view of an AC-130H Spectre with the weapon barrels prominent.

and its length-to-diameter ratio was 15:1. This round was tested for US Air Force service as the 40mm PGU-31/B, the first deliveries being made during 1991. It was not accepted for full scale service.

The end of the Vietnam conflict marked the gradual withdrawal of the AC-130A and AC-130E Spectre from operational service but by that time further development had resulted in the AC-130H Spectre with more powerful engines. On this gunship the armament became even more formidable for the two 7.62mm Miniguns were replaced by a 105mm M102 howitzer, selected as it employed a firing system that operated with the barrel out of battery ('soft' or differential recoil) so recoil forces were significantly reduced, as were the weapon and mounting weights. (This 105mm howitzer was also retrofitted to some AC-130E Spectre gunships, replacing one of the Bofors Guns.) The two Bofors Guns were retained and the target acquisition and other associated systems were improved. Flight trials began in 1989 so the first examples were ready for the First Gulf War in 1991. They also participated in operations in Somalia during 2006 and were also used in action during the Panama, former Yugoslavia and Iraq campaigns.

The AC-130H Spectre has been joined by the AC-130U Spooky originally with the same armament as before but with a fully-computerised fire-control, target acquisition and sighting suite that results in one of the most advanced electronic installations ever placed aboard an aircraft. An in-flight refuelling facility was added and air conditioning was provided in the main cargo/armament compartment for crew comfort. Armament modifications have resulted in the installation of a M137A1 105mm howitzer (a modified version of the M102 howitzer) in a semi-flexible mounting, the replacement of the 20mm M61A1 cannon with a 25mm GAU-12/U Gatling, and one Bofors Gun has been retained. There are indications that all existing 20mm, 25mm and 40mm AC-130U Spooky gun installations will, in time, be replaced by a four-gun battery of 30mm Bushmaster II cannon. The flight testing of one such installation began during early 2007.

Brown Water

The gunships were not the only involvement of the 40mm Bofors Gun in the Vietnam conflict. There was also the part it played with the so-called Brown Water Navy that assumed many of the riverine warfare roles formerly adopted by the South Vietnamese forces and before them the French with their *Dinassaut* (see Chapter 6). As before the intention was to use small river craft to patrol rivers and coastal waters to disrupt enemy movements and supply missions.

The Brown Water Navy came into official being in December 1965 when the US Navy adopted a number of craft, some of them 'specials' based on shallow draught landing craft, and a mixture of local river vessels from the South Vietnamese. They also adapted their established operating procedures

One of the specialised (and much modified) landing craft known as monitors operating with the American Brown Water Navy on the Mekong River during the Vietnam War and armed with a Bofors Gun in the forward turret.

largely without alteration. In time a number of light vessels custom-designed for river warfare appeared, including the PBR (Patrol Boat River), with an armament of machine guns and 40mm grenade launchers. The nippy PRBs had glass fibre hulls and frequently required fire support to enable them to operate in hostile areas so this was provided by specialised armed landing craft known as monitors. From time to time the monitors also provided mobile fire support for US Army units operating close to rivers.

It was here that the Bofors Guns reappeared on monitors. Some of them, equipped to act as command and control craft, were armed with a single Bofors Gun mounted in an armoured turret as well as numerous machine guns and grenade launchers. The turret was located forward of the landing craft cargo-carrying area (usually covered by steel plate) over an added-on pointed bow section grafted onto the normally blunt landing ramp section of the landing craft. This improved handling and speed through the water but top speed (powered by two 220hp Detroit Diesels) was only 8.5 knots, or 6 knots over sustained periods. As well as the Bofors Gun the turrets could also carry co-axial 0.30 or 0.50/12.7mm machine guns. Extra protection was often provided by arrays of slat armour. Some vessels had the Bofors Gun replaced by flamethrowers (the 'Zippo' boats) while others had high-pressure water jet projectors that could be very effective in demolishing river bank structures and bunkers. A few monitors mounted a single 105mm howitzer in place of the 40mm gun. Whatever the armament, the usual length of a monitor was about 18.6m.

American Brown Water Navy activities were conducted in some strength and with a high degree of success until 1970 when operations were handed back to the South Vietnamese. Thereafter American interest in riverine warfare lapsed until 2006 when it was decided to form such units again, this time for operations on the River Euphrates and its subsidiaries in Iraq. The Bofors Gun was not scheduled for participation in those proceedings, however.

What must be one of the very last manifestations of the American Bofors Gun saga is this early 2000s attempt to place Second World War-era L/60 Bofors Guns on a much revised pattern of towed carriage developed by and for the Philippine Marine Corps. Apparently only three such equipments were produced. (Gordon Arthur)

Chapter 6

L/60 Licences and Exports

As mentioned in Chapter 1, the flood of export orders that flowed into the AB Bofors workshops at Karlskoga during the late 1930s was such that the in-house manufacturing facilities were soon overwhelmed. In 1935 plans had been made to establish a production line turning out twenty-five guns a month but this provision rapidly became inadequate, with little capacity available for any expansion. Some respite could be achieved by the sale of manufacturing licences, which suited many potential customers for by manufacturing their own guns not only could they learn the very latest design and manufacturing techniques, they could also generate local income and jobs as well as using, in many cases, their own raw materials.

Countries known to have negotiated with AB Bofors for manufacturing licences included the United Kingdom and the United States, two nations where Bofors Gun production was on such a scale that they merit their own chapters (see Chapters 5 and 6). Other licensee nations included Austria, Belgium, Czechoslovakia, Denmark, Finland, France, Greece, Norway, Poland and Portugal. As will be outlined later in this chapter, some of these countries were destined never to actually manufacture guns. Into this latter category came Czechoslovakia, Denmark, France, Portugal and Greece. For various reasons the latter two eventually manufactured only 40mm ammunition, although not until well after 1945, by which time neither country had any need to manufacture their own guns. In addition to this list of licence producers, the 40mm Bofors Gun also touched the fortunes of other nations without official sanction from AB Bofors, namely Germany, Japan, the Soviet Union and the People's Republic of China.

Most of the licence arrangements entered into between AB Bofors and the various interested concerns involved a set, or sets, of working drawings, perhaps a few special machine tools, technical information and, in most cases, technical or training assistance in the form of Bofors personnel who remained with the licensee for an arranged period while production lines were being established. Most licences involved a down payment for permission to proceed plus the payment of royalty fees on each gun manufactured, although there were variations on this theme. Some contracts also specified who the end users could or could not be, thereby specifying areas where export restrictions might apply.

The first export guns, the five twin-barrel naval mountings ordered by The Netherlands to provided air defence for the cruiser De Ruyter, *sunk in February 1942 while defending the Dutch East Indies.*

One of the staple products that formed pre-war AB Bofors export sales was this model of twin-barrelled naval mounting, complete with a manually-stabilised system operated from a position in front of the mounting.

Two of the very first licence production agreements made during 1935 became important during the pre-war and war years, namely those agreements with Poland and Hungary. They will be dealt with first.

Poland

The first Bofors Guns sold to Poland were six twin-barrel naval mountings purchased in 1934, two during May and four in December. At least two of these twin-barrel mountings were of the 43-calibre type (see Chapter 1). These two mountings (40mm/43 M37) were installed on the destroyer *Blyskawica* ('Lightning'), one of the two *Grom* ('Thunder') class destroyers delivered to Poland from the United Kingdom in 1937. To prevent the likelihood of their being lost to the Germans, as soon as hostilities commenced in September 1939 these two destroyers, with other Polish vessels, sailed to the United Kingdom where they redeployed and operated alongside the Royal Navy. The *Grom* was lost at Narvik on 5 May 1940 but the *Blyskawica* served throughout the war years, acquiring the pennant number H34. At some stage the vessel's L/43 guns were replaced by standard L/60 guns that did not require the special low propellant charge ammunition demanded by the L/43 barrels. It is known that all the original on-board ammunition had been expended as early as May 1940. If they had not already been replaced by then the guns would certainly have been replaced during a refit carried out in mid-1941 when the original main armament of 120mm/50 Bofors M34/36 guns was replaced by British 4in guns. The *Blyskawica* returned to Poland after the war and is now a museum ship at Gdynia.

Apart from the *Grom* and the *Blyskawica*, other Polish Navy vessels known to have been provided with Bofors Guns in 1939 included the minelayer *Gryf* ('Griffon', two twin-barrel mountings), and the submarines *Orzel* ('Eagle') and *Sęp* ('Vulture'), each with two guns. A lack of differentiation between barrel lengths in accessible surviving references makes it impossible to determine how many of these latter installations might have had L/43 rather than L/60 barrels.

In December 1935 the first order for sixty land service guns was placed with AB Bofors and at the same time a licence was obtained to manufacture guns and ammunition. The Polish guns were produced at the Polish State Arsenal at Starachowice, with the immediate output being directed toward supplying the Polish Army. By the time the Germans invaded Poland on 1 September 1939 the Polish Army had received 306 land service Bofors Guns distributed among thirty-five batteries.

The Polish designation for their Bofors Guns was *40mm armata przeciwlotnicza wzor 36*. At one stage the Bofors Gun was considered to be suitable for deployment as an anti-tank weapon but in the event the Polish Army adopted the Bofors 37mm Model 1934 anti-tank gun instead. During the September 1939 campaign Bofors Guns were employed as anti-armour weapons

A battery of Polish Army Bofors Guns coming into action during a training exercise.

Despite its poor quality this photograph is unusual in that it shows the Polish-manufactured version of the Browning Automatic Rifle (7.92mm Reczny Karabin Maszynowy wz 28) strapped to the barrel for use as a sub-calibre training gun.

firing locally-developed armour-piercing (AP) ammunition, but in a secondary role rather than as a dedicated weapon.

Most of the Polish guns ended up in German hands after September 1939 but at that time the Germans did not retain them for their own purposes. They considered the war would not last long and that German resources already to hand were sufficient to meet all forecast needs. Sixty captured Polish guns were therefore sold to Sweden during 1940 (see Chapter 3). Later that same year another ninety-two captured guns, many of them ex-Polish, were sold to Finland by Germany at a time when Finland was deemed as coming under the German sphere of influence (see later in this chapter).

The Poles also licence-manufactured Bofors Guns for export. In all some 168 guns were exported to the United Kingdom, France, Romania and The Netherlands. Plans were made to sell an unknown quantity of guns to Spain to participate in the Spanish Civil War on the Nationalist side but only a few, enough to equip a static coastal battery, actually arrived before the war ended. However, the Poles also supplied the Republicans with twenty-four guns and 50,000 rounds of ammunition in mid-1938, and there are indications that forty more guns were ordered. Whatever the case, the delivered guns eventually fell into Nationalist hands and were retained by the coast artillery and concentrated around the northern port of El Ferrol for many years after 1939. As late as 1958 there were still fourteen of these guns in Spanish Army service, three static and eleven on field carriages.

Some Polish-manufactured guns intended for The Netherlands and the United Kingdom were stranded in Sweden after January 1939 due to the imposition of Swedish neutrality laws, even though the commencement of conflict was still months in the future. They ended up with the Swedish armed forces (see Chapter 3), but twenty-four guns had been delivered to their intended recipients before the neutrality law restrictions were fully applied.

The Poles made some modifications to the Bofors Gun carriage, the most significant being the removal of all fittings that involved receiving fire control from a central point. This trend towards independent operation under field conditions even extended to some guns lacking the Polish equivalent of the Bofors Corrector Sight. Polish technicians developed some enhancements to this accessory but the sight was sometimes removed from the mounting and in some cases it was never even installed. Other Polish engineering changes in the planning stage were destined never to see the light of day. They involved a general simplification of the entire gun and carriage with a view to making both easier to manufacture and maintain. This work was far from completion when the Germans invaded.

One further Polish modification to the Bofors Gun carriage was the so-called 'semi-permanent' version. As its name implies this was primarily intended for static emplacements but it was possible to transport the gun and carriage by

One of the few surviving illustrations of a Polish 'semi-permanent' mounting taken in the aftermath of the 1939 campaign.

towing it on a single two-wheeled axle. Once at the selected site the axle and wheels were removed to allow the gun and carriage to rest on three stabiliser legs. When on the move these legs were arranged to point to the rear, the same direction as the barrel. Exactly how many of these 'semi-permanent' carriages were produced is not known but it cannot have been many. Illustrations of them are now rare.

The British armed forces received a number of Polish-manufactured Bofors Guns between 1937 and 1939 and many of these saw action during the early war years. Some of them ended up in German hands after the Battle of France during May and June 1940.

Hungary

The Hungarians obtained their first production licence in 1935 without apparently obtaining a gun from AB Bofors for the usual trials and familiarisation. The following year they obtained a further licence to manufacture guns originally ordered from AB Bofors but which had to be sub-contracted as the Swedish concern was not in a position to meet demand. A further licence to manufacture ammunition was negotiated during 1935.

In Hungary the Bofors Gun (*36M*) was manufactured by MAVAG (*Magyar Királyi Államvasutak Gépgyára*), the Hungarian State Railways factory. The main MAVAG centre was at Diosgyor and until mid-1943 all Hungarian artillery production, including artillery other than the Bofors Gun, was centred there. After mid-1943 production was dispersed to a consortium of twenty-two workshops where gun and carriage sub-assemblies were manufactured using jigs provided by MAVAG. Final assembly and testing continued to be centred at Diosgyor. By March 1944 production totals had reached forty guns a month.

MAVAG production was primarily directed to the Hungarian *Honvedelmi Miniszterium* (HM), the Ministry of Defence, who controlled weapon supplies for the Hungarian armed forces. Although final production figures cannot be confirmed, records indicate that the HM received at least 767 guns on field mountings, 135 guns for mounting on *40M Nimrod* self-propelled mountings (see Chapter 10), and thirty guns for installing on *Me 210 Ca* aircraft (see below). In addition to the above, 440 spare barrels were also supplied. MAVAG also delivered at least 262 guns to the German armed forces (including seventeen originally ordered by The Netherlands) and 735 spare barrels. During 1944 an uncertain number of guns were passed by the Germans to their Romanian allies who knew their equipments as the *36 M könnyü légvédelmi ágyú*.

MAVAG technicians demonstrating one of the first Bofors Guns manufactured by them for the Hungarian Army.

A Hungarian Army Bofors Gun crew ready for action.

The Netherlands ordered fifty guns from MAVAG after their Swedish and Polish sources had been cut off but only ten guns had been delivered before the German invasion of the Low Countries in May 1940. Thirty-six guns went to Finland and at least another thirty guns were destined for the United Kingdom via Sweden. More guns were sent to Egypt (thirty-two), China (eight guns for the defence of Canton, 1937) and Latvia, the latter guns eventually ending up in Soviet hands. During early 1940 twenty-five guns were ordered by Norway but, although the guns were completed, their delivery was prevented by the German invasion of Norway in April 1940. Components as well as complete guns were supplied to AB Bofors as part of their contract for the Swedish Army. MAVAG records mention at least 1,276 completed guns although the full total was probably in excess of 1,300.

Hungarian involvement in the Bofors Gun story was thus very important numerically but the Hungarians were also involved in the technical development of the gun. One Hungarian innovation was the introduction of improved gearing that almost doubled the rate at which the gun barrel could be traversed.

Another Hungarian innovation was an on-carriage predictor sight known as the *34/38 M Juhasz-Gamma Loelemkepzo* manufactured by R T Gamma of Budapest. This was a mechanical analogue calculator similar to the Bofors Corrector Sight but it involved inertial compensation and an optical system that projected a graticule onto the reflex sight glass. All the on-carriage sight operator had to do was enter the target range obtained from an optical rangefinder off the carriage and the predictor sight did the rest. This sight was fitted to all field carriages produced by MAVAG for the Hungarian armed forces but was not installed on most export guns so is now little known outside Hungary. However, MAVAG-manufactured guns that ended up in Finland did have this sight installed.

The thirty modified Bofors Guns supplied for air-to-ground installation on Hungarian Air Force (*Magyar Kiralyi Legiero*) *Me 210 Ca* strike aircraft were the first of their kind to be employed as aircraft armament. The project was part of the Hungarian defence industry's attempts to establish an indigenous aircraft industry. Licence production of the *Bf 109G* fighter led to a *Me 210C* production line at the *Dunai Repülögépgyár* (Danube Aircraft Factory) at Tököl and some of these aircraft were modified to act as tank destroyers. By most accounts the twin-engined *Me 210* was one of the German aircraft industry's least successful ventures but the Hungarians found it serviceable enough. On the *Me 210 Ca* the gun was installed under the aircraft nose with the muzzle protruding some way forward from the housing enclosing the gun. Only a few aircraft were fitted

The layout of the 34/38 M Juhasz-Gamma Loelemkepzo *predictor sight mounted on a Bofors Gun sent to Finland.*
(T. J. Gander)

with the 40mm gun and they saw action on the Eastern Front during 1944. No details of the installation or ammunition feed involved appear to have survived.

One offshoot of the Hungarian involvement with the Bofors Gun was the adaptation of the machinery for manufacturing gun barrels to be employed as anti-tank gun barrels. Prior to 1939 the Hungarian Army obtained a number of 3.7cm PaK 35/36 anti-tank guns from Rheinmetall-Borsig AG of Germany but by 1940 more such guns were required at a time when the German defence industry was in no position to supply them. As a result MAVAG machine tools normally engaged in manufacturing 40mm gun barrels were employed to bore out and rifle 40mm 51-calibre anti-tank gun barrels to be mounted on copies of the German carriage. The result became the *40mm 36M* and served until the Hungarian Army dropped out of the war during early 1945. There was one further manifestation of this gun as a tank gun. In 1941 the *40mm 36M* barrel was placed on the mounting for a licence-manufactured *Škoda A17* tank gun to create the *40mm 41M*, the main armament of the *Turan I* tank. All these MAVAG derived anti-armour guns fired the same ammunition as the 40mm Bofors air-defence guns.

Austria

Austria was one of the first countries to negotiate a manufacturing licence for the Bofors Gun and its ammunition. That was in 1935, the same year that the Austrian Army also ordered eight guns direct from AB Bofors to equip the cadre of the Austrian anti-aircraft corps that was to be formed at Kagran during 1936. As signed, the licence permitted the manufacture of 132 guns and their ammunition, but in the event the final production total was far less. Although the Army had plans to organise the first thirty-six guns into six six-gun batteries, at the time of the 1938 *Anschluss* only sixteen had been completed and fielded. A further twenty-six guns were almost complete and were finished after the German occupation so the Austrian gun total was fifty-two, eight delivered from Sweden and forty-four of local manufacture. In addition, 48,000 rounds of ammunition had been ordered from the *Enserfelder-Metallwerken*, although only 8,000 rounds had been delivered before the Germans marched into Austria.

The guns were manufactured in Austria at two centres. Much of the barrel manufacture and heavy component fabrication was carried out by the *Gebrüder Böhler* at their Kapfenberg steelworks. The carriage and the final assembly and testing were completed at the *Österreichischen Staatsfabrik*, the state-owned arsenal in Vienna. The production rate was relatively sedate as the modest resources of the Vienna arsenal were also assembling infantry guns and mountain artillery.

Once in service the Austrian guns became the *4cm M.36-Fliegerabwehr maschinenkanone (4cm M.36 FlaMKa)*. They were virtually identical to the Bofors Model 1934 other than they were provided with reflex sight units from

An Austrian Army 4cm M.36-Fliegerabwehrmaschinenkanone *on tow behind a Steyr 340 6 x 4 truck.*

Goerz of Bratislava in Czechoslovakia, and for some reason the firing pedal was on the right-hand side only. The Goerz sights were coupled to a mechanical analogue computer that operated along much the same lines as the Bofors Course and Speed Sight.

The Austrian guns were destined for only a short service life with their original owners. After the March 1938 *Anschluss* the guns, along with the rest of the personnel and equipment of the Austrian armed forces, were assimilated into the German fold as the 4cm FlaK (ö), although by May 1939 that designation had been altered to 4cm FlaK 28. It soon transpired that the Bofors Guns did not fit into any convenient slot in the German armoury. They were therefore set aside until some use could be found for them and that use came in 1939 when forty-two were sold to Sweden (see Chapter 3) in exchange for raw materials. In their turn, thirty of the 'Swedish' guns were later passed 'on loan' to Finland to take part in the 1939–1940 Winter War.

Belgium

Belgium was among the very first customers for the 40mm gun as the Belgian Government ordered its first eight guns from AB Bofors in August 1935 with another twenty being ordered in February the following year, all of them intended for issue to defence forces in the Belgian Congo (*La Force Publique*). A licence agreement to manufacture Bofors Guns and ammunition was taken out in 1936, the plan being that production would be undertaken by *Fabrique Nationale* (FN) in their facilities at Herstal, Liége. The intention was apparently part of a scheme to diversify FN output away from the production of small arms, motor cars and motorcycles and expand the national export capability base, for a fair proportion of the guns produced by FN were destined for export to France and Norway. There were plans to export guns to the United Kingdom but those plans were overtaken by the start of the war, a war in which Belgium declared itself to be neutral. There were also plans to export guns to Czechoslovakia but the German take-over of that country in 1938 and 1939 put an end to that project (see below).

According to a history of FN the initial reluctance on the part of the Belgian Army to obtain more Bofors Guns (due mainly to other defence spending commitments) was eventually overcome so by the time the Germans invaded some 150 guns had been accepted. At least thirty-six guns were deployed by the field army and eighteen were allotted for airfield defence. More guns were emplaced around the major Belgian population centres, the largest number (twelve) going to Brussels. Other defended areas included Antwerp (ten), Liége (eight), Ghent (six), Namur (six) and Charleroi (six). These totals were clearly deemed insufficient, since during 1939 an order was placed with AB Bofors for a further 106 land service guns, an order destined to come to naught.

After May 1940, what was left of the Bofors production line at FN was apparently of little interest to the Germans, mainly because, again according to the FN account, most of the machine tools used on the line had been dispersed to other manufacturing centres all over Belgium as a precaution against any German invasion. The line was not fully reconstituted and only limited Bofors Gun production, apart from a restricted number of spare parts, ensued in Belgium.

In about 1980 FN proposed an L/60 update programme involving an Italian *Officene Galileo* computerised sight, an on-carriage power generator and an Oerlikon-pattern drum magazine holding thirty-two rounds, plus some other gun and carriage enhancements. A prototype was modified accordingly but the project lapsed due to the company experiencing financial difficulties leading to a period of product rationalisation.

Czechoslovakia

Any account of the Bofors Gun's association with Czechoslovakia is bound to be short. A licence agreement to manufacture guns in Czechoslovakia was not completed until just before the Germans took over the nation's Sudetenland defences as one result of the Munich Agreement of September 1938. The period of upheaval that followed the loss of so much national territory was such that there was no chance of a Bofors Gun production line being established. In March 1939 the Germans took over what was left of Czechoslovakia anyway, so plans to obtain guns direct from FN in Belgium were again fruitless.

Denmark

Although the transaction does not feature in any readily-available reference, during 1937 the Danish Navy ordered ten 40mm Bofors Guns to form the main armament of their five submarines of the planned 'H' class. By 1939 seven of these guns (*40mm rekylkanon L/60 M/37*) were mounted on four submarines of the *Havmanden* class. The *Havmanden* (H1), *Havfruen* (H2) and *Havkalen* (H3) had two guns each while the *Havhesten* (H4), still not fully operational in 1939, was provided with only one. (A planned fifth submarine was not completed.) During 1940 the number of Bofors Guns per submarine was reduced to just one each, at least two of the guns so released being assigned to the coast defence ship *Peder Skram*. Two guns were apparently due to be installed on the coast defence ship *Niels Juel* but as far as can be determined this never happened. All these guns became non-operational on 29 August 1943 when most of the Danish fleet was scuttled by their crews rather than allow the vessels to pass into German hands.

In addition to the above Denmark arranged a licence from AB Bofors to produce Bofors Guns for the Royal Danish Navy (*Sövernet*) for incorporation into coast defences. Two statically-mounted guns were ordered direct from AB Bofors during 1939, apparently at around the same time as the manufacturing licence agreement was signed, but they were never delivered. The planned licence production never took place as the Germans marched into Denmark, unopposed, on 9 April 1940.

After 1949 Bofors Guns once again featured in the Danish inventory, this time in the form of ex-American guns supplied as part of the NATO Military Aid Programme (MAP). They became the *40mm maskinkanon M/36*. Among the guns supplied were twin-barrel naval mountings, not all of which ended up on Danish Navy vessels. A significant number of the MAP guns were diverted to the air defence of various fortifications and coastal defence installations. In 1957 the Danish Coast Artillery had no less than forty-three twin-barrel mountings in static emplacements to defend the following locations:

```
Bangsbo Fort (6)
Lynetten (4)
Middlgrund Fort (9)
Flak Fort (6)
Dragør Fort (3)
Kongelundsfort (3)
Stevns Fort (6)
Langelands Fort (6).
```

The Netherlands

As mentioned elsewhere, The Netherlands were among the first customers for the Bofors Gun and they maintained a steady rate of orders with AB Bofors throughout the late 1930s. The first five twin-barrel, manually-stabilised naval

An AB Bofors archive photograph of a factory-fresh 40mm Bofors Gun intended for export to The Netherlands.

mountings delivered from Karlskoga were mounted on the cruiser *De Ruyter*, later sunk during February 1942 while defending the Dutch East Indies.

A manufacturing licence was not negotiated until 1939, by which time deliveries had begun to be affected by the Swedish neutrality laws. Only twelve land service guns had been delivered from Karlskoga before deliveries ceased and by then manufacturing facilities had yet to be established in The Netherlands.

It was therefore time for the usual recourse of ordering Bofors Guns from Poland and Hungary. The Polish order was virtually an open request to provide as many guns as possible but just twenty-four had been delivered by the time the Germans invaded Poland. A total of fifty guns were ordered from Hungary but again the German intervention of May 1940 interrupted deliveries after only ten guns had arrived in The Netherlands. Thus in May 1940 the home-based Dutch armed forces had just forty-five land service guns available, organised into fifteen three-gun batteries, all of them subsequently lost or captured. The guns delivered to the Dutch East Indies were either destroyed or fell into Japanese hands.

After 1945 the Dutch armed forces acquired Bofors L/60 guns of British,

Canadian and United States origin. By 1954 they held 214 guns of British manufacture plus fifty-four guns from Canada (many on truck chassis) and 200 guns from the United States.

The 1939 Dutch term for their Bofors Guns was *40mm Tegen Luchdoelen Bofors*. While the land service guns did not make much impact on the events of May 1940 the Dutch naval guns were to gain an importance out of all proportion to their numbers. It was a Dutch naval mounting that was to give rise to the Royal Navy's Hazemeyer mounting (see Chapter 4) while Dutch guns (and their working drawings) played a major role in the adoption of the Bofors Gun by the US Navy (see Chapter 5).

Finland

Finland took an early interest in the 40mm Bofors Gun but it was not until December 1937 that a manufacturing licence was purchased along with an order for a single land service gun. The intention was that local production would be undertaken at the state-owned armaments factory (the *Valtion Tykkitehdas* (VTT) at Jyväskylä) but the commencement of production was beset by delays, as was the delivery of the single gun ordered from Sweden.

During December 1938 an order for a further thirty land service guns was placed with AB Bofors but by then there was no prospect of that order being delivered direct from Karlskoga. However, AB Bofors were able to deliver a

*One of the single Bofors Gun mounts on the Finnish Navy's coast defence vessels (*Panssarlaiva) Ilmarinen *or* Väinämöinen.

small batch of naval guns, two twin-barrel and four single-barrel mountings. By the time the Winter War began in late 1939 these guns had been delivered and installed on the Finnish Navy's two most powerful warships, the coast defence vessels *Ilmarinen* and *Väinämöinen* where they replaced Vickers 2-pounder Pom-Poms. Each vessel had one twin-barrelled mounting and two singles. During the Winter War these two vessels guarded the Åland Islands and later provided anti-aircraft cover for the port of Turku. The *Ilmarinen* was sunk by sea mines on 13 September 1941 while the *Väinämöinen* survived the war only to be ceded to the Soviet Union as part of war reparations during 1947.

To return to the pre-war period, back in 1939 the international situation was worsening and Finland's leaders became painfully aware that trouble loomed with the neighbouring Soviet Union over a number of territorial issues. By the time the so-called Winter War started in late November 1939 the Finnish Bofors Gun holdings stood at fifty-three.

Those fifty-three guns came from a variety of sources, mainly Sweden and Hungary, the guns from Hungary barely making the journey due to German interventions. Forty-two guns were ordered from MAVAG of which twenty-four arrived during December 1939. Another batch of twelve was delayed by the Germans but released to arrive in January 1940. All these guns had the *34/38 M Juhasz-Gamma Loelemkepzo* predictor sight unit as issued to the Hungarian armed forces. The final six guns ordered from MAVAG never reached Finland.

The bulk of the Swedish guns did not come direct from AB Bofors but from Swedish Army stocks, along with 100,000 rounds of ammunition. In an unusual deviation from the traditional national stance of neutrality the guns were 'loaned' by Sweden to Finland on such a scale that by the time the Winter War ended in March 1940 the Finnish Bofors Gun total was about 100. During 1941 at least four guns became part of the armament of Armoured Trains Nos 1 and 2 (*Pansarijuna 1 ja 2*), with two or three guns for each train. Some components of *Pansarijuna 1* survive at the *Pansarmuseo* (Tank Museum) at Parola in Finland.

Some eighteen of the guns from Sweden were apparently originally ordered by the United Kingdom but, stranded in Sweden by that nation's neutrality stance they were released by the British Government to be passed to Finland along with 10,000 rounds of ammunition. Some of these guns, including naval models, did not arrive in Finland until after 1945. The full total of Bofors Guns delivered from Sweden to Finland totalled seventy-six, along with 144,000 rounds of ammunition.

The March 1940 total was later enlarged by the purchase of ninety-two guns from Germany, one result of the so-called Interim Peace Agreement between Finland and Germany. The guns involved in this purchase were booty from several sources including forty-two that originated in Austria, the remainder coming from The Netherlands and Poland. By 1945 the number of Bofors Guns in Finnish service had grown to 288.

All this varied procurement was necessary because the planned licence production by VTT did not commence until 1941 and even then the output was slow and sporadic, mainly due to the erratic availability of the necessary raw materials and the burden of other weapons-related repair and manufacturing work at VTT. Just twelve guns were completed during 1941, forty-three during 1942, none during 1943, fourteen during 1944 and six more in 1945 (i.e. after what the Finns called the 'Continuation War' had ended), making a grand total of seventy-five 'Finnish' Bofors Guns. Steel blanks for the barrels were supplied by Lokomo Oy at Tampere while the Turku shipyards of Crichton-Vulcan Oy supplied components for the carriages. Ammunition for Finnish guns (and for post-war export sales) was eventually manufactured by Sako Ltd at Jyväskylä and/or Tampella of Tampere (now Patria Vammas Oy).

During the war years the Finnish armed forces employed the cover-all designation of *40 ItK/38* for all their assorted Bofors Guns but after 1945 the logistic situation was clarified by the issue of differentiating designations. They were as follows:

40 ItK/35 B. Former Netherlands guns manufactured by either AB Bofors or in Poland.
40 ItK/36 B. Bofors-manufactured Model 1934 – same as Swedish Army Model 1936.
40 ItK/36 BK2. Naval twin-barrel static mounting manufactured by AB Bofors.
40 ItK/37 B. Naval single-barrel static mounting manufactured by AB Bofors.
40 ItK/38 B. Licence-manufactured model from VTT.
40 ItK/38 U. Hungarian guns from MAVAG.
40 ItK/38 S. Guns purchased from Germany of Austrian and Polish origin.
40 ItK/39 B. Guns released by the British in 1939 and after 1945. Both land service and naval models involved.
40 ItK/36-59 B. Updated variant introduced from late 1959 onwards (see following paragraph).

The Finnish L/60 guns soldiered on until well into the 1990s, the service lives of some being prolonged by an updating programme introduced during 1959 and mainly involving the installation of the Italian *Officine Galileo P36* computerised sighting system incorporating laser rangefinding, and the addition of hydraulically-powered drives. Power was produced by a battery charged by an on-carriage generator driven by a 6hp Lambretta two-stroke engine. This updated model was known as the *40 ItK/36-59 B*, the conversions being based on the *40 ItK/38 S* pattern guns. A total of forty-three conversions were made, the final example being issued in 1964. The last examples of these updated guns were not officially retired until 2000.

France

During the 1930s the French ordnance industry was kept in being by limited government orders intended to either keep existing production facilities functioning or to gradually prepare for the future. Light air defence guns were included in these small-scale programmes with guns having calibres of 13.2mm, 20mm, 25mm and 37mm all being produced in small batches. From this group a 37mm gun (*le canon de 37mm contre avions Schneider*) was selected to be the standard French light anti-aircraft gun although series production was not planned until some time in 1941, mainly due to a shortage of suitable production facilities. Only twenty 37mm guns were available in May 1940.

In September 1937 the French Army decided to forestall future shortages of light air defence guns by ordering thirty-four 40mm guns from AB Bofors, and at the same time they purchased a licence to manufacture more guns and ammunition in France. These actions were remarkable in that they marked the first procurement of a foreign artillery piece by the French since the seventeenth century. The main problem for the French Army was that although they had the licence they did not have a suitable production facility to manufacture the guns, and there was no immediate prospect of one becoming available.

In the long term the Bofors Gun was never manufactured in France. The French Army obtained the relatively few guns they did own in 1940 either direct from AB Bofors or from the line established by FN in Belgium.

There were two French versions of the Bofors Gun. The first was the *Canon Automatique de 40mm modèle 1938*; twenty-eight were procured to be organised into seven batteries. The guns involved were virtually identical to the Swedish Model 1934 while a second batch of fourteen became the *Canon Automatique de 40mm modèle 1939*. This second batch differed from the first in having a different *Précision* sighting system. By May 1940 all forty-two guns formed part of the air defences around Paris.

None of the French Bofors Guns appear to have survived the events of May and June 1940. At the time of the French collapse there were plans to manufacture 100 Bofors Guns a month but exactly where and how had not been determined before the entire scheme was terminated by the German invasion.

From 1942 onwards Free French forces were supplied with 448 Lend-Lease Bofors Guns manufactured in the USA. Many of these guns served in Indo-China during the years following the Second World War, some of them mounted on trucks (see Chapter 10) while others became part of the armament of improvised armoured trains. In both roles the guns were deployed against ground targets since the Viet Minh opposition did not have any aircraft.

Bofors Guns also served the French in another capacity during their Indo-China campaigns. As waterways were often of more use as transport routes than the few roads available, they became involved in the French campaigns against the Viet Minh insurgents as supply and reinforcement routes, acting as a way of taking conflict to the enemy, and for the constant patrolling to prevent insurgents using the waterways themselves. Almost as soon as the French returned to the area in 1945 Army and Navy personnel combined to form a number of *ad hoc* units that used rivers and coastal waters to police and patrol large areas.

The vessels involved with these *ad hoc* units were gradually grouped into more formal flotillas known as *Divisions navales d'assaut*, soon generally known as *Dinassaut*. By 1954 there were ten *Dinassaut* units based at various locations around Indo-China and equipped with a motley array of vessels. The bulk of them were former British and American landing craft of various sizes to suit the shallow inland waters involved but also included were barges, motorised junks, light launches, and so on. Most of the vessels received a measure of armoured protection plus armament in one form or another ranging from former Japanese machine guns and cannon up to 75mm field guns. Included on some vessels were 40mm Bofors Guns but it has to be stressed that all the various armament installations were dependent on availability and mountings could vary accordingly. Most Bofors Guns were mounted on standard naval mountings with, perhaps, an added gun shield, although land service mountings were sometimes encountered. The vessels so involved, usually the larger tank-landing craft, were often designated as monitors.

When the French left Indo-China in 1954 these riverine combat vessels were handed over to the South Vietnamese Navy who continued to operate them for many years and even added to their scope and functions. It was the South Vietnamese who maintained the riverine combat and mobility techniques learned by the French so that when the Americans became involved in Viet-Nam during the 1960s they were in a position to rapidly assume what was for them a novel form of warfare (see Chapter 5).

Norway

Norway was traditionally one of AB Bofors' best customers for military hardware so when the 40mm Bofors Gun first appeared they soon took note of its potential. Their first involvement with the gun came with an order for three single-barrel naval guns placed during April 1936. The guns were intended to be the main anti-aircraft gun armament of the three torpedo boats of the *Sleipner* class, each vessel having a single Bofors Gun. The *Sleipner* was one of the Royal Norwegian Navy vessels that escaped to the United Kingdom after the 1940 Norway campaign and served on with the Allies throughout the war. Each of the three follow-on vessels of the *Odin* class (regarded by the Norwegian Navy as part of the *Sleipner* class) should have had a single 40mm gun but they were not armed when the Germans invaded in 1940. After 1945 the *Sleipner* and the surviving *Gyller* were rebuilt as frigates, each with two 40mm guns, as were the three *Odin* class vessels.

1939, and a team of Norwegian gunners demonstrate their newly-acquired Bofors Gun.

Returning to the pre-war years, a Norwegian manufacturing licence involving Bofors Guns and ammunition was signed in July 1937. As it would take time to establish a new production line, the Royal Norwegian Ministry of Defence placed an order for eight guns with AB Bofors in April 1938. This time the order was for land service guns for the Army, to be known as the *Luftvernmaskinkanon/60 M/1937 (40mm Lvmk/60 M1937)*, a designation later applied to all Norwegian L/60 land service guns, whatever their origin.

The eight-gun order was switched by AB Bofors to FN of Belgium. When they arrived in Norway four of the guns were issued to a light anti-aircraft battery at Narvik in the north of the country, while the other four were transferred to the Coast Artillery. Two of the latter guns were used to defend the Drøbak Narrows and the other two defended Rauøy Fort in the Oslofjord.

At the same time as the eight-gun order was arranged a further order was placed, this time by a civilian concern. The concern was *Norsk Hydro*, a large industrial and power-generating conglomerate, which ordered ten guns on field mountings, the order once again being sub-contracted by AB Bofors to FN of Belgium. *Norsk Hydro* used their guns to defend a few of their prime facilities, four guns being deployed to Rjukan where they defended the famous heavy water production plant at Vemork (the only such plant in Europe at that time). Two *Norsk Hydro* guns defended an industrial site at Herøya and the other four ended up at an anti-aircraft gunnery school at Staven. Only the latter four guns retained their field carriages, the other guns being emplaced in fixed positions. Although these ten guns were paid for by *Norsk Hydro* they were crewed by the military.

By 1939 the Norwegian Bofors Gun production line was still not ready so as an interim measure the Norwegians placed an urgent repeat order for twenty-two guns with AB Bofors in January 1940, an order later increased to twenty-five. That order was transferred to MAVAG who were able to process the order rapidly by diverting guns from another customer. By 15 March 1940 the first batch of ten guns for Norway was ready for test at the MAVAG factory. They were never delivered for the Germans invaded Norway on 9 April 1940.

By that date Norwegian production was just beginning. It was located at the *Kongsberg Våpenfabrik* in the Buskerud district, where it took nearly thirty months to prepare the line, a line much larger than that establishment had ever been called upon to organise. A batch of forty guns was planned, to be followed by another forty, Norwegian technicians being sent to AB Bofors at Karlskoga to train and prepare for the task. Production plans were that the first four guns would be delivered by the Spring of 1940, sixteen more by the end of July 1940, and the remaining twenty by November 1940. The second forty would follow later at an undetermined date.

The German invasion interrupted those plans just as the first four Norwegian-manufactured guns were almost complete. For a few months the line remained dormant until the Germans decided to restart production. Repairs were also to be carried out on damaged Bofors Guns that had fallen into German hands from various sources. The *Kongsberg Våpenfabrik* thus became the *Waffenfabrik Kongsberg* as the Germans arranged to manufacture new guns at a rate of twelve a month, later rising to a planned thirty a month. The Norwegian staff did their best to slow things down, the actual output being an average of just five guns a month. Most of the resulting guns were issued to the *Kriegsmarine*.

All work ended abruptly on 17 September 1943 when a raid by the Norwegian Resistance destroyed the facilities (and four completed guns) so thoroughly that no further production was possible for the remainder of the war. The total output of the *Waffenfabrik Kongsberg* was about 200 guns (to which repaired and refurbished guns should be added), each gun costing the German war economy a nominal 47,000 *Reichsmarks*. This cost was worked out partially

The Bofors Guns seen mounted here aboard a German cruiser may have been manufactured at the Waffenfabrik Kongsberg *in Norway.*

on the assumption that each gun demanded 6,000 man hours to manufacture. (The equivalent German 3.7cm FlaK 36 demanded 4,200 man hours and cost 24,000 *Reichsmarks*.)

When the German forces in Norway surrendered in May 1945 there were large numbers of German 4cm FlaK 28 guns with varying origins scattered around the nation. The Norwegian armed forces simply took them over to the extent that a 1948 Army inventory mentioned a holding of 164 guns, all of them ex-German. That number was soon enlarged considerably for when NATO was formed in 1949 Norway, a founder member, became a recipient of armaments issued under the Military Aid Programme (MAP). From 1950 onwards Norway received no less than 444 Bofors Guns from this source. Most of them were American M1 guns on M2A1 carriages but some guns had Canadian origins and others were for naval applications. Eventually the anti-aircraft artillery arm fielded 332 Bofors Guns and the Coast Artillery thirty-two. The rest were issued to the Norwegian Army who continued to operate a number of ex-German guns.

By 1958 the Norwegian Coast Artillery had 226 L/60 Bofors Guns distributed as follows:

Oscarsborg fortress	12 guns
Oslofjord fortress	26 guns
Kristiansand fortress	28 guns
Stavanger fortress	28 guns
Bergen fortress	28 guns
Agdenes fortress	28 guns
Narvik fortress	28 guns
Harstad fortress	48 guns

By the mid-1970s the Coast Artillery still had about 120 L/60 guns in their inventory. Over the following years the numbers of Norwegian L/60 Bofors Guns gradually dwindled as they were replaced by more modern equipments but L/60 guns remained in service with the Coast Artillery and some local militia units until the mid-1990s.

Post-war training for Norwegian Army gunners on a Bofors Gun with any number of possible origins.

Germany

The old chestnut regarding German involvement in the development of the Bofors Gun was covered in Chapter 1. In that chapter it was noted that although the Rheinmetall-Borsig 3.7cm FlaK series bore a passing resemblance to the Bofors Gun, completely different loading and operating systems were involved. In addition, prior to 1939 almost the only European nation that did not display some interest in the Bofors Gun was Germany. That was not for the want of trying by AB Bofors for they produced highly-detailed descriptive sales literature written in German relating to the merits of their gun.

Once Hitler's *NSDAP* came to power in 1933 there commenced a period during which the German armed forces rapidly expanded and re-armed. Almost all the weapons concerned with this expansion phase came from German industry for it was inherent in *NSDAP* philosophy that a major European territorial and political reorganisation in Germany's favour was going to have to be imposed by military means and the German armed forces wanted to be dependent on their own national resources to as great an extent as could be achieved. As time was to show, not even the German industrial infrastructure was able to supply the ever-growing needs of their armed forces, but that was not apparent during the 1930s.

This independent stance excluded the 40mm Bofors Gun from early consideration, although some attention was paid to it purely from a technical standpoint. At one stage, exactly when is not clear, Krupp AG of Essen spent some time on a project involving a 45mm anti-aircraft gun that was based, visually at least, on the Bofors Gun. It seems that the project did not proceed very far and appears not to have passed the wooden model stage.

Although it was never manufactured, Krupp AG of Essen spent some time on a project involving a 45mm anti-aircraft gun with obvious affiliations to the Bofors Gun. It never got past the wooden model stage.

An unusual view of a Canadian Boffin naval mounting.

The simple twin-barrelled Mark 5 naval mounting widely known as the 'Utility'.

The M2 Bofors Gun installation on an AC-130H Spectre.

A Lend-Lease 40mm Bofors Gun now on display at the Artillery Museum in St. Petersburg and equipped with Soviet pattern sights. (T. J. Gander)

If any doubts remain as to the influence of the 40mm Bofors Gun on the design of the Soviet-era 37mm Model 1939 (61-K) this close-up of the autoloader area should dispel them once and for all. (T. J Gander)

Detail of a gate guardian Bofors L/70 showing the revised location of the equilibrator tubes to the vertical position just behind the shield. (T. J. Gander)

Outline and cross-section of the projectile for the Bofors L/70 MPT round.

Segmented front-sabot

Triple sectioned sabot

Slipping driving band

Primer

The new APFSDS-T Mark 2 round as developed by QinetiQ and Bofors.

The highly-advanced Bofors L/70 3P projectile.

An M247 Sergeant York Air Defense Gun System on the move.

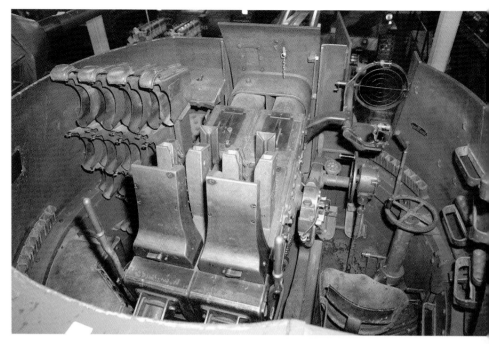

Internal view of the combat compartment on the Landsverk Lvkv 43 *once on display at the* Pansarmuseet *at Axvall in Sweden.* (S. Wiiger Olsen)

CV4090 in a typical Swedish winter environment.

The Bofors Gun came to German attention after the Austrian *Anschluss* of March 1938 and the September 1939 campaign in Poland. German technicians cast their eyes over captured guns to discover what they could and came to the conclusion that the Swedish product was better than their own equivalents. But there was no chance that the Germans would switch their allegiance to the Bofors product. It was considered that as Rheinmetall-Borsig already had well-established production lines churning out the 3.7cm FlaK 36 and 37, there was no need to change anything. The German design was deemed serviceable enough so to disrupt busy production lines when light anti-aircraft guns were sorely needed would be to court trouble.

Captured Bofors Guns were therefore surplus to requirements and were accordingly sold to Sweden in exchange for various raw materials. In 1941 more went to Finland to cement what promised to be a useful relationship during the planned invasion of the Soviet Union. These transfer ventures (see above and Chapter 3) did not exhaust the stock of captured guns but those remaining in German hands were cleaned up and stockpiled against some future contingency.

That contingency eventually arose after the 1940 campaigns resulted in yet more Bofors Guns falling into German hands. They were captured from Belgium, France, Norway and the United Kingdom, so many that the German armed forces could not overlook such potentially valuable assets. For instance, the total British losses in Northern France included 101 Bofors Guns (not all in a serviceable state). More guns entered the German fold from Greece and

A fully-manned 4cm FlaK 28, which appears to be of Hungarian origin.

German personnel manning a captured 40mm Bofors Gun in the North African desert. Note the vegetation applied around the barrel to break up its distinctive outline.

According to the rings painted around the barrel of this 4cm FlaK 28 it has been credited with nine 'kills'.

A FlaK 28 emplaced somewhere in France.

Yugoslavia during 1941. It was therefore decided to adopt the Bofors Gun, which, from May 1939 onwards, had become known to German ordnance personnel as the 4cm FlaK 28.

If the 1940 totals were considerable they were about to swell. Production at the *Waffenfabrik Kongsberg* in Norway was restarted (see above) and the same facility was also used to repair damaged guns, as many captured weapons had been rendered unserviceable to some extent or another by their former owners. Ammunition production was also resumed at the *Waffenfabrik Kongsberg*, limited to two high explosive natures (HE and HEI), although in the short term sufficient captured stocks were on hand to meet immediate needs. Most of the *Waffenfabrik Kongsberg* gun output went to the *Kriegsmarine* even though the guns retained their non-stabilised field carriages in most cases. Single-barrel installations were fitted on the cruisers *Admiral Hipper* and *Prinz Eugen*, and the guns were also mounted on several types of *Schnellboote*.

From 1941 onwards Germany had another source of Bofors Guns, this time MAVAG of Hungary (see above), which eventually manufactured at least 262 guns for the German armed forces (including seventeen that had originally been ordered by The Netherlands) and 735 spare barrels.

The Norwegian and Hungarian facilities enabled the Bofors Gun to become a standard German weapon. By March 1942 the *Luftwaffe* alone had 615 guns, and by July 1941 the *Kriegsmarine* already had 247. After the end of 1942 the numbers in service began to gradually dwindle for various reasons, ranging from combat losses to general wear and tear. As one example, by February 1945, the last month for which reliable figures can be obtained, the number of 4cm FlaK 28 guns remaining available to the *Luftwaffe* to defend the *Reich* was listed as just thirty-four.

A Luftwaffe *crew pose with their 4cm Flak 28.*

Japan

The Japanese had never been particularly interested in obtaining 40mm Bofors Guns although prior to 1941 they had frequently observed them being used against their own aircraft by the Chinese. After 1942 they were to learn exactly how effective the weapons could be whenever they attempted to attack American ships or land installations. However, the Japanese armed forces' successes in their early 1942 campaigns in the Dutch East Indies and against the British in Malaya and Singapore brought many Bofors Guns into their gun parks. At Singapore alone the British lost 100 Bofors Guns that had been shipped from United Kingdom stocks originally earmarked for Home Defence. Of these twenty-four were found by the Japanese to be in perfect condition and another fifty-six were rendered serviceable after repairs. They were then retained by the Japanese Army for the rest of the war, as were any of the Dutch East Indies guns they captured.

The Japanese produced their own version of the Bofors Gun by making a direct copy of one of the guns captured at Singapore. Progress on the project was slow as a general shortage of proper machine tools meant that almost every component had to be shaped by hand. During 1943 a Japanese prototype underwent firing trials at the Torigaski range belonging to the Yokosuka Naval Arsenal but it was apparent that further improvement was needed, especially relating to quality control. Nevertheless, limited production began before the end of 1943 and an output rate of five to seven units a month was being achieved by late 1944 at Yokosuka and the Hitachi Manufacturing Company. Some post-war reports mention the involvement of the Kokura Arsenal. Due to its unreliability, mainly inflicted by the poor manufacturing standards involved, the Bofors Gun clone was never formally accepted as a general service weapon by the Japanese but such was the general dearth of Japanese war materiel by 1945 those few available had to be pressed into service.

The 'production' guns, mostly single-barrel naval-pattern mountings known as the 40mm/60 Type 5, differed from the original Bofors Gun in numerous respects, not the least being the poor standard of finish and component inter-action. On the Type 5 the barrel length was increased to a true 60 calibres by being 2.4m long, while the barrel was provided with a non-standard flash hider of German Rheinmetall-Borsig design.

Soviet Union

The Soviet Union was another of the unplanned users of the Bofors Gun but the guns involved were not Bofors Guns at all but derivatives of them. Although the Soviet guns were produced in 37mm calibre, and not in 40mm, their designs were so obviously based upon AB Bofors originals that they are included here to complete the overall picture.

The basis for the Soviet guns was an AB Bofors design but not the 40mm

Bofors Gun. Instead the original was the 25mm naval gun developed during the early 1930s as one possible alternative to the 40mm gun. It was mentioned in Chapter 1 as it incorporated the loading mechanism and general operating principles developed for the 40mm gun, while a land service carriage also had many features in common with the larger equivalent.

The Soviets evinced some interest in the 25mm land service version and eventually took out a licence to manufacture the gun and its ammunition, the latter involving a 25 x 205mm round. For various reasons production did not commence until 1940 when it went into what was, for the Soviet Union, relatively limited production as the 25mm Model 1940 (72-K). A twin-barrel land service version, the 94-KM, also appeared, as did a self-propelled twin-barrel version, the ZSU-25. The latter was based on a tracked SU-76M self-propelled 76.2mm gun chassis during late 1944 but only a few were built.

Once they had obtained the 25mm gun drawings from AB Bofors Soviet technicians at first used them not only as the starting point for production but as something with which they could experiment. One of their first courses of action was to enlarge the calibre to 45mm and scale up all the associated components accordingly. The result was an air defence gun known as the 45mm Model 1939, or 49-K, a gun clearly proclaiming its Bofors origins but one which was not accepted for service. Instead, the Soviets decided to select another scaled up version of the 25mm gun, this time firing a 37 x 250mm round loaded in five-round chargers. Once again the mechanisms and operating principles were almost exactly the same as on the AB Bofors 25mm original.

During 1939 the 37mm gun went into production at Artillery Plant No 8 at Kaliningrad, near Moscow. The design of this gun, known as the 37mm Model 1939, or 61-K, was attributed to L. A. Loktev and M. N. Loginov, both members of the design staff at Kaliningrad.

While the 37mm Model 1939 demonstrated its close affinity to its Swedish design origins in many ways, the standards of machining and finishing were nowhere near as refined as on their Western counterparts and the cyclic rate of fire was increased to between 160 and 180rpm. A full crew involved eight gunners although this number was often less. The field carriage was much more basic than that of the Bofors Model 1934 in having a turntable in place of the platform frame of the Swedish design. The gun laying controls involved wheels rather than cranked handles and the field sights were almost rudimentary, although a mechanical analogue calculator system along similar (but simpler) lines to that of the Bofors Course and Speed Sight could be incorporated. There was also provision for centralised or predictor fire control although it seems to have been little used. A shield, weighing about 1,000kg, was available but was frequently left off.

The ammunition developed for the 37mm Model 1939 appears to have been based on that developed in the United States for the 37mm M1 Colt/Browning air defence gun and so carried over its general lack of overall ballistic performance compared to the more highly-powered 40mm ammunition. Numerous variants of HE and AP rounds were developed and produced over the years, the AP projectile being able to penetrate 47mm of armour at 500m.

In addition to the production at Kaliningrad, production was also carried out at Artillery Plant No 4 at Krasnoyarsk and Artillery Plant No 586 at Kolomna. War year production totals were as follows:

1942	3,896
1943	5,477
1944	5,998
1945	1,545

To keep these figures in proportion it should not be forgotten that the number of American-produced 40mm Bofors Guns assigned on Lend-Lease terms to the Soviet Union was 5,511. An unknown number from this latter total were doubtless lost *en route* to the Soviet Union but what the Soviets did with the guns they received is not easy to discover. Little pictorial evidence seems to have survived showing Bofors Guns in service with any of the Soviet armed forces. However, it is known that once in service with the Soviets many Lend-Lease guns were provided with Soviet pattern sights and on-carriage predictor units to allow gunners familiar with 37mm Model 39 guns to utilise their new equipments with a minimum of conversion training.

The 37mm Model 1939 proved to be a rugged and reliable weapon and a twin-barrelled variant, the B-47, was also manufactured. Another twin-barrelled version, known as the B-11-M and with water-cooled barrels, was produced for the Soviet Navy, as was a single-barrel naval mounting, the 70-K.

Two self-propelled platforms carrying the 37mm Model 1939 appeared during 1944 but only in relatively small numbers as their turret traverse rates proved to be inadequate; they had been withdrawn by the end of 1946. Both were based on the SU-76 or SU-76M tracked chassis, the ZSU-37-1 carrying a single Model 1939 gun and the rarely-encountered ZSU-37-2 carrying two. Rudimentary self-propelled platforms were also created by placing a single Model 1939 on the back of a ZiS-42 half-tracked truck or a GAZ AAA 6 × 4 cargo truck. The 37mm Model 1939 was also mounted on armoured trains.

Captured Model 1939 guns were employed by the Germans as their 3.7cm FlaK M 39a(r). On 1 March 1944 the *Luftwaffe* fielded 138 of these battlefield trophies organised into twelve batteries.

The Model 1939 is no longer in front line service with any of the former Warsaw Pact nations but may still be retained by a few reserve or militia units. Many guns are still in service all around the world with nations who once came under the Soviet sphere of influence or who received Soviet military aid; at one stage the Model 39 was in service in forty-one countries. Their numbers are now dwindling, although 37mm Model 1939s were still deployed by nations such as Somalia as late as the end of 2006.

DATA FOR 37MM MODEL 1939 (61-K)	
Length of barrel	2.729m
Length of bore	2.468m
Weight travelling	2,100kg
Length travelling	6.036m
Width travelling	1.937m
Height travelling	2.105m
Axis of bore	1.1m
Track	1.545m
Ground clearance	360mm
Max towing speed	35km/h
Rate of fire (cyclic)	160–180rpm
Elevation	-5° to +85°
Traverse	360°
Max range, horizontal	9,500m
Max effective AA range	3,000m
Ammunition feed	5-round charger
Muzzle velocity	880m/s
Round weight (typical)	
HE	1.48kg
AP	1.5kg
Projectile weight (typical)	
HE	732g
AP	780g

People's Republic of China

As late as 2006 the 37mm Model 1939 (61-K) was still being marketed by the People's Republic of China (PRC) as the 37mm Type 55, a direct copy of what was once a Soviet-supplied gift (the 37mm Model 1939) and a model known to be still in service in China as well as with many other nations. Production is now on an 'as required' basis by a number of factories under the control of NORINCO, the China North Industries Corporation headquartered in Beijing. Apart from the 37mm Type 55, NORINCO also marketed a twin-barrel variant known as the Type 65. Another twin-barrelled model with an on-carriage generator to power the carriage is known as the Type 74, while there is yet another twin-barrelled and powered carriage model, this time with the addition of an optronic fire-control system. This latter model is the 37mm Type P793.

There was also a twin-barrelled self-propelled variant with Type 55 guns in an open-topped turret on a T-34 tank chassis. Produced in limited numbers only, this variant has been withdrawn from Chinese service. A potential replacement appeared in 1988, again carrying two Type 55 guns, this time in an enclosed turret mounted on a modified Type 69 tank chassis, the latter being a Chinese development of the Soviet T-54. As far as is known this variant did not enter production and neither did a later (1997) and more advanced model with the usual optronic fire-control system augmented by a roof-mounted target surveillance radar.

Naval versions of the later 37mm Model 1939/Type 55 weapon variants have been produced in the PRC during the recent past and may still be marketed. At least some of these later production naval guns are chambered for a 37 x 240mm round.

Chapter 7

Bofors L/70

When the Second World War ended, armed forces all over the world seemed to be over-equipped with light anti-aircraft guns. The massive production totals of the war years meant that there were more than enough guns to equip air defence units and navies for years to come so the future sales prospects for the 40mm L/60 Bofors Gun looked unpromising. Even so, between 1945 and 1954 AB Bofors manufactured thirty-eight L/60 guns to complete contracts for the Swedish armed forces while outstanding export orders totalled 460. Production of the L/60 ceased at Karlskoga in 1954.

Yet AB Bofors marketing and planning staffs were canny enough to realise that a potential market for air defence guns still existed. The L/60 had been designed to counter a past generation of military aircraft but by 1945 strike aircraft had become even more potent with the appearance of jet propulsion. Guns such as the L/60 could no longer deal comfortably with the high speed targets that jet-propelled aircraft presented. Something better was needed so the AB Bofors design staff set to work.

An early example of the Bofors L/70 undergoing land firing trials with the Swedish Army during the early 1950s.

They arrived at two solutions. One was to develop an all-round improvement of the existing 40mm gun. The second solution was to enlarge the existing gun to a calibre of 57mm. Both courses of action had their attractions so in the end AB Bofors executives decided to follow both. One result was the L/60 57mm Bofors Gun (*m/54*) which was subsequently produced in both naval and land service forms, but that is another story. What concerns the 40mm saga is that a new model of 40mm Bofors Gun was ready for testing as early as 1947.

The new model displayed several innovations, all incorporated to boost all-round gun performance. Barrel length was increased from a nominal 60 calibres to 70 calibres, giving rise to the designation of 40mm L/70, often referred to as the 40/70. Internally the number of barrel rifling grooves remained at 16 although the rifling increased from one complete twist in 46 calibres at the chamber to one twist in 27 calibres at the muzzle.

One major innovation to the gun that increased the cyclic rate of fire to 300rpm was a revised method of ejecting spent cases. Rather than dragging the spent case from the breech and ejecting it rearwards (and then forwards via a curved chute) before a fresh round could be loaded, as on the L/60 gun, each spent case was deflected downwards by a deflection plate as soon as it was clear of the breech ring. Once the case had cleared the breech ring the deflection plate flipped down to enable a fresh round, carried on top of the plate, to be chambered from its position in a direct line behind the breech. This simple modification enabled gunners to put more than twice as many projectiles into the air within a given time period compared to the L/60 Model 1934 and its ilk, so even fleeting targets could be usefully engaged. The increased rate of fire coupled with new, more powerful ammunition having a higher muzzle velocity meant that, from the outset, the L/70 would be able to remain a viable air defence weapon well into the immediate future.

The increase in barrel length was introduced to obtain the maximum ballistic performance from a new and more powerful ammunition family. While the new 40mm round was based on existing L/60 outlines, it featured a longer propellant case (365mm as opposed to the earlier 310.8mm) to contain a more powerful propellant charge that increased the muzzle velocity to around 1,025m/s compared to the 850–890m/s of the L/60. Also increased was the muzzle energy which became a nominal 461,000 joules compared to 345,000 joules for the L/60 rounds. The projectiles at first remained much the same as before although marginally heavier and with a revised outline that improved the aerodynamic shape. At the same time (and where appropriate) the projectile's high explosive payload was increased.

The new barrel and ammunition were not the only innovations on the L/70 for a new method of gun control was introduced as well. Away went the manual two-man laying operations of the L/60 to be replaced by a single layer and an on-carriage power control system. AB Bofors had anticipated the future

40/70 PFHE

Three of the Bofors L/70 projectiles available during the mid- to late 1970s. More modern L/70 ammunition details are provided later in this chapter.

40/70 HET

40/70 APCT

40mm Bofors L/70 rounds complete with the four-round chargers.

requirements of light anti-aircraft defence weapon systems as early as 1944 when jet aircraft made their operational debut. Attempts to utilise the two-man, hand-operated laying system against such high-speed targets would have been problematic, at best, so a single layer operating a powered carriage was seen as the solution. It could provide high barrel traverse and elevation acceleration rates, allowing the layer to acquire and follow aircraft targets flying at very high speeds. By introducing a gyro-stabilised reflex sight unit with integral predictor capabilities the gunner could have a very good chance of obtaining a lethal hit on almost any low-flying aircraft likely to be encountered for years to come.

Thus the 1947 L/70 prototype was in nearly every aspect of its design some way ahead of its time, to the extent that the prototype's appearance aroused almost as much international interest as its 1932 predecessor. Once again, AB Bofors had anticipated an operational requirement and produced their optimum solution and, once again, the market responded with a flood of orders and licence agreements, even though it was the end of 1948 before the Bofors L/70 was ready to be marketed. By 1951 the land service gun was in service with the Swedish Army (as the *40mm Luftvärnsautomatkanon m/48 – 40mm Lvakan m/48*).

AB Bofors went on to produce the L/70 in a variety of forms, including naval mountings with powered and stabilised controls, of which more later. By the late 1950s the number of artillery products emanating from Karlskoga, although still extensive, had diminished compared to the late 1930s levels so more attention could be devoted in in-house production. As a result AB Bofors were able to manufacture 454 L/70 land service guns for the Swedish armed forces and 401 for export sales. Between them, the Norwegian Kongsberg organisation and AB Bofors were able to co-operate in manufacturing another 268 land service guns. When it came to naval models of the L/70 AB Bofors manufactured 311 guns for Sweden and 411 for export. Once again Kongsberg and AB Bofors co-operated to manufacture a further 302 guns for naval applications.

One oddity regarding the L/70 was that a few early production guns for Swedish service were provided with barrels and other calibre-related components to enable them to fire L/60 ammunition in order to utilise existing (and extensive) ammunition stockpiles for training purposes, conserving the newer and more costly L/70 rounds to build up combat stocks. Guns in this category, known as the *40mm Lvakan m/36-48*, were later brought up to full *40mm Lvakan m/48* standard. The Dutch implemented a similar programme after they adopted the L/70 in 1957 as their *40mm Tegen Luchdoelen L/70*. By 1963 all their L/60 ammunition stocks had been expended so the hybrid guns could be brought up to full L/70 ammunition standard.

The Swedish *m/48 C* was an improved *m/48*, while the main production variant (and the most numerous land service model) became the *Lvakan m/48*

D. There was also a *Lvakan m/48 R* but it differed only in electrical power supply details.

Description

Two basic factory versions of the land service Bofors L/70 were produced, the Type A and the Type B, differing only in the means of obtaining an electrical power supply. The Type A took its power from a remote power generator or some form of mains supply. On the Type B the power source, a generator delivering three-phase 220V at 50Hz, was located on the carriage in an auxiliary power unit (APU). Various types of APU have been employed, typical being a BMW 425 air-cooled petrol engine developing between 10.5 and 15.7hp. A battery was provided for engine starting, a typical complete APU installation weighing 350kg.

The Bofors L/70 introduced an autoloader system very similar to that of the Model 1934 although above the loading assembly the ammunition guides could be elongated in an arc to accommodate a loading system capable of holding up to twenty-six rounds, still in their usual four-round chargers; on some guns the capacity was limited to sixteen rounds. The extra capacity guides could be folded forward and over the barrel when not required. This enlarged ammunition capacity allowed the layer to open fire for a useful period even when the two loaders were not in their positions on the carriage. If they were in position the loaders took turns to feed clips into the autoloader by taking fresh chargers from two ready-use ammunition racks arranged each side of the rear gun platform

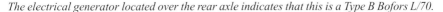

The electrical generator located over the rear axle indicates that this is a Type B Bofors L/70.

A head-on view of an unusual Bofors L/70 utilised by AB Bofors for trials and demonstrations and employing a two-layer aiming system. (T. J. Gander)

and holding ninety-six rounds, although some racks had a lesser capacity. Off-carriage ammunition handlers continually replaced any chargers removed from these racks by the on-carriage loaders to ensure an ammunition supply was maintained ready for loading into the gun. The traverse acceleration rates on the L/70 were such that the on-carriage loaders had to be supported in their positions by padded hip support rings rigidly secured to the gun platform. A typical land service gun crew numbered six or seven.

The layer's position was to the left of the gun. For local control a joystick arrangement operated by both hands (and with wrist supports) was provided although on some later models (especially naval models) this was replaced by a faster-to-operate rolling ball arrangement actuated by the thumbs. If for any reason power was not available, or in an emergency, provision was made to revert to manual operation using the usual cranked handles, in which case an extra layer and sight unit was required on the mounting. Various sight units could be employed, typical being a NIFE SRS-5 close-range reflex sight unit with an integral predictor capability. Firing limit provisions could be involved.

Overall, the lower field carriage was similar in principle to that of the Model 1934 but suitably strengthened and enlarged as necessary to accommodate the increased weights and operating stresses. Many of the short cuts introduced during the war years by others than AB Bofors to speed L/60 carriage production rates were simply disregarded, so features such as Ackermann steering, independent wheel suspension, air brakes, and so on, were retained. If required, and once the carriage was in position, the axle units could be completely removed from the carriage. One L/70 innovation was the introduction of front and side gun shields made from steel plate 5mm thick. Another change to the carriage was the elimination of the two horizontal equilibrators used on the L/60 land service guns. In their place came two vertical equilibrators linked to the elevating mass by steel cables.

An L/70 once kept by AB Bofors for live firing trials and demonstrations. (T. J. Gander)

DATA FOR BOFORS 40/70	
Length of barrel	2.8m
Length of barrel with flash hider	3.1m
Rifling twist	1 in 46 to 1 in 27 cal
Number of grooves	16
Max gas pressure	3,250kg/cm²
Weight of gun, Type A	5,150kg
Weight of gun, Type B	4,800kg
Weight of complete barrel	174.6kg
Length on tow	7.29m
Height on tow	2.35m
Width on tow	2.225m
Length of recoil	230mm
Height, axis of bore firing	1.335m
Wheelbase	4.025m
Track	1.8m
Ground clearance	390mm
Turning radius	8m
Rate of fire (cyclic)	>300rpm
Max towing speed	32km/h
Elevation	-4° to +90°
Traverse	360°
Elevating speed	45°/s
Traversing speed	85°/s
Elevating acceleration	135°/s
Traversing acceleration	127°/s
Power supply	220V, 50Hz
Power consumption, min/max	5/12kW
Max range, horizontal	12,620m
Max effective AA range	3,000–4,000m
Number of rounds in racks	>96
Number of rounds in loader	>26

The list of known land service L/70 user nations is a long one especially as in November 1953 the L/70 became the standard NATO light anti-aircraft gun. Not all the users mentioned in the list retain their L/70 guns on a front line basis as many have been placed in reserve or replaced by air defence missile systems. The list is as follows: Argentina, Austria (*4cm Fliegerabwehrmaschinenkanone 55/57*), Bahrain, Brazil, Chile, Columbia, Denmark (naval, *40mm maskinkanon Mk M/48 LvSa*), Djibouti, Ecuador, Estonia, Finland, Gabon, West Germany,

Greece, India, Indonesia, Iran, Ireland (thirty guns), Israel, Italy, Kenya, South Korea, Kuwait, Latvia, Libya, Lithuania, Malaysia, Malta, The Netherlands (*40L70G luchtdoelkanon*), New Zealand, Nigeria, Oman, Peru, Saudi Arabia (seventy-two guns manufactured by SA de Placenia de las Armas of Spain), Singapore, South Africa, Spain, Sri Lanka, Sweden, Taiwan, Thailand, Turkey, Uruguay, Venezuela, and some of the states that once formed Yugoslavia.

Naval Guns

When it came to naval versions of the L/70 production must have been greatly assisted by the upper carriage, including the ordnance and 5mm thick armoured shield, being much the same for both naval and land service models. Naval L/70 barrels manufactured by AB Bofors were air-cooled and only single-barrel mountings made their appearance.

There were three main models known to AB Bofors as the SAK 40/70-315, 40/70-350 and 40/70-520. SAK is the abbreviation for *Skepps Automat Kanon* (automatic naval gun).

The SAK 40/70-315 was the simplest by having manual controls. Total weight was originally 2,870kg. Ammunition racks for ninety-six rounds were provided.

By contrast the SAK 40/70-350 employed electro-hydraulic power drives that could be controlled from a central fire-control system. A gyro-stabilised

The Swedish Navy carried out a programme to remove the power controls for a number of their naval Bofors L/70 guns so that they could be manually controlled in time-honoured fashion on light patrol vessels.

system was also involved, with a set of manual laying cranks for emergency use.

Similar in overall configuration was the SAK 40/70-520 but with the addition of an Automatic Feed Device (AFD) which increased the total weight to 3,450kg but reduced the crew requirement to two. Also available was an optional (but usually installed) fibreglass cupola over the gun and mounting to act as a sea spray and weather shield. This shield, which weighed 150kg, could also be installed on other SAK 40/70 models.

By the 1990s some of the Swedish Navy powered-drive models had been extensively modified by removing the power controls and installing the original L/60 two-man laying system involving manually-cranked handles. This was an economy measure using surplus powered mountings that could then be installed on smaller vessels such as light coastal patrol craft.

Intercontrol AS of Norway has developed an upgrade package for single-barrel L/70 naval guns based around electrical rather than hydraulic drives. The outline details for this package are provided below in this chapter.

Ammunition fired from naval L/70 guns remains the same as that fired from land service guns (see below).

A Bofors SAK 40/70-350 naval gun complete with cupola.

DATA FOR SAK 40/70-350	
Length of barrel	2.8m
Rifling twist	1 in 46 to 1 in 27 cal
Number of grooves	16
Max gas pressure	$3,250kg/cm^2$
Weight of gun	2,870kg
Weight of complete barrel	174.6kg
Length of recoil	230mm
Swept radius	3.315m
Rate of fire (cyclic)	>300rpm
Elevation	-10° to +90°
Traverse	360°
Elevating speed	45°/s
Traversing speed	85°/s
Elevating acceleration	35°/s
Traversing acceleration	127°/s
Power supply	440V, 60Hz
Power consumption, min/max	4.5/10kW
Max range, horizontal	12,620m
Max effective AA range	3,000–4,000m
Number of rounds in racks	>96
Number of rounds in loader	>18

As with their land-based equivalents the list of L/70 naval gun users is a long one. The vessels involved are mainly patrol boats, mine-hunters and similar light vessels. The list may be regarded as current at the end of 2012, although some users obtained their guns from licence manufacturers such as OTO Melara SpA (see below): Algeria, Argentina, Bahrain, Bangladesh, Brazil, Cameroon, Chile, Columbia, Croatia, Ecuador, Egypt, Finland, Germany, Ghana, Greece, Indonesia, Iran, Ireland, Italy, Ivory Coast, Kazakhstan, South Korea, Kuwait, Latvia, Libya, Lithuania, Malaysia, Mexico, Montenegro, Morocco, Nigeria, Norway, Oman, Peru, Portugal, Qatar, Saudi Arabia, Senegal, Singapore, Sweden, Taiwan, Thailand, Trinidad/Tobago, Tunisia, Turkey, United Arab Emirates and Uruguay.

Licences and Orders

One of the very first countries to arrange a licence manufacturing agreement for local manufacture of the land service L/70 was the United Kingdom. During the early 1950s the British Army's low-level air defence batteries were still mainly equipped with the Bristol Bofors (see Chapter 4) that in overall operation and concept was very similar to the Bofors L/70. However, the Bristol Bofors retained the L/60 barrel and fired the previous generation of ammunition that imparted an overall performance significantly lower than the L/70.

In the United Kingdom the L/70 was manufactured at the then Royal Ordnance Factory at Nottingham (now closed) and well over 1,000 land service guns were produced, some for export to nations such as Nigeria. L/70s were also manufactured (and repaired) at The Royal Arsenal, Woolwich, prior to its closure. The L/70 was introduced into British Army service during 1953 and more were issued to the Royal Air Force Regiment to defend airfields and bases. The British designation was Gun Equipment, 40/70 AA, L3. British L/70 guns differed from most others in having an 'official' cyclic fire rate of 240rpm.

British L/70 guns fired only one type of operational round, the Round 40/70 HE L40A1. This round contained a tracer element and a self-destruct feature, the nose-mounted fuze being the Fuze Percussion DA L41A1, with the DA denoting Direct Action. An earlier round, the Round 40/70 HE L22A1 was withdrawn to be used only for training purposes. Available for training were the Cartridge 40/70 Blank L30A1, and the inert Drill Round 40/70 L20A1.

A Royal Air Force Regiment Bofors L/70 firing during a practice shoot held at Belize Airport.

A Royal Artillery Bofors L/70 in action on the Larkhill ranges in Wiltshire. The gunner hanging precariously from the left side of the gun is a range safety officer. (T. J. Gander)

Gunners of the Gibraltar Regiment during a practice shoot on the Rock. (T. J. Gander)

A Royal Artillery Bofors L/70 under wraps and on tow behind a FV 11002 Tractor, 10-ton, 6 x 6, GS, AEC Militant Mark 1. (T. J. Gander)

Familiarisation training with a Royal Artillery Gun Equipment, 40/70 A.A., L3. (T. J. Gander)

British L/70s remained in constant British service until March 1979 when the last of them was retired after a parade held to mark their passing at Kirton in Lindsey, Scotland. They were replaced by the Rapier missile system. Even then some of the 'British' guns soldiered on. A batch of forty-eight refurbished L/70s was sold to Thailand in 1987, while the Gibraltar Regiment did not hand in their guns until 1983.

There were plans for the Royal Navy to acquire L/70 guns on single-, twin- and six-barrel mountings. The single-barrel mounting would have been the Mark 10, the twin the Mark 11 and the six-barrel mounting the Mark 12. None actually appeared as all were cancelled in 1957 in favour of the Seacat guided-missile system.

Another major L/70 Bofors Gun licensee was India where a reported 1,000 or so guns were manufactured at the Gun Carriage Factory at Jabalpur. Exactly how many of this reported total were actually completed is uncertain but it is known that the Indian Ordnance Factory Board marketed their L/70 and its ammunition for possible export sales. Nepal may have been one customer but this cannot be confirmed.

Other licensed manufacturing nations were Brazil, Indonesia, Italy, The Netherlands (the first nation to negotiate a L/70 licensing agreement), Norway and Spain (by SA de Placenia de las Armas who manufactured about 400 guns for the Spanish Army plus more for the Spanish Navy and export sales). Of

An Indian Army Bofors L/70.

these the Italian Breda Meccanica Bresciana SpA (later OTO Melara SpA) was the most prolific developer and innovator and is deserving of a mention in its own right (see below).

A total of 132 L/70 guns for The Netherlands armed forces were licence manufactured by Bronswerk-Feijenord at Schiedam, while their lower carriage construction was sub-contracted to FN of Belgium. During 2001 thirty of these guns were withdrawn and sold to Ireland (together with eight Signaal Flycatcher radars) where they replaced twenty-four L/60 guns, four of which had been in the Irish inventory since 1939. At the time of writing (2013) twenty-four of the Irish L/70 guns were still in service organised in four six-gun batteries, plus six guns held in reserve.

OTO Melara Guns

L/70 guns manufactured in Italy by Breda Meccanica SpA (later OTOBREDA and then OTO Melara SpA) at its Brescia facility were mainly for naval applications although land service guns for the Italian and Greek armies were also produced, the first during 1969. Part of the early Breda output was formed from licence-manufactured versions of AB Bofors designs but Breda introduced and developed some novel mountings of their own. They were particularly innovative regarding ammunition feed devices and systems.

One early naval mounting was the Breda Type 105, a twin-barrel mounting with two 32-round magazines. Another twin-barrel powered mount, the Type 106, could be controlled from a remote station or from on the mounting using either a *Mirasole* or NIFE type SRS-5 sight unit. The Type 107 was a single-barrel version of this mounting.

The Breda Type 64 also involved a twin-barrel mounting but with twin 100-round magazines. Capable of very high rates of barrel acceleration, the Type 64 also had automatic fuze-setting arrangements. An upgrade package for this model was introduced during 1990, the main change being the replacement of the hydraulic drives by a digitised electric servo system. A fibreglass cupola formed part of the package

Also developed by Breda was the Type 520R, basically an updated version of the L/70 naval gun with the addition of a 144-round, ready-to-feed ammunition feed device (AFD), digital servo-mechanisms and a fibreglass cupola. It was at one time in service with South Korea and Morocco. Due to the incorporation of the powered magazine system the barrel elevation limits were -9° to +83°.

A single-barrel mounting that was long in production by Breda/OTO Melara was the Type 564, also known as the Breda/Bofors 350P. It differed from the previous Type 520R in having a revised digital servo drive system. There was also a compact AFD holding 144 rounds, a system also produced under licence by Empresa Nacional Bazan (now Navantia FABA Systems) at San Fernando, Spain, for the Spanish Navy. This system could be retrofitted to existing L/70 land service guns and was essentially the same as the ammunition feed system installed on the Breda Type 520R (see above).

One of the more important of the Breda/OTO Melara models, in both numerical and technical terms, was the Twin 40L70 Compact, originally known as the Breda Type 70 and at one time in service with over twenty navies. This surprisingly small mounting for its firepower (the cyclic rate of fire from both barrels was 600rpm) had two barrels set 300mm apart. All operations could be fully automatic and contained within a dome-like turret. There was no need for personnel to enter the turret during firing as control came from a remote fire-control system; internal access was normally only required for maintenance. The Type A Compact had a rotary magazine under the mounting holding 736 rounds arranged in seven layers, while the Type B held 444 rounds.

The two feed systems, driven by the gun recoil, comprised the magazine, two lower elevators, two upper elevators and two fan-shaped 'shifters' to actually feed the guns. The magazine was under the training platform and could

The Breda Twin 40L70 Compact naval mounting.

be located either above or below deck level. Magazine loading was carried out manually using the usual four-round chargers and could be carried out before an action or during intervals in firing. With the gun in action ammunition automatically entered the lower elevators to rotate eventually to the upper elevators. From there the rounds proceeded to the shifters oscillating on the trunnion axis level to adapt to the barrel elevation angle. In their turn the shifters led to the usual loading mechanism systems. Each gun had its own feed system.

The Compact is no longer in series production having been superseded by the Fast Forty (see below). Examples serve on in the Italian, Argentina, Saudi Arabian and South Korean navies, plus several others.

DATA FOR 40L70 COMPACT	
Length of barrels	2.8m
Separation between barrels	300mm
Rifling twist	1 in 46 cal to 1 in 27 cal
Number of grooves	16
Weight of mounting	
Without ammunition	Type A, 5,600kg; Type B, 5,400kg
With ammunition	Type A, 7,400kg; Type B, 6,500kg
Height above deck	2.4m
Intrusion below deck	Type A, 1.3m; Type B, 920mm
Diameter of deck intrusion	2.4m
Axis of bore above deck	1.37m
Swept radius	2.902m
Rate of fire (cyclic)	600rpm (2 x 300rpm)
Elevation	-13° to +85°
Traverse	360°
Elevating speed	90°/s
Traversing speed	60°/s
Elevating acceleration	120°/s
Traversing acceleration	120°/s
Max range, horizontal	12,500m
Max range, height	8,700m
Number of rounds in system	Type A, 736 rounds; Type B, 444 rounds

The potential of the 40L70 Compact mounting led to the development of a land version, the Twin 40L70 Field Mounting. This was a virtually unaltered naval Type B (444-round) mounting placed on a towed land carriage with two folding outrigger arms each side to impart extra stability when firing. The land mounting was not intended to operate in isolation but as part of an air defence system known as Guardian in which the gun operated under the control of a central fire-control system. When it originally appeared the Guardian system involved the Hollandse Signaalapparaten BV Flycatcher radar-based system capable of controlling two mountings at the same time. A batch of thirty-six Twin 40L70 Field Mountings was sold to Venezuela before production ceased during the mid-1990s.

As mentioned above, the Compact was replaced in series production by the so-called Fast Forty from the early 1990s onwards. Outwardly, the Fast Forty and the Compact are almost identical for the Compact mounting can be upgraded to Fast Forty standard by a kit. Produced in both single- and twin-barrel forms, the guns involved with the Fast Forty were considerably modified to produce a cyclic fire rate of 450rpm, the twin-barrel mountings thus being able to produce a combined cyclic fire rate of 900rpm. This firing rate increase involved a drastic revision of some parts of the loading and breech mechanisms and the introduction of some exotic materials such as titanium. Ammunition magazine and feed arrangements remain much the same as for the Compact but operate at a higher speed. To take full advantage of the enhanced fire rate the barrel training and acceleration rates were increased, the latter to no less than a possible 130°/s, while to enhance firing accuracy the barrel, or barrels, are secured in a barrel guidance frame. Accuracy is so enhanced that the Fast Forty is claimed to have an anti-missile capability from a range of about 3,000m downwards. To enhance the close-in lethality it is possible to configure the fire control to automatically switch the ammunition feed to APFSDS (see under Ammunition below) once a target approaches to within 1,000m of the firing platform. The twin-barrel Fast Forty replaced the Compact mounting on some Italian Navy vessels.

Single-barrel Fast Forty mountings are available in three forms to enable them to be installed on a variety of light vessels. In each case the on-mounting

A Breda Twin Fast Forty naval mounting capable of churning out a cyclic rate of fire of 900rpm.

ammunition capacity is 144 rounds. The Type A is an unmanned mounting with all operations under remote control. By contrast the Type B is controlled and aimed by an on-carriage operator. The Type C incorporates what is described as an integral Micro Fire Control System, or MFCS, on which all the operator has to do is designate a target and all subsequent tracking and fire-control computations are then completely automatic. Also available is an optional 'Stealth' cupola that provided a significant reduction in the radar cross-section of the mounting. Single-barrel Fast Forty mountings were sold to Kuwait.

Also developed was a land-based Twin Fast Forty Field Mounting, basically a land service development of the 40L70 Field Mounting. A prototype was completed during the early 1990s but did not attract a customer. Another proposal was a fully enclosed L/70 Bofors Gun turret for one or two guns that could be mounted in place of the usual open turret twin L/60 mounting on a M42 or M42A1 Duster tracked air defence vehicle chassis (see Chapter 10), but it was never built.

As mentioned above, one further Breda/OTO Melara venture was the 144-round Automatic Feed Device (AFD) from the naval Type 564 as a retrofit package for the land service L/70. Also developed was a version of the L/70 with a 32-round autoloader known as the AL-100.

For many years Breda/OTO Melara and Daewoo of South Korea had a form of mutual manufacturing agreement that eventually came to an end in 1992. Using the experience and knowledge gained from the agreement and from experience of the Breda/OTO Melara Compact, Daewoo decided to develop their own twin-barrel 40mm L/70 naval mounting known as the Vespa 40mm L/70 K(T). Using ammunition feed techniques derived from Breda/OTO Melara designs, the magazine and feed capacity was 768 rounds. They were installed on the South Korean minelayer *Won San* and the fast frigate *Ulsan*. It is understood that about fifteen equipments were produced.

South Korea was not the only nation to develop a Breda/OTO Melara Compact derivative. During 2009 it was announced that Iran had introduced an indigenous version under the name of *Fath* ('Victory') and had installed a gun on at least one fast frigate, the *Jamaran*.

Fire Control

The L/70 was designed from the outset to be incorporated into a remote fire-control system based on radar or any other form of target-acquisition and tracking system. To this end the land-based L/70 originally featured an innovative AB Bofors precision remote-control system that eventually featured solid-state circuit amplifiers, but many other such systems appeared. Most of them operated along much the same lines so one example will suffice to outline the rest.

By 1958 the British Army had developed a fire-control system that employed three main components, namely a target-warning radar, a fire-control equipment, and the gun or guns.

The radar involved was the Radar AA No 4 Mark 7/1 or 7/3 which searched the surrounding air space at an antenna rate of 15revs/min to watch for the approach of a target. The radar incorporated an identification friend or foe (IFF) system. Maximum target acquisition range was about 15,500m with a target-tracking function cutting in at about 8,200m. Once a target was detected the target data was passed on to the fire-control equipment via cables.

The British Army adopted the Fire Control Equipment No 7 Mark 4. Developed by EMI Electronics at Hayes, Middlesex, and code named 'Yellow Fever', this was a fire-control cabin on a field carriage equipped with the same traverse controls as the L/70 mounting. As target data was received from the warning radar the cabin traversed towards the target so that a roof-mounted Radar AA No 7 searched for the target and, once it was acquired, began to track the target and calculate its position and track. At the same time the on-board radar pointed a visual sight towards the target. Using an on-board computer the equipment was then able to use radar and visual data to continually predict the target's future position and range and transmit the resultant data via cables to the gun or guns to power the electro-hydraulic drive units on the mountings and point the barrel(s) accordingly. If necessary, each gun could revert to its own powered control, relying on the on-board sight units for aiming. Should power

Radar AA No 4 Mark 7/1 or 7/3 target-warning radar. (T. J. Gander)

Fire Control Equipment No 7 Mark 4, code named 'Yellow Fever'. (T. J. Gander)

The power source for the Royal Artillery's Bofors L/70 guns, the Generating Set 27.5kVA (Meadows) No 1 Mark 1. (T. J. Gander)

be somehow lost it was also possible to keep the gun in action using the cranked control handles.

The above-mentioned centralised fire-control system was employed by British Regular Army air defence batteries. Their part-time Territorial Army counterparts relied on the on-carriage reflex sight units only.

As the British Army employed the Type A L/70 Bofors Gun, power for all these equipments was delivered from a towed generator, the Generating Set 27.5kVA (Meadows) No 1 Mark 1, which weighed 4,420kg.

Other nations employed generally similar remote-control fire-control systems that operated along similar lines but often differed considerably in detail. For instance, Switzerland offered the widely-acquired Oerlikon-Contraves Fledermaus, Super-Fledermaus or (later) Skyguard systems. The French introduced a system known as the Eldorado-Mirador while the Netherlands selected their locally-devised Hollandse Signaalaparaten L4/5 (no longer in service) and a later Signaal product known as Flycatcher. The Swedish Army had a system known as the PS-04/R. Many other such systems were and still are on offer, along with a seemingly never-ending array of improvement packages.

LVS

During 1994 and following intensive trials the Swedish Army ordered 215 LVS sight units from Saab Instruments (later Saab Dynamics AB) to update their L/70 guns not already involved with centralised fire-control systems. The first examples entered service during 1995, some of them being issued to Swedish coastal defence units.

The LVS system is easily retrofitted to 40mm L/70 guns. On the L/70 the layer's position is to the right of the gun, leaving the existing sight system and controls as a back-up, should they ever be required. There are two main components; the Target Acquisition and Tracking Unit (TAU), and the Computer and Control Unit (CCU). The system is completed by several other black boxes.

In operation the gunner acquires and tracks a target with the TAU which contains a ×7 telescopic sight combined with a laser rangefinder. Using underslung control bars, the gunner lays the sight graticule on the target and commences the engagement by firing a series of laser pulses to determine the target range. Angular movements of the line of sight are measured by gyros so that three-dimensional target speed and position are constantly computed inside the CCU. The system calculates the aim-off angle and controls the gun-laying system, all the while entering corrections for wind, temperature, atmospheric pressure, type of ammunition and muzzle velocity. These variables are automatically considered during the calculation of the aim-off angle. Different operating modes are available for moving and stationary targets. Normally the

LVS is a day-only sight but it is possible to fit an image intensifier or thermal imager for night or poor visibility fire missions.

Thailand upgraded their L/70 guns with LVS sight units in 1998. The LVS system has been installed on several other types of light air defence gun as it was designed for the 20mm to 60mm calibre powered gun carriage categories.

Retro Tech

One proposed update programme introduced for the L/70 during 1989 came under the general AB Bofors sales name of Retro Tech. The overall intention was that by the addition of some all-round improvements to the land service gun and its fire-control system the revised equipment could become part of a system that would enable the L/70 to remain a viable air defence weapon against the latest generation of strike aircraft, helicopters and even guided missiles. By the addition of some fire-control features derived from the BOFI programme (see following chapter) the gun could be controlled from a computer-controlled target acquisition and tracking radar (the Super-Fledermaus produced by what was then SATT Communications was the preferred option) or from an on-carriage Universal Tank and Anti-Aircraft Sight (UTAAS), an optronic unit from Bofors Aerotronics AB (later part of Saab Systems), complete with a laser rangefinder and fire-control computer.

Few Retro Tech changes were to be made to the gun itself although the magazine capacity could be increased to twenty-two rounds by the provision of lengthened feed rails. Limitations imposed by the UTAAS system restricted the maximum barrel elevation to +80° while an on-carriage power supply unit became a fixture. No changes were made to the ammunition, the intention being that the proximity-fuzed PFHE (see below in this chapter) would become the most frequently used air defence round.

The scope of the Retro Tech programme was expanded to include land service L/60 guns. In many ways the updating of the L/60 gun and carriage was far more extensive than for the L/70 as the old manual controls were replaced by hydraulically-powered drives involving just one layer. The conversion included the provision of an off-carriage electrical power supply unit and an on-carriage power supply slip ring to transmit electric power to the various drive and control systems. The cyclic rate of fire was increased to 200rpm. Many of the improvements introduced to the L/70 guns were extended to include the older L/60 guns to the extent of the introduction of an L/60 PFHE round, plus the introduction of on-carriage, ready-use ammunition racks capable of holding an extra twenty-four rounds (the autoloader capacity could be increased to twenty rounds). While it would have been possible to link an updated L/60 to a target-acquisition radar, the proposed fire-control solution was the introduction of the UTAAS pattern sight, plus the introduction of an optical target indicator as employed with the BOFI system (see following

The optical target indicator, originally introduced with the BOFI, that can be utilised with the Bofors L/70 fire-control system. (T. J. Gander)

chapter), the latter being yet another target acquisition option for updated Retro Tech L/70 guns.

The AB Bofors Retro Tech programme offered much in cost-effectiveness and tactical capability terms but one problem emerged. There were no takers and the Retro Tech programme lapsed.

L/70 REMO

Following on from the Retrotech exercise, during 2006 AB Bofors produced another update for existing 40mm L/70 guns to extend their efficiency and service lives. Known as the L/70 Renovation and Modernisation (L/70 REMO) package the intention was to utilise several aspects of a 1989 upgrade programme carried out by RDM Technology of the Netherlands for the Netherlands Army and Air Force which allowed the guns to fire PFHE rounds (see below). The components to carry out this programme were supplied by AB Bofors.

Perhaps the main aspect of the 2006 L/70 REMO programme was the installation of a Proximity Fuze Programmer (PFP) to permit programmable 3P rounds (see below in this chapter) to be utilised. Power for drive and control systems could be provided by an on-carriage diesel-powered auxiliary power unit (APU). The conversion could be carried out by AB Bofors or at the user's own facilities.

Following a thorough overhaul and renovation exercise the fire-control system was updated and enhanced by the introduction of an on-carriage UTAAS optronic sight unit proposed as part of the Retro Tech project (see above). Other upgrade options included revised ready-use ammunition racks accommodating ninety-six rounds and autoloader feed guides holding up to twenty-six rounds.

As far as is known the L/70 REMO package did not find any takers.

Intercontrol AS

Intercontrol AS of Os, Norway, has developed an upgrade package for hydraulically-driven L/70 naval mountings. Known as the SAK 40 N67 El the main upgrade features include the replacement of electro-hydraulic drives by all-electric components. These changes result in a gun and mounting weight saving of about 900kg, improved barrel pointing speed rates and precision, a significant reduction in maintenance demands and costs, and improved reliability. It has been stated that once modified the potential service life of the guns involved could be extended by an extra twenty years.

No changes have been made to the gun itself other than the introduction of electrical firing control circuits rather than the existing electro-mechanical linkages. The main changes are to the lower carriage where the electro-hydraulic drive mechanisms are replaced by electrical components. In general these are reliable, readily available off-the-shelf units. Some mechanical parts are replaced by new and simpler equivalents and much use is made of low maintenance materials such as stainless steel.

After modification the barrel elevation speed is 45°/s with elevation limits of from -10° to +90°. Barrel traverse is unlimited at a training speed of 65°/s and it is possible to programme training limits over prescribed arcs for safety reasons. If necessary it remains possible to utilise two-man manual crank controls.

Fire control can be either remote or on-carriage. For the latter the layer/operator is seated to the left of the gun to operate a fixed control unit via a joystick.

Ammunition

When the Bofors 40mm L/70 was first produced the only ammunition natures available were those already in production for L/60 guns, namely high explosive with a tracer element (HE-T), armour-piercing (AP) and a training/practice round, with or without a tracer element (TP or TP-T). While these natures were carried over to the L/70 family, the new rounds featured slightly enlarged projectiles with an improved payload capacity and longer cases to accommodate more propellant. Since the early days of the 40mm L/70 and its ammunition, the latter has been the subject of considerable attentions, resulting in many significant advances in ammunition technology.

HE-T Often referred to as HEI (high explosive incendiary) or HEI-T, this round was one of the most frequently fired of all 40mm operational rounds, dating back to the early days of the L/60 models. By the 1990s AB Bofors regarded HE-T as outmoded, having been replaced by more efficient types of projectile, but in 2008 L/70 HE-T rounds remained available from at least twenty-one manufacturers.

Although slight variations exist between manufacturers the L/70 HE-T projectile is a hollow special steel forging with a boat-tailed base and a streamlined ogive. A copper or cupro-nickel drive band encircles the projectile body just above the crimped cartridge/projectile junction, this crimping being common to all L/70 rounds. The AB Bofors filling is 100g of Hexotonal, a rapid action explosive comprising 42 per cent TNT, 40 per cent RDX, 15 per cent aluminium powder and 3 per cent desensitiser. Many other alternative explosive fillings have been employed. The base of the projectile contains a tracer element which burns for at least four seconds after firing.

The drawn 70:30 brass propellant case has a semi-rimmed base and is fitted with a percussion primer; case length is 365mm. Propellant loads may vary but the AB Bofors 40mm L/70 HE-T uses approximately 485g of a flash-reduced, low erosion, single base, nitrocellulose powder (NC 1066). These propellant details can be taken as typical for all other rounds (other than APFSDS-T) in the AB Bofors L/70 ammunition family.

The projectile for the Bofors 40mm L/70 HE-T round.

Swedish-manufactured fuzes for the L/70 HE-T include the nose-mounted, mechanical super-quick LI 472 and LI 473 produced by Lindesbergs Industri AB (LIAB). While the LI 472 is primarily intended for employment against aircraft targets, the LI 473 incorporates a post-impact delay element to be more effective against lightly armoured targets. Each type of fuze can have a self-destruct element functioning after about 12 seconds. An early alternative to these two fuzes was the delayed-action Bofors Fz104 M12.

The latest generation of HE-T and similar rounds incorporate Low Vulnerability Ammunition (LOVA – also known as Insensitive Munition (IM)) techniques relating to the case primers, igniters and propellant. The intention is that the shock or heat created by incoming artillery fragments or explosive detonations nearby will not cause the normally sensitive propellant to conflagrate, thereby enhancing ammunition safety under extreme combat conditions. LOVA measures can be incorporated into all L/70 ammunition.

HCHE HCHE stands for High Capacity High Explosive and is a development of HE-T. It differs mainly in employing a special grade of steel for the projectile body to enable it to penetrate armour plate up to 20mm thick without excessive deformation. Only after this degree of penetration will the nose-mounted Fz104 M12 point-detonating fuze function to detonate the 165g Octonal payload. The delay ensures the maximum blast, fragmentation and incendiary effects both on and inside a target. HCHE has rather fallen out of favour in favour of more recent developments such as MPT (see below) and was withdrawn from production by AB Bofors, although it remained available from some other manufacturers.

MPT MPT stands for Multi-Purpose Tracer, a novel type of ammunition developed jointly during the 1980s by AB Bofors and Raufoss Technology A/S of Norway (now Nammo Raufoss A/S, part of the Nordic Ammunition Company (Nammo)). It involves an operating principle introduced by Raufoss during the 1970s whereby the projectile detonates on impact without the involvement of a fuze. Instead the MPT relies on a pyrotechnic train device that is totally safe to handle; the round can be dropped nose down onto a hard surface from a height of 15m without functioning.

The pyrotechnic ignition train in the MPT projectile nose will activate only on firing and becomes fully sensitive during the projectile trajectory. On impact with even lightly armoured targets the pyrotechnic element ignites with a post impact delay of 0.3ms. Penetration levels can be up to 25mm of armour plate. Each projectile has an incendiary charge inside the nose cap and the forward part of the projectile body while the explosive payload located towards the base is 105g of Composition A4. The incendiary element has the longest burning time so on detonation the chances of creating a conflagration inside a target are much enhanced, while the explosive creates a cone of body fragments to be dispersed into the target to inflict more damage. A tracer element is located in the projectile base and burns for at least four seconds before initiating a self-destruct train that functions after 8.5 seconds.

The destructive power and handling advantages of the MPT round are such that AB Bofors promoted it as much more lethal and effective than HE-T and HCHE rounds.

The AB Bofors MPT and PFHE rounds are ballistically matched so no alternative fire-control changes need to be introduced when both are in use.

PFHE When it first appeared in 1975 the 40mm PFHE round (also written as PF-HE) was regarded as a significant technological breakthrough. PFHE stands for Pre Fragmented High Explosive, a projectile and proximity fuze combination that can be highly effective against low-flying aircraft, helicopters and guided missiles. (The term PFHE can also denote Proximity-Fuzed High Explosive.) This round had been accepted for Royal Swedish Navy service by the end of 1975.

The proximity fuze was one of the more important technological advances to emerge from the Second World War. Developed in the United States using principles originating in the United Kingdom, the proximity fuze operates on the Doppler Principle using reflected radio energy from a target to detonate the fuze at a pre-determined distance from the target. In this way the projectile does not have to impact with a target – a near miss is good enough.

Making such a fuze small enough to install in the nose of a 40mm projectile was a considerable achievement in its own right, the development being successfully completed by AB Bofors and Philips Electronik-Industrie AB (later Bofors Electronics AB) when many others had yet to succeed. An improved Mark 2 fuze appeared in 1983 and further enhancements have been introduced

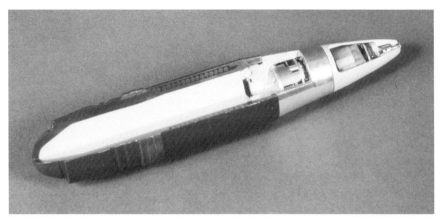

Cross-section of the projectile for the Bofors L/70 PFHE round.

since then. By 1985 well over one million PFHE fuzes had been produced for delivery to about thirty countries and production, including licence production, continues. Other manufacturers than AB Bofors have since developed their equivalent 40mm PFHE fuzes and projectiles, notably Borletti of Italy and what was then Thomson CSF (later Thales) of France. A more recent arrival in the field has been the Ji-Ning Machinery Corporation of Taiwan.

With the Bofors L/70 PFHE projectile the fragmentation created by the high-fragmentation steel body is augmented by an internal layer of 650 tungsten pellets, each 3mm in diameter, that travel outwards at velocities of up to 1,500m/s to inflict their destructive kinetic effects at distances of several metres from the burst. Each pellet can penetrate up to 18mm of Dural. The pellet layer is located around the inside of the projectile wall, the projectile base having a 'duck tail' curved contour to form an improved aerodynamic outline and create a rearwards fragmentation effect in the case of a delayed burst. The explosive content is 120g of Octol, a high energy mixture of HMX and TNT capable of creating approximately 2,400 viable projectile fragments, including the 650 pellets.

The PFHE fuze is located in the nose of the projectile and incorporates an automatic sensitivity control to prevent initiation by surface clutter returns at low altitudes. There is also a sensitive impact function and an electronic self-destruct feature (after 8.5s), together with delayed arming and bore and muzzle safeties. There are also electronic counter-counter-measure (ECCM) circuits to combat jamming.

When fired against aircraft targets the fuze triggering distance is from 6.5m to 7m, or 4m to 7m against helicopters. Against guided missiles the distance is about 4.5m. These performances considerably increase the equivalent target area compared to conventional projectiles. For instance the PFHE projectile increases the equivalent target area by a factor of about 50 while against missiles that figure could be as high as 500. In this manner a single PFHE projectile can carry out the destructive task of far larger numbers of conventional rounds.

The AB Bofors PFHE and MPT rounds are ballistically matched so no alternative fire-control changes need to be introduced when both are in use.

3P If the 40mm PFHE projectile was one significant leap in ammunition technology, the Bofors 3P was another. The technology involved was originally developed as part of the Trinity programme (see Chapter 9) but by 1990 the principles involved were expanded to include the L/70 ammunition family. The first 3P deliveries were made during 1996, covering a supply of the rounds for the 40/70B gun for the CV9040 IFV and the TriAD air defence vehicle (see Chapter 11). Other applications for 3P include the BAE Systems Bofors 40mm Mark 3 and Mark 4 naval gun systems (see Chapter 9) and, potentially, the L/70 REMO programme (see above).

3P denotes Prefragmented Programmable Proximity. A 3P projectile contains all the PFHE features mentioned previously but with the addition of an additional programmable function. By means of a Proximity Fuze Programmer (PFP) connected to a gun-control computer each 3P fuze can be individually programmed by induction as it enters the gun chamber, so this round can only

A batch of Bofors L/70 PFHE rounds fresh off the production line.

be fired from suitably-equipped guns (the programming facility can be retrofitted to most existing L/70 guns). Programming is carried out in two steps. The first actuates the fuze circuitry and sets the required programme to suit the target. The second step is carried out while the round is actually in the gun chamber and only milliseconds before firing, where the range and hence the predicted time of flight to the target is fed into the fuze. Six fuze functions can be programmed. They are:

- Auto mode 1. A range gated proximity function with an impact function and self-destruct at the end of the gate. All other signals, including attempted jamming, are ignored until the fuze comes to the gate.
- Auto mode 2. A range gated proximity function with impact priority and self-destruct at the end of the gate. All other signals, including attempted jamming, are ignored until the fuze comes to the gate.
- Time. A highly accurate time function, capable of producing air bursts over a target area.
- Impact. An impact function with a post-impact delay of 0.3ms and self-destruct after about 15 seconds.
- Anti-armour. An armour penetration function.
- Proximity. The normal proximity function with an impact function and self-destruct after about 15 seconds.

If none of the above is programmed or the range to the target is not determined the 3P fuze will act as a normal proximity fuze with an impact function and self-destruct after about 15 seconds. Power for all the associated circuitry is derived from an internal battery initiated by firing setback. The battery also provides power for several safety-associated circuits and a central clock that times the programmed gates and other functions.

Apart from the fuze the 3P projectile is similar in construction to that of the PFHE but the number of pre-fragmented tungsten pellets is increased to about 1,100. Each pellet travels outwards at a velocity of 1,200–1,500m/s and can penetrate up to 18mm of Dural. The payload is 120g of a polymer-bonded explosive (PBX) based on a mixture of HMX and TNT with LOVA properties.

AP-T Compared to the high-tech 3P round the L/70 AP-T is very much a relic of a past era. It is a purely kinetic energy hole-punching round intended for use against armour so the projectile is a hardened solid steel penetrator with a thin steel nose cap (or windshield) crimped over the nose to improve the aerodynamics. A tracer element is screwed into the base and burns for four seconds after firing. The L/70 AP-T can penetrate from 40–50mm of armour plate set at an angle of 60° at a range of from 100–150m.

At one stage AB Bofors introduced an alternative armour-piercing round known as APHC-T, or Armour Piercing High Capacity Tracer. It consisted of an aluminium body enclosing a sub-calibre heavy metal core. It did not find much favour and was withdrawn from production. There was also an APC-T, or APCT, with a hardened steel penetrator with a soft steel cap to improve penetration (hence Armour Piercing Capped Tracer) but it had been withdrawn from production by the late 1970s.

APFSDS-T The abbreviation APFSDS-T denotes Armour-Piercing, Fin-Stabilised, Discarding Sabot Tracer, and refers to a kinetic energy armour-penetrating round where the penetrator is an arrow-like, sub-calibre projectile that combines mass, velocity and density to perform the actual armour penetration. It was developed specifically for one gun, the 40/70B gun developed for the CV9040 MICV (see Chapter 11) operated by the Swedish Army. As this vehicle would have to be deployed against vehicles as well protected and armed as itself it needed a better armour penetration capability than the standard AP-T, so the APFSDS-T was developed and first demonstrated during 1988.

The sub-calibre penetrator rod for the 40mm APFSDS-T weighs 200g and is 200mm long. It is fin-stabilised in flight at the relatively high muzzle velocity of from 1,470–1,480m/s. As the penetrator rod is made from a dense tungsten alloy it can penetrate more than 120mm of armour at 1,000m. The round is handled and loaded in exactly the same manner as all other L/70 ammunition and can be fired at the full cyclic fire rate.

At the instant of firing the penetrator rod is held in a light alloy sabot with a windshield over the front. There are three sabot segments wrapped around the rod, the complete assembly being crimped onto the brass propellant case. The drive band is plastic and the entire rod and sabot assembly remains as a single unit until it leaves the muzzle. The drive band then breaks up and the windshield and the sabot segments separate and fall away from the rod, leaving the finned rod to travel at high velocity in a flat trajectory. Time of flight to 1,500m, the maximum effective combat range of the 40mm APFSDS-T, is less than 1.1 seconds. A tracer element in the base of the rod burns until a range of about 2,000m is reached.

To obtain the high velocity required for this round the propellant employed is 540g of a single-base, high energy propellant known as NC 1289, plus an anti-barrel wear additive.

A special training round had to be developed for this round as the APFSDS-T rod can travel considerable distances before it expends its momentum and falls to the ground. Distances of well over 40,000m can be quoted so special range safety provisions have to be made when firing the operational APFSDS-T during training. A 40mm TPDS-T (Training Practice Discarding Sabot Tracer) round was therefore developed, the penetrator rod being steel to reduce costs. In place of the usual fins the tail is a hollow cone which has no effect on

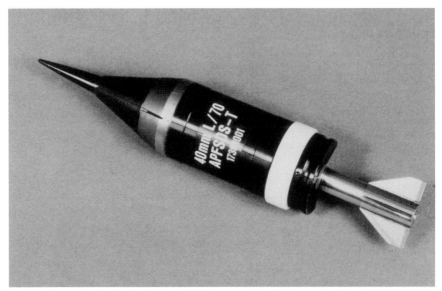

Produced specifically for the Bofors 40/70B armoured vehicle gun, the 40mm L/70 APFSDS-T projectile.

performance until about 800m from the muzzle is reached so up to that range the external ballistics of the APFSDS-T and TPDS-T are identical. Beyond that range the conical tail starts to create drag-inducing eddies that slow down the rod considerably until it loses its momentum, becomes unstable and falls to earth at about 6,000m. Due to the reduced weight of the projectile assembly the muzzle velocity of this round is increased to 1,540m/s.

Bofors were not the only concern to develop a 40mm L/70 APFSDS-T round. During the 1980s the Italian SNIA BPD Difesa e Spazio (later Simmel Difesa SpA) developed a APFSDS to be fired from the Breda/OTO Melara Fast Forty (see above) but it did not enter anything more than token production. However, it was marketed sporadically over several years. In 2006 the Ji-Ning Machinery Corporation of Taiwan revealed that they too were manufacturing a 40mm APFSDS round (see Chapter 9).

Not content with the performance of their existing APFSDS-T round, which was based on a past generation of technology, Bofors Defence, (now part of BAE Systems Bofors AB) allied with QinetiQ of the United Kingdom to develop an updated round with an improved ballistic and penetration performance. The new round, also intended to be fired from the 40/70B gun, is known as the APFSDS-T Mark 2 and incorporates the latest LOVA (IM) techniques. The muzzle velocity is about 1,500m/s and the disclosed armour penetration at 1,000m is 'well in excess of 150mm', enabling it to penetrate the side armour of most main battle tanks. Among the projectile design

On the left is a 40mm APFSDS-T round introduced by the Italian SNIA BPD Difesa e Spazio (later Simmel Difesa SpA) to be fired from the Breda Fast Forty. (T. J. Gander)

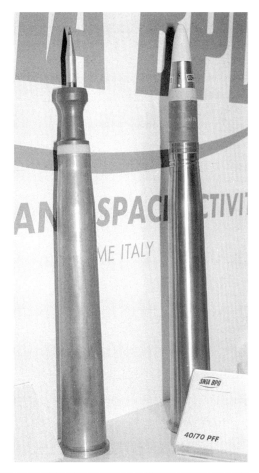

The most frequently fired of all Bofors 40mm L/70 projectiles, the TP-T.

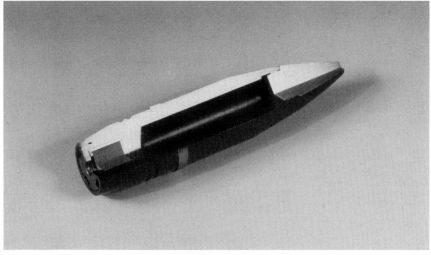

DATA FOR AMMUNITION

Type	HE-T	HCHE	MPT
Weight			
Complete round	2.5kg	2.4kg	2.5kg
Projectile	960g	870g	940g
Explosive	100g	165g	105g
Length			
Complete round	534mm	534mm	534mm
Case	365mm	365mm	365mm
Tracer burn time	4s	4s	4s
Muzzle velocity	1,005m/s	1,030m/s	1,025m/s

Type	PFHE	3P	AP-T
Weight			
Complete round	2.4kg	2.5kg	2.45kg
Projectile	880g	975g	930g
Explosive	120g	120g	none
Length			
Complete round	534.4mm	534.4mm	497mm
Case	365mm	365mm	365mm
Tracer burn time	4s	none	4s
Muzzle velocity	1,025m/s	1,012m/s	1,025m/s

Type	APFSDS-T	TP-T	Break-Up
Weight			
complete round	2.3kg	2.5kg	2.2kg
projectile	200g	960g	770g
explosive	none	none	none
Length			
complete round	520mm	534mm	534mm
case	365mm	365mm	365mm
Tracer burn time	to 2,000m	4s	none
Muzzle velocity	1,470–1,480m/s	1,025m/s	n/app

improvements introduced is an improved slipping drive band and a revised triple-sectioned segmented front sabot that will improve ramming as well as separation once past the muzzle. A complete APFSDS-T Mark 2 round is 520mm long and weighs 2.5kg. The projectile weighs 500g, as does the propellant load, the latter being ignited by an extended primer.

TP-T Of all the rounds ever fired from 40mm L/70 guns the most numerous has to be TP-T (Training Practice Tracer) due to its relatively low cost compared to operational rounds. Expended during training and live fire functional testing, the L/70 TP-T is identical in outline, weight and dimensions to the L/70 HE-T other than that the filling is inert and a dummy fuze or some other form of inert plug is secured to the projectile nose. A tracer element is normally threaded into the base of the projectile but is not always fitted.

Break-Up Break-Up training rounds were originally produced by the Netherlands concern of NWM De Kruithorn BV before the sales rights were taken over by Oerlikon-Contraves Pyrotec, now part of Rheinmetall DeTec AG. These rounds can be fired in relatively enclosed areas where safety ranges can be as short as 100m, the rounds producing the recoil, firing noise and flash of an operational round in relative safety. The rounds can even be fired against live aircraft or other targets with no danger of the target being harmed in any way.

The Break-Up projectile has a thin plastic body while the nose is filled with light polystyrene foam. The body interior contains three pellets of pressed iron powder while the drive band is nylon. As the projectile proceeds down the barrel after firing the rotation imparted by the rifling causes the iron powder to migrate outwards but the barrel walls prevent any outward movement. Due to internal stresses created by this migration and once the projectile is clear of the muzzle the plastic walls of the projectile split along fluted serrations so that the iron powder and the plastic body fragments fall to the ground within a cone-shaped area extending to 80m from the muzzle. The cartridge case involved with this round can be re-cycled several times to reduce costs.

Break-Up ammunition is produced for many calibres other than 40mm so is not specific to the 40mm L/70. It is also available for Bofors L/60 guns.

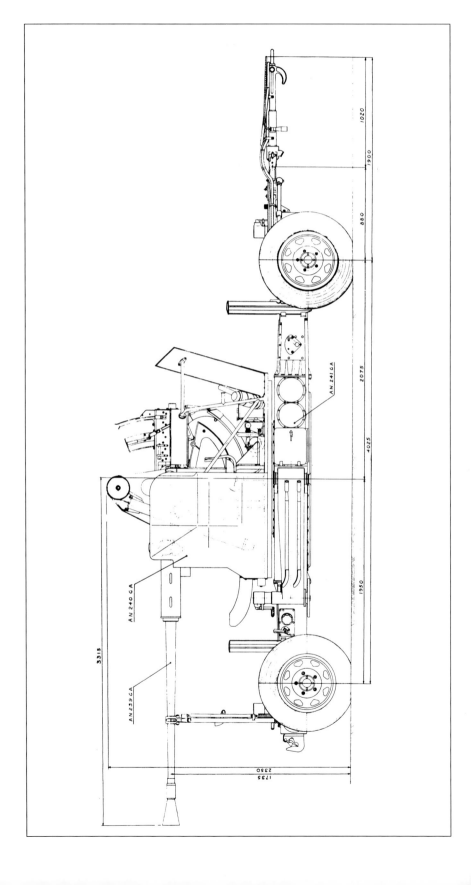

AN 239 GA

AN 240 GA

AN 241 GA

3315

1735

2350

1950

4025

2075

880

1900

1020

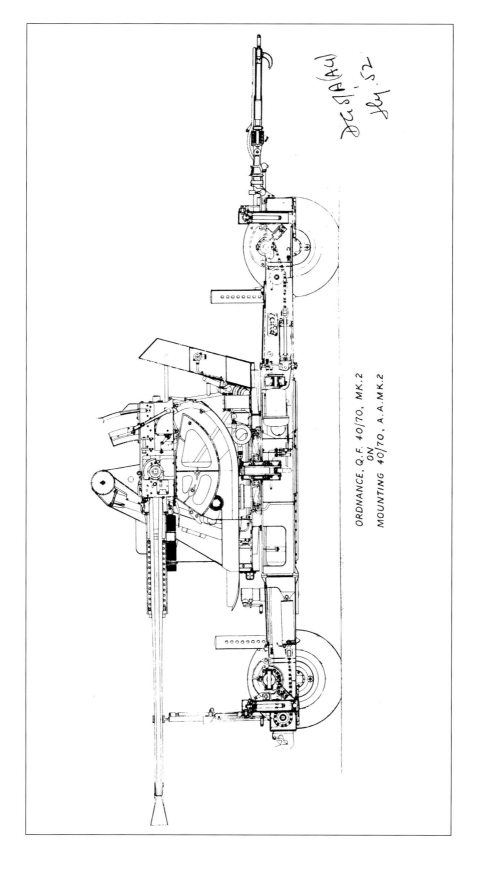

DaslA(A4)
fly. 52

ORDNANCE, Q.F. 40/70, MK.2
ON
MOUNTING 40/70, A.A.MK.2

Chapter 8

BOFI

By the early 1970s the AB Bofors design team was ready to contemplate the next step in the Bofors Gun story. The Bofors L/70 was then still in series production and selling well, usually in a form where a fire-control system was able to control a number of guns. One factor that emerged from land-based installations was that it often took a significant amount of time to install and prepare multi-gun batteries and their central fire-control positions and make them ready for action. To offset this time constraint the employment of a fire-control position capable of tracking targets and pointing the guns under remote power control could be very efficient. Even so, multi-gun installations could be expensive and many potential L/70 customers could not foresee that they would ever require such complex air defence arrangements.

From these factors it came as a logical step that efficiency of the L/70 could be increased by providing each gun with its own on-carriage fire-control sensor and control system. The facility to operate within a centralised system could be retained but the main objective was to make each gun its own completely autonomous air defence system that could be brought into action within the minimum possible time period.

The first trials with components of this new configuration were conducted from about 1972 onwards and by 1975 the first full equipment was ready for demonstration. It was then known as the Bofors 40mm System 75 which went into production the following year, 1976. The System 75 was essentially a combination of a partially-modified L/70 gun, an optronic fire-control system and the then new PFHE ammunition. The towed gun remained basically unchanged but a petrol-driven generator located over the rear carriage axle became a standard fixture to power the on-board drive controls, optronics and associated electronics. The layer's position was enclosed within a cab to the left of the gun, the cab also containing the gun controls, a computer and other system components.

The System 75 optronic fire-control system was later renamed as BOFI, denoting Bofors Optronic Fire-control Instrument. In time this early BOFI system became known as the BOFI fair weather gun system to differentiate it from what was to follow. Whatever the name, the system included a combined day and night sight, a laser rangefinder and a computer. Using a constant supply

An early outing for BOFI at the Farnborough Air Show. (T. J. Gander)

of laser-derived range data and the angular positioning of the target, the computer could calculate the target's future position and barrel aim-off for firing.

The day and night sight were combined in the same vision scope unit, with both vision devices mechanically fixed so that they remained in the same plane as the barrel. The passive night sight originally used was a second-generation image intensifier with a field of view of 7° and a magnification of ×8. Under clear visibility conditions on a star-lit night the maximum range was approximately 7,000m. The day sight had a magnification of ×7.

The laser rangefinder was also connected mechanically to the sight unit. The laser receiver contained optics that focussed the laser energy reflected from the target for amplification and signal processing. Registered range was converted into digital form before passing to the system computer. In order to prevent spurious returns from trees and other nearby objects the laser incorporated a blocking device calibrated at 500m. Another computer-controlled blocking device came into action when the first reflected laser signals came from a target. When the computer received the first range signals it blocked the receiver for all other input signals other than those immediately around the target, meaning that it continued to process range data from only one aircraft in a loose formation.

When the layer/operator pressed the foot pedal to fire the gun the computer added the calculated aim-off data components to the respective position coordinates and the gun barrel moved to the calculated aim-off point and firing could commence against that point. As the continued movement of the target was being constantly predicted the aim-off point was also continually calculated throughout the entire firing sequence. When firing ceased the barrel automatically returned to the target's predicted position. Also calculated and introduced were corrections for various factors such as wind drift, muzzle velocity variations and atmospheric factors, all entered into the computer via the control panel inside the layer's cab.

Another feature of the BOFI system computer allowed the gun and sight to be pointed towards an oncoming target by external means from an optical target indicator that was part of the original System 75. Positioned close to the gun,

The large radome gave BOFI a distinctive appearance. (T. J. Gander)

the optical target indicator involved a pistol-aimed arm, or pointing stick, aimed manually by the operator. Synchros within the target indicator transmitted aiming information to the gun via a cable so when the aiming arm was pointing directly at the target the operator pressed a trigger on the pistol grip. This lit a lamp on the layer's control panel and a buzzer sounded. On receipt of these signals the layer pressed a button and the gun slewed onto the target, after which the tracker mode selected could commence.

The BOFI fair weather gun system found customers in Malaysia, the former Yugoslavia and perhaps some others, but it was only a step towards the full potential of BOFI. Being an optronics-based fire-control arrangement the BOFI fair weather system depended on the visual acquisition and tracking of a target. Under poor visibility or bad weather conditions the optronic BOFI was limited in what it could do and the only way that BOFI could be converted into an all-weather system was to introduce some form of on-carriage tracking radar. By 1979 this had been achieved.

AB Bofors introduced the term BOFI all-weather gun system, also known as BOFI-R, to denote the introduction of the on-carriage radar, heralding the integration of gun, fire control and ammunition that would later go one stage further with Trinity (see Chapter 9). But back in 1979 the Bofors Gun story had taken one more step in its technical progression away from the simple manually-controlled actions of the Model 1934.

With the BOFI-R the system had a choice of on-carriage sensors that enabled it to track aircraft targets under all weather and visibility conditions, including under extreme electronic warfare conditions. Its performance with PFHE ammunition was such that the gun could be realistically called upon the engage targets such as low-flying guided missiles.

The all-important radar was a product of Bofors Electronics AB. Mounted over the barrel and mechanically aligned with it, a monopulse tracking radar operated in the Ku-band (J-band), normally operating on a fixed frequency during the target acquisition phase and automatically switching over to frequency agility (frequency hopping) during target tracking. This frequency agility provided improved accuracy and resistance to jamming while retaining the ability to detect small targets such as guided missiles or surveillance drones. Against small targets the radar range could be up to 8,000m; against full-size aircraft this increased to 22,000m. Other radar features included automatic target acquisition and moving target indication (MTI).

Introducing the radar meant that BOFI could be operated in four modes:

• Autotrack. Automatic tracking in elevation, traverse and range using the tracking radar. This was the normal operating mode with the layer supervising the tracking through the day or night sight.
• Noise track or ECCM mode. Employed when a target was employing

electronic counter-measures. The radar switched to passive tracking of the jammer in elevation and traverse and the laser rangefinder determined the target range.

• Manual laser. This involved using the original BOFI optronic system as the day or night sights were employed for semi-automatic tracking with the layer tracking the target using the control joystick until the computer had sufficient data to assume control. The layer then supervised the tracking using the day or night sight.

• Manual radar. Essentially the same as manual laser but the tracking radar was employed to obtain target range data.

These operating modes provided BOFI with the ability to operate under a wide range of conditions. Having the ability to switch rapidly from radar to optronic control enabled the BOFI to remain in action even under severe electronic warfare conditions and, by varying the modes, a gun commander could effectively counter most of the countermeasures any enemy might introduce.

Other sensors that could be employed with BOFI included a Doppler muzzle-velocity radar, transmitting data to a display unit inside the on-carriage cab ready to be inserted into the BOFI computer. It was also possible to insert an identification-friend-or-foe (IFF) unit into the system.

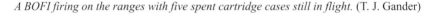

A BOFI firing on the ranges with five spent cartridge cases still in flight. (T. J. Gander)

A BOFI demonstrator on the firing ranges. (T. J. Gander)

For rapid target acquisition the BOFI computer could be fed with target indication data from a central search radar via a target data receiver (TDR). The computer transformed the target indication data into the bearing from the gun so that the servo system could swing the barrel towards the target. Multiple BOFI firing units could be connected to a central search radar from any number of such systems, each capable of acting as combat command centres. The widely deployed Ericsson Giraffe was typical of such radars. Radars could also be arranged in such a fashion that the BOFI tracking radar did not need to be switched on until required, thereby assisting in the concealment of the gun position until the last possible moment.

When firing PFHE ammunition a BOFI gun firing at a strike aircraft flying at a speed of 300m/s could open fire at a range of between 3,000–4,000m with a 50 to 60 per cent chance of obtaining a hit when firing a ten-round burst. As the range decreased the chances of a hit increased so that between 2,000 and 3,000m the chances of a hit with a ten-round burst increased to between 60 and 80 per cent. At ranges below 2,000m the chances were even higher.

The gun used with BOFI was a standard L/70 with 118 rounds on the gun (twenty-six in the autoloader and ninety-two in ready-use racks at the gun platform rear). A gun crew could be as few as four; gun commander, layer/operator, a loader on the gun platform and the operator for the optical target indicator. More personnel could be on hand to top up the ready-use ammunition racks. Time into action could be as low as two minutes when just the on-carriage fire-control equipment was involved.

One BOFI-related off-shoot of the Trinity programme was a Brazilian project that involved a BOFI-based fire-control system. The system was placed in a modified Armoured Trinity turret (see Chapter 9) known as the EB-3 and set on a Moto Pecas Charrua II armoured personnel carrier chassis. The project did not get past the mock-up stage.

The BOFI all-weather system failed to find favour with customers even though numerous technical enhancements to improve the overall performance were planned or actually introduced. When Trinity arrived BOFI continued to remain on offer for a while but it gradually faded from the scene. Its main part in the Bofors Gun story was as a major stepping-stone to the ultimate Bofors Gun – Trinity.

DATA FOR BOFI	
Weight	5,500kg
Wheelbase	4.025m
Track	1.8m
Ground clearance	390mm
Rate of fire	300rpm
Rounds on gun	118
System accuracy	3mrad
Elevation	-4° to +90°
Traverse	360°
Ammunition stowage	
Autoloader	26
Racks	92
Generator engine	2-cyl petrol
Voltage output	3-phase 220V, 50Hz
Power	7.5kVA

Chapter 9

Trinity and After

By the early 1980s it appeared to many observers of the air defence world that the gun no longer had much part to play in a tactical scene seemingly dominated by the guided missile. Air defence guns were increasingly being replaced by missile systems of all shapes and sizes but, despite prophesies to the contrary, it emerged that the gun still retained a viable role.

One reason for the survival of the air defence gun remains cost. Missile systems are expensive, with even basic shoulder-launched systems costing up to tens of thousands of dollars. Many nations lack the funds to deploy such missile systems in anything other than token numbers and once those token numbers have been expended they are gone for good. Under such circumstances the air defence gun lives on, for in cost terms most gun systems are still relatively inexpensive to procure and maintain and they will continue to provide a measure of defence for as long as the ammunition lasts. While ammunition with proximity or programmable fuzes might be relatively costly compared to conventional rounds, their performance can still be regarded as economic since fewer rounds have to be expended against most targets, and even the most advanced gun ammunition remains a much less expensive proposition than most guided missiles.

Another reason for the survival of the gun is that guided missiles have their limitations. High speed strike aircraft targets can arrive and depart at bewildering speeds, especially when low-flying aircraft are concerned, and few missile systems can realistically deal with such challenges. Many gun systems might also find it difficult to deal with such targets, but there is one particular threat against which any air defence guided missile system has severe limitations, namely the wave-hugging anti-ship missile.

Small and moving at high speed, the anti-ship missile presents a difficult target that often cannot be detected until it is very close, often too close for guided missile systems to be employed effectively. Although this threat had been appreciated for some years before then, it was the Falkland Islands campaign of 1982 that forced home the message that missiles such as the air-launched Exocet could be deadly against surface vessels.

It was soon realised that the gun could be far more responsive and accurate than the guided missile against such targets, leading to a rapid renewal in interest in the air defence gun. Soon after 1982 many navies began to assess their requirements for guns capable of producing accurate and rapid fire against wave-hopping targets, requirements expanded by the appearance of attack helicopters with lethal capabilities no less dangerous than missiles.

AB Bofors had never lost its faith in the gun as an air defence weapon, one example being the introduction of the BOFI gun system (see Chapter 8) at a time when it seemed to be unfashionable to even think in terms of air defence guns. As ever, AB Bofors planners had been busy surveying the military scene and analysing future trends and, despite the success of the BOFI, they formulated ideas that indicated that further improvements to the 40mm gun could be introduced by following the synergy principle. This approach considered that as the gun was already part of a weapon system, improvements in all aspects of the system could result in an end result greater than the sum of their individual effects. BOFI had already combined the gun, ammunition and fire control. It was time to go one better by improving all three elements, hence the name Trinity.

When the AB Bofors design teams set about creating their future weapon, using the guide designation of SAK 40L/70-600, they decided at an early stage that all fire-control sensors would have to be integrated on the weapon mount. In addition, by utilising various forms of mathematical model they determined

The basic outline of a Trinity naval mounting.

that the then-current trend of producing a large shower of gun-delivered projectiles, such as with the American 20mm Phalanx or Soviet 30mm AK-230, could not be as efficient as a much smaller number of projectiles fired with extreme accuracy. At an early stage they also accepted that the ranges of any future gun system would have to be increased beyond existing values by a considerable margin. Using these basic parameters design work began during the early 1980s, resulting in Trinity.

Trinity was unveiled to the public during the 1984 Farnborough Air Show. By 1985 the assembling and testing of the first examples of hardware had taken place and qualifying testing followed throughout 1986 and into 1987. By 1988 two naval prototypes were undergoing trials and the first land platform, Armoured Trinity, was functioning. The first sea trials were conducted during May 1988 on board the Royal Swedish Navy's *Vinga*, a *Landsort* class minesweeper.

Ammunition

Once it had been decided to retain the 40mm calibre work could commence on the ammunition. Projectile weight was increased to 1.1kg and the muzzle velocity was increased to 1,100m/s, the intention being to reduce the time of flight to a target while retaining maximum accuracy. Improvements in projectile aerodynamics were introduced to reduce the effects of drift-inducing side winds, further enhancing accuracy.

Perhaps the greatest innovation came with the introduction of a programmable fuze that combined a proximity function with time and point contact modes in such a manner that the fuze operating mode could be selected, programmed and set when the round was in the chamber and almost at the instant of firing. This resulted in the 3P round already mentioned in connection with L/70 ammunition in Chapter 7. The Trinity designation was 3P-HV, the HV denoting High Velocity and differentiating the Trinity round from the L/70 round which arrived on the scene later as it was an off-shoot of the Trinity programme.

A 40mm Trinity round. (T. J. Gander)

A comprehensive description of the modes and functions of the L/70 3P projectile is provided in Chapter 7. The Trinity 3P-HV explosive payload was 140g of Octol surrounded by 1,100 tungsten pellets, each 3mm in diameter, to add to the usual projectile case fragmentation on detonation. For Trinity the brass propellant case remained the same length as for the L/70 guns, namely 365mm, but the propellant contents were marginally increased to provide the extra muzzle velocity.

The effective proximity fuze triggering distance against a sea-skimming guided missile was about 3m while against an aircraft target this could increase to as much as 12m.

Gun and Mounting

At first sight the Trinity gun bore little resemblance to any of the earlier 40mm Bofors Guns but some components from the earlier models were carried over, including the basic operating and final loading mechanisms. The heavy barrel weighing approximately 200kg (as opposed to 163kg for the usual L/70 barrel) retained a nominal length of 70 calibres but the introduction of the 3P-HV ammunition converted the gun into a super-accuracy weapon. As mentioned above, with the new ammunition the muzzle energy was increased, producing greater recoil forces that were kept to an acceptable level by the introduction of a Solothurn pattern 'pepperpot' muzzle brake.

One Trinity innovation was a slight increase in the cyclic rate of fire to 330rpm, delivering 5.5 rounds per second. Any further increase would have caused trunnion loading problems that would have acted to the detriment of accuracy. Accuracy was such that Trinity remained a single-barrel weapon. Introducing another barrel, or barrels, onto a mounting was deemed as inherently inaccurate due to the extra stresses and vibrations that would result.

For Trinity a new magazine was introduced to hold up to 100 rounds. The magazine was so arranged that there were forty-five rounds to the left of the gun and fifty-four to the right, the odd round being loaded in the feed system. Rounds were stacked in eleven vertical rows of nine, all loaded as single rounds so the former chargers were no longer involved. Modifications later enlarged the ammunition capacity to 101 rounds. It was possible to load two different types of ammunition, one type to each side of the gun, and switch between the two as required. Reloading the magazine was a manual operation intended to be carried out during lulls in action or before action was expected. On a typical naval installation the barrel was elevated to +75° to assist the loading process. When firing the outer vertical column on one side emptied first. Assuming that between five and fifteen rounds would be used for each target engagement the magazine capacity was considered sufficient for between six and twelve engagements.

The Trinity mounting made much use of aluminium to keep weight to a minimum and also to reduce the weapon's magnetic signature to enable the weapon to be installed on vessels such as minehunters where magnetic signatures could be dangerous. Naval mountings employing gyro-stabilisation or heading reference systems normally had them mounted on the lower gun mounting to stabilise the gun barrel against ship movements while at the same time eliminating the effects of any hull flexing on the accuracy of the fire-control system. No part of the Trinity system needed to be below deck level other than perhaps a fire-control computer or computers or, as Trinity could be deployed in either manned or remote forms, a control panel.

A typical Trinity naval gun and mounting with a full load of ammunition weighed approximately 4,075kg.

Fire Control

One of the basic components of any modern fire-control system is the digital microprocessor yet when the AB Bofors designers examined various existing military-purpose microprocessors they decided that none came close enough to their performance and radiation protection requirements, so they developed their own. It emerged as the mBOF 8016, originally employed with the Bofors 57mm

This outline block drawing provides only an indication of the complexity of the Trinity weapon system.

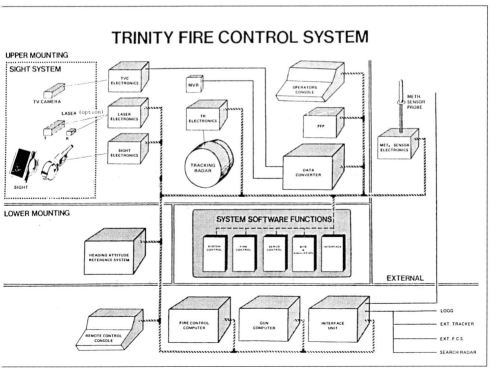

Mark 2 naval gun. With Trinity, the number of mBOFs could vary to suit any particular application but in a typical naval installation they could be used for the central fire-control computer, the gun computer, an interface with the vessel's log, for handling data from external radar systems or fire-control computers, and other functions. More could be involved for the overall system control, interface administration, servo controls, built-in test equipment (BITE), and simulation for training purposes.

The Trinity fire-control system was designed to be modular to enable it to suit any particular naval or land requirement. As a result the system could accommodate all manner of sensors and functions including target-acquisition and tracking radars, laser rangefinding, optical day and night sights, video or infra-red tracking, a gyro reference system, muzzle velocity radars, and fire-control computers. To these could be added remote sensor or control systems and fire directors, to the extent that Trinity could be integrated with a central search radar and fire-control system. In short, the Trinity approach was to combine as many fire-control functions as possible.

On Trinity the sight was a reflex optical unit through which all the optical sensors could pass their information. From a gyro-stabilised, servo-controlled mirror, the ingoing light passed to a beam splitter that reflected some of the light into the operator's eyepiece. The rest of the field of vision passed through the beam splitter to a channel employed for some form of image intensifier for night vision, or for an infra-red or thermal imaging detector. If a video camera was involved a portion of the main light channel to the operator was reflected by another beam splitter into a camera above the sight unit. Since the image intensifier channel also reflected back into the main channel to the operator, a night picture could be seen on a monitor screen. Pulsed laser light from the laser rangefinder was reflected in the outer field of the main beam splitter and then via the aiming mirror. This gyro-stabilised and servo-controlled mirror served to isolate the sight from vibrations present in any military environment. It also disconnected the sight from any mechanical linkage that could introduce sighting errors and it could also permit aim-off to be applied before firing instead of at the instant of firing. One further advantage of the integrated sight system was that the line of sight of all the sensors involved left the sight co-axially.

Associated with the Trinity sight was the operator's panel, usually located beneath the sight in two units, a keyboard and a visual monitor capable of displaying the sight image. The keyboard could be used to call up all manner of sight information in numerical and symbolic form and could also be employed to display simulated combat information during training or for trouble-shooting. In front of the keyboard were two handles for the operator, one of which was purely for operator support when the gun mount was traversing at high degrees of acceleration. The right-hand handle contained a thumb joystick for the manual mode and to over-ride the Auto-Combat mode (see below).

Trinity had five operating modes: Start/Stop, Operation, Alignment, Test and Simulation. For combat the Operation mode was selected and was attained automatically once the Stop/Start mode had been completed. When the Operation mode was ready two sub-modes could be selected, Auto-Combat and Manual.

Once in the Auto-Combat mode any target designated by a search radar or an optical target designator was engaged fully automatically, including selection of the ammunition type, proximity fuze setting, length of bursts, and the actual command to open fire. All the operator had to do was monitor the operations and override them if necessary.

Manual selection involved operator control. In this mode a number of selectable variables were displayed on the monitor and the operator used several buttons to change the data to suit the choice of action. The operator could command target indication and start the tracking radar, laser rangefinder and the automatic tracking unit (ATU) if they were included in the installation.

Once a target had been acquired the operator could choose to switch sensors for any number of reasons but mainly to suit the type of target and the tactical situation. But the main import was that once an action had commenced the on-board computers could make decisions at a speed that no human brain could match. The Trinity fire-control computer could carry out its own target evaluation using just the system sensors. It could evaluate the type of target presented (missile, strike aircraft or whatever), determine the number of rounds to be fired, the fuze setting for the optimum effect, when to fire to ensure a certain level of hit probability (usually greater than 60 per cent), and the burst pattern. The latter was an indication of the gun and mounting accuracy for bursts could be fired to circle the target or, if a sea-skimming missile was involved, in a fan-shaped 'half moon' above the target. It has to be stressed that every round was aimed individually, even during bursts. Such was the degree of automation that if a more threatening target appeared the fire-control computer could be over-ruled by the detecting sensor. Once a programmed burst had been fired the gun could slew to a new target, if there was one, or return to the first target track to engage it again if necessary.

Results

For a large aircraft target the effective range of Trinity could be as much as 6,000m. Smaller targets such as a head-on strike fighter could be effectively engaged at between 2,000m and 3,000m. For low-level guided missiles the effective range was determined more by detection than by the gun system precision but could be of the order of 2,500m.

The Trinity mount had a laying precision of 0.3mrad but the overall system of the fire control/gun/ammunition was more important as any shortcomings in one affected the others. With radar tracking of an aircraft target the system polar dispersion could be as little as 3mrad at 6,000m and 1.7mrad at 2,000m. Against a low-flying guided missile using optronic tracking the system accuracy was 1.5mrad at 2,500m down to 1.3mrad at 1,000m. Trinity needed only two seconds to fire a programmed burst and then switch to another target. Time of flight of a Trinity projectile to 2,500m was three seconds and once on an aircraft target the greatest lethal hit probability was at a radial miss distance of 2.5m. Against missiles it was somewhat lower.

Armoured Trinity

To take full advantage of Trinity it was planned to introduce land-based, self-propelled platforms. One test installation was extensively trialled on a Swiss MOWAG Shark 8 × 8 weapons carrier, although other platforms were investigated. It was intended that the Trinity gun and its sensors would be carried in an enclosed turret although early trials involved an open installation. The trials were never completed.

The intended ultimate form of Armoured Trinity on a MOWAG Shark 8 x 8 chassis.

What might have been – an impression of a proposed Armoured Trinity turret on an Austrian Steyr 4K 7FA G127 armoured personnel carrier chassis.

Aftermath

It was originally intended that Trinity would be developed into four naval configurations. The most basic was the 011, also known as Trinity Spartan, a direct replacement for the L/70 naval gun with no sensors on the mounting as fire control would be from the carrier ship's central fire-control system. The 012 would be similar but with the addition of a proximity fuze programmer capability coupled to the fire-control system. With the E11 the fire control was basically optronic and on the mounting, including a video tracker, infra-red sensors and laser rangefinding. The E12 had all the features of the E11 but with the addition of an on-mounting fire-control radar. These four were base configurations, all of them modular, so sensor sub-system components could be added or taken off as required.

There were also plans to introduce a Stealth Trinity that would become the main self-defence armament of a proposed Swedish Navy surface-effects ship, the stealth factor arising from the introduction of radar-reflecting surfaces, materials and general configuration, as well as infra-red signature suppression and careful camouflage colouring, all of which would assist in concealing the presence of a warship or generally reduce its background contrast under combat situations. By introducing similar techniques to the Stealth Trinity turret outline the gun would be able to add to the overall concealment effect. Even the barrel was lowered into the deck to add to concealment, the barrel only elevating to the firing position the instant before firing. Work in Sweden began on such a project during the 1980s resulting in the construction of a twin-hulled technology demonstrator vessel that was to become HMS *Smyge* at its launch during 1991.

The *Smyge* underwent numerous technical and tactical trials but did not prosper for various reasons, one being that its twin hull configuration was not as efficient as had been hoped and, despite all the radar-return reduction measures and other stealth factors, the vessel was seen as being too large overall. Many of the lessons learned with the *Smyge* were incorporated into the YS2000 general purpose corvettes, the first of which was the *Visby* (K31), a single-hulled vessel launched in June 2000.

By the time the *Visby* had been launched a decision had been taken that the vessel's main armament was to be the Bofors 57mm Mark 3, so there was no longer any call for a 40mm Stealth Trinity. In fact it emerged that there was no longer any need for any form of Trinity and the entire project foundered. For some time costs had been escalating during a period when the Cold War years were becoming a distant memory and while the gun side of the system presented few problems, it emerged that other parameters such as target engagement range and firepower could be better served using a heavier gun calibre, hence the selection of the 57mm Mark 3 gun for future naval applications. With the withdrawal of Trinity from what was once seen as its main future employment the entire programme came to a halt.

That left one potential Trinity customer out on a limb, namely the Finnish Navy. They had decided to adopt Trinity as the main gun armament of their *Hamina* class missile-armed fast patrol craft under the Bofors factory designation of SAK 40/70-600(E). Fortunately for the Finns their vessels could easily accommodate the slightly larger Bofors 57mm Mark 3 so they decided to follow the Royal Swedish Navy lead and adopt the larger-calibre gun. The only craft out of the class of four actually fitted with Trinity, the *Hamina*, was eventually retrofitted with the 57mm Mark 3 gun.

The Trinity programme was far from being a loss. Much knowledge, technical data and experience was gleaned from the programme. Some off-shoots from Trinity found applications elsewhere, one example being the utilisation of the 100-round magazine on existing L/70 naval guns. What was then the West German Navy commenced a magazine retrofit programme for the L/70 guns on their Type SM 343 and MJ 332 minehunters. Brazil adopted a kit of Trinity-related components that enabled them to upgrade some of their existing L/70 guns to near 40mm Mark 3 standard (see below) on the *Niteroi* class of frigates, the first vessel being so equipped being the *Liberal*. The fire-control system for the Bofors 57mm Mark 3 gun retains many characteristics gleaned from the Trinity programme, including the employment of a 57mm 3P round.

Out East

Needless to say, AB Bofors' progress with Trinity attracted a great deal of attention from many sources, some of them following the programme to see what they could utilise for their own ends. One such organisation was Allied Ordnance of Singapore (AOS) who used many of the Trinity specifications to develop their own equivalent. There were two results with near identical top mountings. They were the Naval Air Defence Mount (NADM) and the Field Air Defence Mount (FADM), both 40mm Trinity-influenced systems having similar fire-control system options and including the 330rpm cyclic fire rate and the 101-round dual compartment magazine. Both have been extensively marketed, the FADM entering low level production during 1996. At least five examples of the NADM were sold to the Brazilian Navy, the last of them scheduled for delivery during 2013. On the NADM the elevating mass weighs 1,400kg; total weight is 3,300kg.

Singapore was not the only country taking note of Trinity developments. During early 2006 it was revealed that another Trinity-inspired air defence system had been developed in Taiwan. Many details of this system remain to be finalised but, developed by The 202nd Arsenal Material Production Center AB at Nankang, the system is known as the 40mm/L70 T92 Air Defence System and is based around a Bofors 40mm L/70 gun up-rated to fire at a cyclic rate of 330rpm. What appeared to be a prototype was mounted on a modified Swiss Oerlikon-Contraves twin 35mm GDF towed anti-aircraft gun carriage of a type already in service with Taiwan.

The magazine used with the T92 appears to be similar to the one developed for Trinity with a capacity of 101 rounds. A new suite of ammunition was developed and manufactured for the system by the Ji-Ning Machinery Corporation of Nangang. Some of the rounds involved are based on existing 40mm L/70 designs but at least two appear to be completely new.

Designation	TC74	TC77	TC93	XTC96
Type	HE-T	PFHE	APC-T	APDS
Round weight	2.5kg	2.4kg	2.5kg	2.3kg
Muzzle velocity	1,005m/s	1,025m/s	1,010m/s	1,300m/s

Designation	XTC97	TC74
Type	APFSDS	TP-T
Round weight	2.1kg	2.5kg
Muzzle velocity	1,400m/s	1,005m/s

Of these the two X-designation armour-piercing rounds appear to be still under development. The XTC96 APDS (armour-piercing discarding sabot) projectile contains a tungsten alloy sub-projectile carried in a light sabot assembly that breaks up soon after leaving the gun muzzle. It can penetrate 80mm of armour at 1,000m. Using a tungsten alloy penetrator rod, the APFSDS round can penetrate 100mm of armour at 1,000m.

For fire control the T92 shown to date has been provided with an optronic sight unit apparently based on the French SAGEM day/night optical sight although the system can be coupled to radar-based fire-control systems of several types.

Within the T92 system the gun itself has a crew of three and the complete gun and mounting, without ammunition, weighs approximately 6 tonnes. During 2006 it was announced that consideration was being given to ordering seventy-six production guns, sufficient to equip two airfield air defence battalions.

Mark 3

The follow-on to Trinity, the Bofors 40mm Mark 3 naval gun, is to all intents and purposes Trinity without the on-carriage fire-control options. Intended from the outset to be configured to utilise any naval vessel's central fire-control system the Mark 3 retains many Trinity features. The up-rated 330rpm gun remains much the same, apart from a few modifications such as a reversion to the cone-shaped flash hider at the muzzle, and it continues to fire 3P ammunition, although as configured for L/70 guns with a muzzle velocity of 1,012m/s. All other types of 40mm L/70 round can be fired from the Mark 3.

As on Trinity, the gun and mounting are capable of firing programmed bursts with each round individually aimed to provide burst patterns to suit the target being engaged. Rounds are stacked in a 101-round capacity dual compartment magazine only slightly modified from that employed with Trinity. The gun turret utilises many of the radar-reflective properties introduced for Stealth Trinity

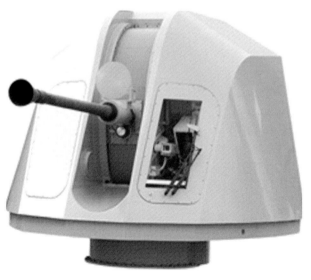

The Bofors 40mm Mark 3 naval gun.

while the gun and mounting continue to incorporate aluminium and other non-magnetic materials.

Very little of the Mark 3 mounting intrudes into a deck although space has to be found for a power distribution rack to supply three-phase 440V, 60Hz, for the gun's power systems. The electro-hydraulic power drives are such that the Mark 3 has faster barrel traverse and elevation rates than the naval Trinity equivalent. In traverse the latter had an acceleration rate of 45°/s. With the Mark 3 this rate is 57°/s. The same applies to the elevation acceleration rate. On the naval Trinity the rate was 85°/s while with the Mark 3 it is 92°/s.

The Bofors 40mm Mark 3 is no longer on offer and it is understood that about 15 systems were ordered for Brazil and the Japanese Coast Guard.

DATA FOR 40MM MARK 3	
Length of barrel	2.8m
Rifling twist	1 in 46 to 1 in 27 cal
Number of grooves	16
Weight of gun and mounting	3,500kg
Weight combat ready	3,750kg
Rate of fire (cyclic)	330rpm
Elevation	-20° to +80°
Traverse	360°
Elevating speed	57°/s
Traversing speed	92°/s
Elevating speed	135°/s
Power supply	3 × 440V, 60Hz
Magazine capacity	101 rounds
Maximum range	12,500m

Mark 4

At one time it was understood that the Bofors 40mm Mark 3 would be the last of the 40mm Bofors Gun line but it was not to be. During 2012 a 40mm Mark 4 materialised following investigations by BAE Systems Bofors AB marketing personnel. Their findings revealed that there remained a requirement for an advanced light naval gun system (NGS) but it had to be lighter, more compact and less expensive than the Bofors Mark 3, especially as the main sales potential for such weapons was foreseen as the main armament of small vessels less than 30m in length.

Compared to the Mark 3 the resultant Mark 4 NGS is claimed to be 40 per cent lighter, 40 per cent less in overall volume and 40 per cent less costly, yet it

The external appearance of the Bofors 40mm Mark 4 naval gun.

retains a Mark 3 level target capability against air, surface and land targets with an extremely rapid target response. Also carried over from Trinity and the Mark 3 is extreme accuracy coupled to computer-controlled burst patterns, with each round individually aimed.

Much of the weight saving compared to the Mark 3 is achieved by the introduction of easier-to-maintain all-electric drives in place of the electro-hydraulics of the Mark 3, the weight of the gun system without ammunition being less than 2,300kg. The gun itself is a variant of the Bofors 40/70B installed on the Swedish Army's CV9040 MICV (see Chapter 11) but optimised for the naval role and with a cyclic fire rate of 300rpm plus single shot and two-, four- or eight-round bursts. The barrel elevating mechanism is the same as for the 40/70B.

The primary magazine under the gun holds thirty rounds with the option of a further intermediate carousel magazine in the lower mounting to hold another seventy rounds. Replenishment of the primary magazine from the intermediate magazine is fully automatic and rapid switching between ammunition types is available. The intermediate magazine can be manually reloaded from beneath deck level. Spent cases are ejected forward to outside the lower part of the mount.

Fire control can be remotely implemented from an on-board gyro-stabilised system via a digital interface. Local control can be from any position on the vessel using a gun-mounted video camera as a sight. As an alternative the gunner/operator can be seated to the left of the gun, operating the gun system using an interface that includes a flat, multi-function screen display and twin hand controls.

The Mark 4 NGS can involve the complete family of L/70 ammunition, including the 3P round which is fired at a muzzle velocity of 1,012m/s. A muzzle velocity radar feeding data into the fire-control system is an add-on option.

A prototype Mark 4 NGS underwent initial range firing trials during early 2012 and was installed on the former HMS *Jägaren* (V150) patrol boat (displacement 140 tonnes) during October 2012, prior to initial sea firing trials.

DATA FOR 40MM MARK 4	
Weight of gun and mounting	<2,300kg
Height	1.99m
Width	2.14m
Rate of fire (cyclic)	300rpm
Elevation	-20° to +80°
Traverse	360° unlimited
Magazine capacity	30 + 70 rounds
Muzzle velocity (3P)	1,012m/s
Maximum range	12,500m
Barrel life	>5,000 rounds

Chapter 10

Self-Propelled Guns

With the exception of naval guns and those devised for static installations most of the 40mm Bofors Guns covered in these pages have been towed. By their very nature towed guns have to be hauled into action by some form of prime mover and, depending on the size and weight of the specific gun model, the prime movers could vary from Jeeps to specialised 6 × 6 trucks provided with facilities for looking after the gun and its crew. Few nations, if any, decided to tow their Bofors Guns with draught animals, a measure resorted to only rarely other than for demonstrations and exercises or, in a few instances in Thailand and the Dutch East Indies, as part of sales demonstrations.

No matter how efficient a gun crew could be, it always took a finite amount of time to bring a towed Bofors Gun into action. Even the best-trained and most experienced gun crews took at least two to three minutes, and often longer, to prepare a gun for action and actually open fire. There was one other disadvantage with towing vehicles and that arose when really rough terrain had to be crossed by wheeled tractors, often a major task even without a gun in tow. In addition to this lack of tactical mobility, difficult terrain usually meant that the prime movers and their towed guns could often not keep pace with the mechanised formations they were meant to support. In addition, if for any reason the prime mover became damaged or unable to move, any Bofors Gun could not be moved very far by manual haulage and so could be rendered immobile.

One solution to these drawbacks was the self-propelled carriage. If the Bofors Gun could be placed on a suitable form of wheeled or tracked self-powered platform it could be carried with relative ease across most types of terrain to the extent that it could travel at the same pace as the formations it was supposed to defend. It would also take less time to get the gun into action if the crew and a viable ready-use ammunition load could be carried on the same platform.

By 1941 numerous attempts to produce such self-propelled carriages for the Bofors Gun were already in progress.

Sweden

Sweden was one of the first countries to attempt to place a Bofors Gun on a self-propelled carriage. Prompted by German developments that placed light air defence guns onto trucks and half-tracks to increase their mobility, during 1941 the Swedish Army installed a Bofors Gun on the flatbed cargo area of a commercial truck chassis. Exactly what truck type was involved is now not known for little information regarding the project seems to have survived. It appears that the truck was protected by sloped armoured plates and provision was made for the gun to be fired against ground targets as well as against aircraft. Against air targets the gun had a full 360° traverse. By all accounts the cross-country performance of the vehicle and gun combination was not very good due to the centre of gravity being rather high, so after some extended trials the project was allowed to lapse.

The next Swedish Army attempt to produce a self-propelled carriage for the 40mm Bofors Gun was more successful. This project commenced around 1941 and involved placing a single Bofors Gun onto a much modified *Stridsvagn L-60* (Strv L-60) tank chassis, adopted during 1939 by the Swedish Army as their *Stridsvagn m/38* (Strv m/38). The Strv L-60 was produced by AB Landsverk, based at Landskona in southern Sweden. AB Landsverk produced its first tank during 1929, a design followed by a line of gradual developments that were, for their time, perfectly serviceable if rather austere. For the air defence role the Strv L-60 chassis was lengthened to accommodate an extra road wheel each side and the turret ring was enlarged to take the large circular, open-topped, sloping-sided turret, designed and manufactured by AB Bofors. This turret

A Finnish Army Landsverk L-62 Anti II.

A Landsverk L-62 Anti II *on display at a demonstration in Finland.*

One of the Landsverk L-62 *Anti II to be seen at the* Pansermuseo *at Parola in Finland.* (M. van Best)

carried a single L/60 gun and a manually-powered mounting. The turret was rather cramped as it had to contain four of the five-man crew (it was occupied by the two layers, a loader and the vehicle commander), while spent cartridge cases had to be ejected backwards through a chute and a slot in the turret rear. Power was provided by a Scania-Vabis 144hp petrol engine that provided a maximum road speed of 40km/h. Armour thickness was limited to 20mm (or as little as 6mm in places) and combat weight was approximately 10,740kg. There was no secondary armament.

The result was the *Luftvärnskanonvagn 40* (Lvkv 40) and after extensive trials it was placed into limited production for the Finnish Army. Just six were manufactured during early 1942 and delivered to Finland minus their armament. After the gun had been installed at the *Valtion Tykkitehdas* (VTT) at Jyväskylä, all six vehicles were delivered to the Finnish Army on 14 May 1942 and organised into a single mobile air defence battery that formed part of the Finnish Army's Armoured Division. All six survived the war after serving alongside the Germans on the Eastern Front, mainly around the Lake Ladoga region where they were credited with shooting down at least ten Soviet aircraft. After 1945 all six served on until 1966, although by then they had been relegated to the training role.

Two examples survive as part of the collection at the *Pansarmuseo* at Parola in Finland, one fully restored and the other in a poor state and minus its gun. A third restored example is located at the Anti-Aircraft Museum at Hyrylä. Another resides in the Tank Museum at Kubinka in Russia.

The Finns knew these vehicles as the *Landsverk L-62 Anti II*, although the initials 40/ITPSV appear in some references.

DATA FOR LANDSVERK L-62 ANTI II	
Crew	5
Weight	10,740kg
Length	5.4m
Width	2.3m
Height	2.3m
Max road speed	40km/h
Road range	200–225km
Fuel capacity	250 litres
Engine	Scania-Vabis L8V/36T 144hp petrol
Gun elevation	-5° to +85°
Gun traverse	360°

The Lvkv 40 was not accepted for Swedish Army service for they considered that mounting just one Bofors Gun on a tracked chassis was a rather costly

One of the turrets for the Landsverk Lvkv 43 *on the Karlskoga ranges in 1945.*

exercise and a waste of potential performance. They wanted a two-gun arrangement, so AB Bofors duly designed a twin-gun turret installation which was ready for testing during 1945, this time on a much-modified *Landsverk Strv m/42* tank chassis with the usual two engines of the tank version replaced by a single 162hp unit. This resulted in the *Luftvärnskanonvagn fm/43* (the *fm* denoted *försöks modell*, or test model), later accepted for service as the Lvkv 43.

On the Lvkv 43 the two guns were mounted close together and side-by-side in a power-controlled turret with a full 360° traverse, the mounting being designated in full as the *40mm luftvärnsautomatkanon m/36-43 i luftvärnsauto-matkanonvagn*. The weight of the guns and their mounting was approximately 3,550kg. For extra protection the two gun barrels were set in a curved shield that rose and fell with barrel elevation. Unusually, the layer sat to the right of the guns behind a hatch that had to be opened for him to utilise the cartwheel sight. Also in the turret were two loaders, one of whom doubled as the vehicle commander. The fourth crew member was the driver seated at the left front of the hull. Stowage space was provided for 326 rounds, 180 of them in chargers stacked in ready-use racks to the left of the guns and the other 146 rounds stowed around the vehicle. Power was initially provided by a single Scania-Vabis L603/3 162hp petrol engine coupled to a Volvo VL-220 five-speed transmission. In 1951 the vehicles were updated by replacing their original engines with German war surplus Maybach HL120 TRM 300hp V-12 petrol engines that increased the road speed to 55km/h.

A total of seventeen Lvkv 43s were produced during 1948 and 1949 and they served until 1968 before being withdrawn. Each Swedish Army armoured brigade was allocated three vehicles. Two examples survive as part of the collection of the Swedish Army *Pansarmuseet*, at one time at Axvall.

DATA FOR LVKV 43	
Crew	4
Weight	approx. 17,000kg
Weight of guns and mounting	approx. 3,550kg
Length	5.79m
Width	2.31m
Height	2.39m
Max road speed	36km/h (later 55km/h)
Engine	Scania-Vabis L603/3 162hp petrol (later Maybach HL120 TRM 300hp V-12 petrol)
Transmission	Volvo VL-220 5-speed manual
Gun elevation	-6° to +88°
Gun traverse	360°
Ammunition stowage	326 rounds

A Landswerk Lvkv 43 *operating under field conditions.*

The next Swedish self-propelled carriage to be produced was one of the first two armoured vehicles designed and manufactured by AB Bofors, the other appearing at around the same time being a 120mm assault gun. The air defence vehicle was known as the *Luftvärnskanonvagn 42* (Lvkv 42), also known as the Lvkv fm/49 and by the AB Bofors design designation of 40 VAK. Produced at the request of the Swedish Army in 1954 the Lvkv 42 mounted a single L/70 gun in an open-topped turret. One unusual feature of the chassis was that the suspension height was adjustable to level the vehicle from within the vehicle before firing commenced. The turret had flat sloping sides while the front and rear were curved. Inside the turret the single layer sat to the left of the gun with the vehicle commander on another seat on the right. Two loaders sat behind them facing inwards. In action the loaders took ammunition from racks holding up to ninety-six rounds in their usual four-round chargers. The driver's position was under a hatch at the front of the hull, with a seat that could be raised to improve his forward vision. The gun was rated to fire at 240rpm with the layer using powered controls and a gyro-stabilised or reflex sight unit. If for any reason the power controls were not available the layer and commander could resort to the usual cranked control handles. It was also possible to utilise some form of remote fire-control system and even to fire the gun from a remote position with no personnel on the carriage other than the loaders.

For various reasons the Lvkv 42 did not get past the prototype stage although it underwent a series of trials and tests. Some of its features were to reappear on later vehicles, one being the adjustable height suspension that was developed

The Lvkv 42, armed with a single Bofors L/70 gun, was one of the first armoured vehicles designed and manufactured by AB Bofors.

Although neat and functional, the Lvkv 42 did not pass beyond the prototype stage.

further for incorporation into the unconventional S-tank, another and later AB Bofors product.

The Lvkv 42 prototype survived as part of the collection of the Swedish Army *Pansarmuseet*.

DATA FOR LVKV 42	
Crew	5
Weight	approx. 13,500kg
Length	5.43m
Width over track	2.4m
Height	2.34m
Ground clearance	320mm
Max road speed	66km/h
Engine	185hp petrol
Gun elevation	-5° to +85°
Gun traverse	360°
Elevating speed	45°/
Traversing speed	70°/
Ammunition stowage	96 rounds

The Bofors VEAK 4062 was based on a tracked chassis similar to that utilised for the adjustable height S-tank and was armed with two 40mm L/70 guns.

The next self-propelled platform for the Bofors Gun appeared in 1956, this time a carriage carrying two L/70 guns. By 1956 the L/70 gun had been developed to the point where a radar-based fire-control system could be contemplated and it seemed to be possible for the radar to be rendered fully mobile along with the gun (or guns) on some form of tracked vehicle. This conclusion was reached after early design work that involved two vehicles, one for the guns and one for the radar. Only the gun platform reached the hardware stage for by 1959 it had been decided to integrate the guns and radar on one vehicle. A prototype, known by the Bofors design designation of VEAK 4062, was duly requested by the Swedish Army, the result being handed over to them during 1965.

The VEAK 4062 was based on a tracked chassis similar to that utilised for the adjustable suspension S-tank, although the chassis also incorporated components from the VK 155 155mm self-propelled gun (the *Bandkanon 1A*), another AB Bofors product. One feature of this chassis was that the hydro-pneumatic suspension could be locked out to provide a more stable platform when firing. Another and very unusual feature of the VEAK 4062 was that the driver was located in the turret along with the vehicle commander and the system operator. This meant that the vehicle had to come to a halt before the driving controls were disconnected and the gun traverse and elevation controls could be brought into play. In practice this procedure usually took well under 30 seconds and often half that time.

After stopping, the search radar started work almost immediately as it was possible to switch on the radar and raise the roof-mounted antenna while the vehicle was still on the move. There were two operating modes, one a 360° search sweep carried out in 1.5 seconds and the other a search over a 90° sector. The radar operated over two frequencies in the X-band and had a maximum range of 20,000m. Within the turret any radar returns were displayed on a monitor screen and, after the system operator had selected a target, all further tracking was automatic. Tracking was followed by an analogue computer inside the turret, the computer calculating the required aim-off for the barrels. Firing was carried out via the usual foot pedal. A full optical tracking system, based on a ×8 periscope and a ball-type control device, was also provided. In addition, the vehicle commander had a joystick for laying the guns, although this was normally employed only when engaging ground targets.

The two L/70 guns were rated to fire at a cyclic rate of 325rpm from each barrel and, while they remained air-cooled, there was provision for cooling them

Although completely successful, the VEAK 4062 was judged to be ahead of its time so it did not pass beyond the prototype phase.

with water from a 100-litre tank located inside the turret. Rounds were fed automatically from a magazine with seven slots for each gun, each slot holding ten rounds. It was intended that on each gun six magazine slots would be filled with HE rounds for firing against aircraft, leaving the seventh slot filled with AP to utilise against ground targets. Apart from the 140 rounds in the magazine, further stowage was provided for another 285 rounds inside the turret.

The VEAK 4062 was destined never to pass the prototype stage, although it was extensively trialled at the Swedish Army's Anti-Aircraft School at Vaddo throughout 1965 and after. The general opinion was that the VEAK 4062 was ahead of its time and, although the overall concept was later shown to be viable, it was really too large, complicated and expensive for the period.

DATA FOR VEAK 4062	
Crew	3
Weight	approx. 35,000kg
Length	6.35m
Width	3.3m
Height, antenna lowered	3.15m
Ground clearance	425mm
Max road speed	60km/h
Engine	240hp Rolls-Royce K60 diesel and 300hp Boeing 502-10MA gas turbine geared together
Gun elevation	-5° to +85°
Gun traverse	360°
Ammunition stowage	
Magazines	140 rounds
Inside turret racks	285 rounds

By the end of 1994 AB Bofors were again investigating the possibilities of mounting a L/70 gun on a self-propelled platform. At that time the Armoured Trinity concept was still in being (see Chapter 9) but the Swedish Army and Navy, the latter including the Coast Artillery arm, retained large numbers of towed L/70 guns with potentially long service lives still before them, while the prospect of personnel shortages loomed ahead. By placing those guns, which were regarded as having a low mobility rating, on some form of relatively inexpensive self-propelled carriage it seemed that fewer personnel would be required while the L/70 guns' useful lives could be extended. At the same time cross-country mobility could be considerably enhanced and in and out of action times could be significantly reduced.

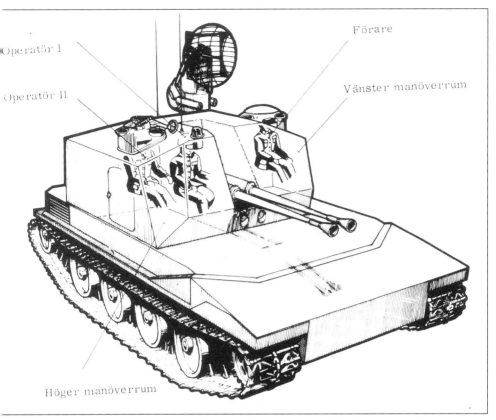

Operatör I

Operatör II

Förare

Vänster manöverrum

Höger manöverrum

Cutaway drawing of a VEAK 4062 showing the driver to the left of the guns and the two radar/weapon operators to the right.

After some investigations there arose the possibility of mounting the gun on a modified Volvo 6 × 6 articulated chassis of the type already in widespread and trouble-free service on numerous construction sites and other such commercial projects. By the end of 1994 a L/70 gun and a Volvo VME 825B 6 x 6 chassis had been brought together to become what could be described as a technology demonstrator and by July 1995 preliminary firing trials to test the viability of the concept in both the ground-to-ground and ground-to-air firing roles had been completed. Mobility trials included driving the vehicle through snow 1m deep. By the end of 1995 a specially-modified L/70 gun with electrically-powered traverse and elevation controls, the EL-40/70, had been placed on another VME 825B chassis for further trials, the revised chassis being more fully equipped for the air defence role and with extra armoured protection applied to the driver and operator cabs. This version became known as Tridon.

Tridon was able to demonstrate that its concept had considerable promise, especially following the demise of Armoured Trinity (see Chapter 9). Four

The Bofors Tridon.

different fire-control and other equipment standards were forecast, the overall approach being modular so that individual user requirements could be easily met. The intention was that each vehicle and gun combination would be capable of acting as an autonomous air defence unit for prolonged periods, using the latest PFHE and 3P ammunition to improve the overall air defence performance.

The simplest proposed version was Tridon 1, a relatively low cost, fair weather system with few frills. Tridon 2 would have extras such as a laser rangefinder and add-on units including a proximity fuze programmer, a muzzle-velocity radar and, possibly, a local-search radar on the system control cabin roof. More optronic target sensors would be involved with Tridon 3, including a fully integrated combat control system, while Tridon 4 would have a full, all-weather sensor suite virtually to Trinity standards, the Tridon 4 gun having a cyclic firing rate of 330rpm and an optional 101-round magazine.

All four Tridon models were to be operated by a crew of five, including the driver. At the front were the driver and the target designator, the latter dismounting to set up and connect his target designator sight. The rest of the crew, the commander, target plotter and gunner, would travel and work in an air-conditioned cab located on the rear articulated unit behind the driver's cab. No crew member needed to be on the gun in action as the gun magazine could contain forty-three rounds, sufficient for eight to twelve engagements. The articulated rear unit had space to carry more ammunition in lockers. Power for all operations could be provided by an auxiliary power unit when the main vehicle engine had been switched off.

Tridon seemed to offer much but once again the entire project came to an end with only prototypes being tested. As the Cold War years receded and defence budgets shrank, the need for a weapon concept along the lines of Tridon faded away. However the Volvo articulated carrier idea, up-rated to a Volvo A30D 6 × 6 chassis, survived in the form of the BAE Systems Project Archer self-propelled 155mm artillery system involving a L/52 version of the Bofors FH-77B howitzer. After a joint Swedish/Norwegian development programme it was ordered by the Swedish Army (twenty-four) and Norwegian Army (twenty-four).

DATA FOR TRIDON	
Crew	5
Weight	approx. 23,000kg
Length	11.5m
Width	3m
Height travelling	3.5m
Ground clearance	455mm
Max road speed	70km/h
Fording	1.5m
Engine	Volvo 255hp diesel
Transmission	ZF automatic
Gun elevation	-10° to +85°
Gun traverse	360°
Ammunition stowage	43 or 101 rounds

The latest Swedish self-propelled 40mm L/70 air defence gun is the air defence model of the CV90 family, the TriAD. Full details are provided in Chapter 11.

Hungary

Until 1940 the only tanks used by the Hungarian Army were a handful of Italian CV-33 two-man tankettes and a few Swedish light tanks. The Swedish tank was the AB Landsverk Strv L-60, first purchased in March 1937 and later licence-manufactured in Hungary by the Manfred Weiss concern of Budapest as the *38M Toldi*. In December 1938 a *Landsverk Strv L-62* light tank, essentially similar to the Strv L-60, was purchased to be converted to an anti-aircraft tank that eventually became known as the *40M Nimrod legvedelmi harlosi*. This

Although of poor quality this photograph is one of the few that shows Hungarian Army Nimrod *air defence vehicles in action.*

vehicle mounted a single L/60 gun licence-produced by MAVAG, the Hungarian state railway manufacturing concern (see Chapter 6).

Conversion work for the *Nimrod* was carried out jointly by MAVAG and Ganz of Budapest, the prototype being delivered to the Hungarian Army during October 1941. In all, 135 Nimrods, including the prototype, were manufactured in two batches, series production commencing with a batch of forty-five vehicles in November 1941. Production of the second batch of eighty-nine commenced during May 1943, the last vehicle being delivered during 1944.

Nimrods were deployed on the Eastern Front, not only as air defence vehicles but also as anti-tank platforms, in which latter role they were not particularly successful. Not only did the gun lack the necessary armour-penetrating power but the vehicle's overall silhouette was high and armoured protection was light, being a maximum of only 28mm at the front and 10mm or less around the turret sides and rear. In the absence of more suitable vehicles Hungarian Army bureaucracy classified the *Nimrod* as a medium tank or tank hunter, even if they did continue to serve in the air defence role. Each Hungarian armoured division had a tank hunter battalion with three *Nimrod* batteries, each with six vehicles. A further eight were held at armoured regiment level.

In many ways the *Nimrod* followed the same lines as the Swedish AB *Landsverk L-62 Anti II* manufactured for Finland (see above), although there were many detail differences, not the least being a turret overhang at the rear. The open-topped, manually-powered turret accommodated a single L/60 gun and four personnel, the fifth crew member being the driver in the hull front. The gun barrel protruded through a vertical slot in the curved armour at the front of the turret and two spring-loaded plates provided protection for the slot. Further

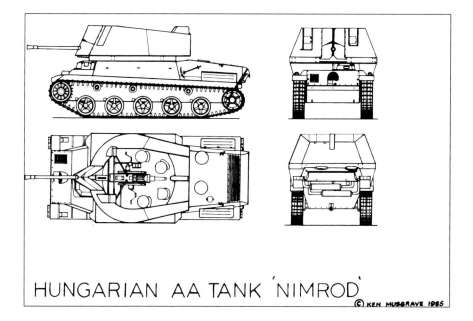

HUNGARIAN AA TANK 'NIMROD'

© KEN MUSGRAVE 1985

slots in the front of the turret acted as vision hatches for the two layers who continued to operate the usual cranked handles. The other two crew members in the turret were the vehicle commander and a loader who took ammunition chargers from various ammunition stowage points around the turret and hull interior. The vehicle commander also operated the *34/38 M Juhasz-Gamma Loelemkepzo* predictor sight as used on the towed Hungarian Bofors Guns.

A surviving *Nimrod* can be seen at the Zrinyl Miklos National Defence University in Budapest. Another is in the Tank Museum at Kubinka in Russia.

Data for *Nimrod*	
Crew	5
Weight	approx. 10,700kg
Length	5.29m
Width	2.31m
Height	2.99m
Ground clearance	350mm
Max road speed	35km/h
Engine	Ganz (Büssing-NAG) VIII VGT 107 150hp petrol
Range	300km
Gun elevation	0° to +80°
Gun traverse	360°
Ammunition stowage	approx. 148 rounds

France

The first mounting of a 40mm L/60 Bofors Gun by the French Army was carried out during 1944, the locally-devised conversions being made when the Free French 22nd Colonial Group joined the 2nd (French) Armoured Division in France. Single guns were lifted off their field carriages to be mounted on armoured Lend-Lease GMC CCKW 353 2½-ton 6 × 6 trucks, the first examples going into action as air defence vehicles during August 1944. These conversions served with a moderate degree of success until the war ended.

Their next period of service began in 1946 when the 2nd Armoured Division was sent to Indo-China where, once again, guns were mounted on armoured GMC 2½-ton 6 × 6 trucks for convoy escort duties, the guns being mounted over the two rear axles, with a 0.50/12.7mm M2 machine gun ring-mounted over the driver's cab. Controls were manual, as on a field mounting, and extra protection was provided for the gun, cargo area and driver by add-on armoured plates. These conversions, carried out in local French Army workshops, were intended to produce fire against ground targets only. They did not remain in use for very long as the weight of the gun and armour over-stressed the chassis and impeded mobility when operating off-road. As a result most of these conversions were relegated to static guard duties. Few illustrations seem to have survived.

A more formal attempt to produce a self-propelled Bofors Gun was carried out in France itself. Starting in May 1949, a requirement was issued for an air defence vehicle to support French Army armoured formations in the field. A design contract was issued to SAMM (*Societé d'Applications des Machines Motrices SA*, located at Biévres) who designed a turret, known as the S 980,

The SAMM S 980 turret mounting a single Bofors 40mm L/70 gun to be mounted on an AMX-13 light tank chassis.

mounting a single L/70 gun, then still fresh on the open market. The open-topped turret was mounted on a virtually unmodified AMX-13 light tank chassis, the turret, gun and chassis combination being known as the AB 380. Being a prototype it appears that no special fire-control arrangements were incorporated other than a reflex sight unit on a raised arm to clear the turret armour walls. The turret carried a crew of two, the vehicle commander was doubled as the loader, and the layer, the driver being located in the hull front.

A hardware order was placed with SAMM during 1951, work on a prototype commencing during 1952. The first (and only) vehicle was finished during January 1954 and underwent a series of trials mainly held at Toulon. However, by 1955 the French Army had decided to adopt an air defence vehicle armed with two 30mm Hispano-Suiza HSS-831A cannon in a SAMM S 401A turret, the turret also being carried on an AMX-13 light tank chassis. Production of that vehicle, the AMX DCA-30, commenced soon after. With that selection the AB 380 prototype no longer had a future but tests and trials with the turret and vehicle continued until April 1957. The project was then terminated and the turret was returned to SAMM.

Data for AB 380	
Crew	3
Weight	approx. 15,000kg
Length	5.13m
Width	2.84m
Height	2.39m
Ground clearance	370mm
Engine	Sofam Model 8Gxb 250hp petrol

While the AB 380 project had come to naught, during the early 1980s SAMM decided to go ahead with an alternative gun turret known as the TTB 140 but this time mounting the 40/70B armoured vehicle gun (see Chapter 11). The two-man TTB 140 turret was fully enclosed and barrel elevation was limited to +50°, an angle providing an anti-helicopter capability. Up to forty rounds could be carried in racks inside the turret. It should be noted that this venture was not intended primarily to be an air defence turret as it was meant to be the main armament component for a light armoured vehicle.

SAMM designed the TTB 140 turret as an add-on module that could be readily grafted onto a wide variety of light armoured vehicles and it is known to have been tested on at least two. One was the Giat Industries (now Nexter) AMX-10 tracked infantry combat vehicle. As far as is known this project

Frontal view of the SAMM TTB 140 turret installed on an AMX-10 tracked infantry combat vehicle.

The SAMM TTB 140 gun turret was also trialled on the Panhard ERC reconnaissance vehicle.

remained at the feasibility stage and did not progress very far after a single trial installation had been completed. A second trial installation seemed to be more promising as it involved a Panhard ERC reconnaissance vehicle, a 6 × 6 armoured car normally armed with a 90mm main gun turret but capable of being configured for numerous turret, gun and missile armament combinations. However, once again the TTB 140 turret option did not prosper and had been withdrawn from the market by 1990.

United Kingdom

United Kingdom defence authorities at first paid little heed to proposals that involved placing Bofors Guns on any form of self-propelled carriage. One of the main reasons for this was that virtually all available facilities had to be fully involved in the manufacture of whatever weapons and vehicles were already in service and for the British that meant as many land or naval Bofors Guns as possible. Self-propelled versions simply had to wait until there were the resources to manufacture them.

Despite this lack of official sanction a few British engineers had foreseen the need for some form of self-propelled platform as early as 1941. During that year a few Nuffield Organisation engineers decided they could assist the Home Guard units formed from among Nuffield Organisation workers by providing them with mobile Bofors Guns mounted on converted Morris Quad artillery tractors, the Quads being already in production by Nuffield to tow 25-pounder field artillery pieces. Although their official status is now impossible to verify, the conversions to carry the Bofors Gun were carried out in Nuffield factories at Birmingham, Oxford and Coventry. After their issue to Nuffield Home Guard units, demonstrations of their capabilities were given to various Army units and authorities including, so the story goes, an unscheduled and uninvited demonstration presented during a display on Horse Guards Parade in London.

Despite the speed with which the Home Guard could get their Bofors Guns into action compared to regular gunners with their towed guns the British Army remained unenthusiastic. But after some persuasion the Nuffield conversion was put into production in time for many to take part in the Normandy D-Day landings of 6 June 1944 and the campaigns thereafter. Some were carried into action in gliders but once the landings were over there was little for these carriers to do as the Allies had by then gained overwhelming air superiority and few *Luftwaffe* aircraft dared to appear. As a result some light anti-aircraft regiments were disbanded to reform as infantry or other units, although others continued to serve until well after the war ended, often in support of ground operations.

The Nuffield carriage for the Bofors Gun was the Platform, Carrier, Morris, 40mm AA Mark 1 (Morris Motors were part of the Nuffield Organisation). The chassis involved was the Morris-Commercial C9/B 30cwt 4 × 4, a development

As the gunners on the Bofors Gun on the Morris Carrier stand by, ready for any eventuality, the rest of the crew take the opportunity to sort out their kit.

Although it is not immediately apparent, the crew of this Morris Bofors Gun Carrier are Luftwaffe *personnel so the vehicle has obviously changed hands following the fortunes of war.*

of the Morris-Commercial C8 FAT (field artillery tractor) or Quad that had been involved with the early Nuffield Home Guard conversions. On this chassis the Bofors Gun Mark 1 or 1* was placed on a special Mark 5 or 5/1 mounting developed specifically for this vehicle. The Mark 5 mounting had provision for power controls while the Mark 5/1 relied upon manual controls only.

Unfortunately for their crews during the harsh European winter of 1944–1945, the mounting on the Morris carrier was completely open, with no cover for the crew of four other than a few canvas weather shields, and the driver's position was also left open. For firing direct from the carrier wheels the rear axle could be locked to the vehicle frame but for more prolonged periods of firing, or when under predictor control, four jacks were lowered onto cones and base plates placed on the ground, the shape of the cones giving rise to the term 'elephants' feet'. Two of the jacks were at the sides with the others under the bonnet and at the rear.

While on the move there was seating for the driver, whose steering wheel could be lowered during firing, and three gunners. Stowage was provided for 120 rounds packed in boxes, and a spare barrel. Various stowage boxes located around the vehicle carried gun accessories, tools and the crew's personal kit. In addition, most vehicles usually carried additional ammunition boxes and other supplies.

To accompany the gun carriers there was another similar vehicle carrying a No 3 (Kerrison) Predictor to control groups of Bofors Guns. This vehicle, based on a Morris-Commercial C8/P chassis, had a driver and a crew of two, the predictor being placed on the open vehicle just behind the driver's position.

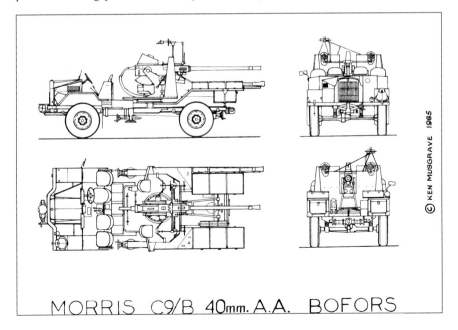

© KEN MUSGRAVE 1985

MORRIS C9/B 40mm. A.A. BOFORS

Only three stabilising jacks were needed for this vehicle, one of them at the rear. These predictor carriers were also meant to be employed as back-up ammunition carriers (often known as limber vehicles) as there was space on the rear for a further 192 rounds, plus two spare wheels. It was as ammunition carriers that these vehicles were primarily employed for by the time they appeared the Kerrison predictor had largely been phased out of service.

Once the need for self-propelled Bofors Guns had been accepted by the British Army they were produced and issued in significant numbers and used in action from 1944 onwards, the usual allocation being at least one self-propelled troop in each light anti-aircraft battery. It was not until the late 1950s that they were withdrawn from British service. Even then, some were retained for a few more years by various Commonwealth armies and nations such as Denmark and The Netherlands.

One of those Commonwealth armies was that of Canada. During 1944 Canadian light air defence units based in the United Kingdom were issued with self-propelled Bofors Guns mounted on Morris chassis but by the end of 1944 many of these carriers had been replaced by alternatives manufactured in Canada. The Canadian carriers closely followed the layout and mounting as employed on the Morris equivalent but the chassis involved was the Ford 3-ton F-60B (C39QB) 4 × 4, the vehicle being known as the Carrier, Self-Propelled, 40mm AA (SP Bofors). The only mounting involved was the C Mark 5, so power for the controls could be derived from a 2.75kVA generator powered from a power take-off on the gearbox. These carriers were employed only by

A post-war photograph of a Morris Carrier crew training with the Bofors Gun in the Egyptian Canal Zone.

The Canadian Carrier, Self-Propelled, 40mm AA (SP Bofors) based on a Ford 3-ton F-60B (C39QB) 4 x 4 chassis.

Canadian Army units operating in North-West Europe and Italy, some ending up in Dutch service after the war.

A virtually identical self-propelled Bofors Gun carrier to that manufactured in Canada and based on a Ford F-60L 4 × 4 chassis was manufactured in Australia but not many were issued.

DATA FOR BRITISH AND CANADIAN CARRIERS		
Model	Morris	Ford
Crew	4	4
Weight	5,792kg	7,061kg
Length	6.15m	6.2m
Width	2.21m	2.38m
Height	2.286m	2.34m
Wheelbase	2.51m	3.4m
Engine	Morris 70hp petrol	Ford V-8 95hp petrol
Gun elevation	-2° to +85°	-2° to +85°
Gun traverse	360°	360°
Ammunition stowage	120 rounds	120 rounds

The only other British self-propelled carriage involving the Bofors Gun was the Crusader III, AA Tank Mark 1. This was a conversion of the Crusader cruiser tank employed by the Royal Armoured Corps, the Crusader III appearing during 1942. As with so many other British tank designs of the early war years the Crusader was prone to technical failures but by the time the Crusader III was taken out of production in January 1943 most of the mechanical troubles had been eliminated. However, by 1943 the Crusader was no longer a viable battle tank as it was too lightly armed and armoured, resulting in a stock of tank chassis with no tactical role to play. As a result, many of them were converted into special-purpose vehicles such as gun tractors or command vehicles.

Some Crusader IIIs were converted into anti-aircraft gun tanks during early 1944 to provide air defence during the period after the planned landings in Normandy later that year. There were three marks of these anti-aircraft tanks, the Mark 1 carrying a single Bofors Gun and the Marks 2 and 3 carrying twin 20mm Oerlikon or Polsten cannon.

The Crusader AA Tank Mark 1 carried its single gun in a rather tall and truncated open-topped turret with the slab sides sloping towards the centre of the vehicle, the original turret having been removed. On a few early conversions there was no protection other than the usual gun shield. The gun involved was the special Mark 6 because the usual method of ejecting a spent propellant case forwards from the mounting would not work with a tank installation. Instead, spent cases were deflected to the rear and upwards. There was also a special-

The Crusader AA Tank Mark 1 armed with a single 40mm Bofors Gun.

*Side view of a
Crusader AA
Tank Mark 1.*

to-role type of autoloader, the Type A* with an adjustable peep-sight located in the rear ammunition guide for when ground targets were encountered. No secondary armament was carried other than the crew's personal weapons.

The Crusader AA Tank Mark 1 had a crew of four, including the driver. Inside the turret were the vehicle commander, a loader and the layer, the latter having a joystick to control the hydraulically-powered mounting. A two-stroke engine located in the combat compartment provided power for the mounting. If for any reason the power failed, the gun could still be controlled by the usual cranked handles carried stowed somewhere in the vehicle.

As with the wheeled Morris and Ford carriers, once the landings in Normandy had been successfully accomplished there was little for the Crusader AA tanks to do for they rarely even encountered, let alone engaged, German aircraft. After a while the AA tanks were withdrawn from front-line duties.

DATA FOR CRUSADER AA TANK MARK 1	
Crew	4
Weight	approx. 19,300kg
Length	6.285m
Width	2.64m
Height	2.38m
Max speed	43.5km/h
Engine	Nuffield Liberty 340hp petrol
Gun elevation	-2° to +85°
Gun traverse	360°
Ammunition stowage	150 rounds HE, 40 rounds AP

United States

When considering the development of self-propelled Bofors Gun carriages in the United States the sequence of events is not so clear-cut and straightforward as the development histories outlined above. This was due almost entirely to the sheer volume of weapon development work carried out in the United States from 1940 onwards when it became painfully obvious to US Army staff planners that they had allowed all aspects of their defence preparations to fall dangerously behind far more advanced programmes being carried out elsewhere. Military observers based in Europe during 1939 and 1940 sent to the United States numerous reports which emphasised the extent to which the American military inventory had been allowed to become at best obsolescent or, in many cases, completely obsolete, to say nothing of the limited levels of all manner of military materiel then maintained.

There followed a frenzied period of all manner of weapon, automotive and armour development into which self-propelled carriers for all kinds of artillery became drawn, and somewhere in that maelstrom of activity came the development of self-propelled carriages for American-produced M1 Bofors Guns.

It is not easy to follow a logical time sequence of all the developments involved so a certain amount of hopping around the time scale has to be involved in the following outline account. It is not even possible to be certain exactly when the sequence of events actually began for by the end of 1940 there were already several 40mm-related projects under way at the same time, even though local series production of Bofors Guns was still in the planning stage. We will therefore start in numerical sequence with the 40mm Gun Motor Carriage T1.

The 'T' designation denoted that the vehicle involved was a trial or experimental vehicle. Once type classified, that is accepted for service, it was given an 'M' designation. With the 40mm Gun Motor Carriage T1 (GMC T1) the story is relatively straightforward for it was first recommended during May 1941 by representatives of the US Army Coast Artillery and the Ordnance Department.

In several ways the GMC T1 was a pioneering vehicle for it was one of the first attempts to place a Bofors Gun on a self-propelled platform that could carry a gun, predictor and the associated power unit all on the same chassis. The chassis selected was produced by the Mack Manufacturing Corporation of Allentown, Pennsylvania, namely the Half-Track Chassis T3. Although officially designated as a half-track the chassis was more of a three-quarters track involving the rear-located track and suspension units taken from the Light Tank M3. After conversion for the Bofors Gun role the vehicle had the 192hp main engine and radiator positioned at the rear, the M1 Bofors Gun was located amidships and the Director M5 (the American-manufactured Kerrison predictor)

The 40mm Gun Motor Carriage T1 using a Mack chassis known as the Half-Track Chassis, T3.

was mounted next to the driver on an open platform of its own. The top of the vehicle was completely open and there was no protection against the elements for the driver or any of the crew travelling on the vehicle. The prototype had no armoured protection either. Combat weight was 9,965kg.

The GMC T1 underwent trials at the Aberdeen Proving Ground in Maryland but the trials demonstrated that the chassis was unsuitable for its intended role, even though there were no mechanical troubles on the vehicle itself. The main shortcoming was that the overall layout proved to be unsatisfactory, the location of the bulky Director M5 often interfering with the intended field of fire, or the gun interfered with the Director's field of view. Another problem was that firing vibrations affected the Director M5 so badly that it often could not interface correctly with the gun. In addition the Director M5 proved to be too slow and cumbersome to operate and deliver useful fire-control results against all except the slowest and most predictable aircraft targets flying at convenient heights. So unsatisfactory was the Director M5's operation that the performance of the Bofors Gun in its self-propelled role was not even commented upon before the GMC T1 project came to a halt. The Half-Track Chassis T3 went on to be developed into several models of lightly-armoured cargo carriers, although few of them were manufactured in any quantity.

Another attempt to render the Bofors Gun mobile was put forward during November 1941 as an offshoot from a project involving the placing of a 75mm anti-aircraft gun and its associated fire-control components on the much modified upper superstructure of a Medium Tank M3. While the 75mm part of the project appears not to have reached the hardware stage an alternative Bofors Gun development went ahead, two prototypes being built. The result was the

The Gun Motor Carriage T36 was armed with a single 40mm Bofors Gun in a complex cast turret mounted on a M3 medium tank chassis.

40mm Gun Motor Carriage T36 (GMC T36), with one prototype being tested at the Aberdeen Proving Ground and the other by the US Army Antiaircraft Artillery Board at various locations. Neither liked what they found for they both decided that the Medium Tank M3 was really too large for the gun involved and both agencies felt that the gun and chassis combination lacked the degree of mobility they desired. The Antiaircraft Artillery Board also criticised the weapon installation as being too complicated and the fire-control system, which included a gear-operated analogue computer, was considered to be too fragile for military use. Another factor was that the large cast turret, regarded as a technological achievement of its type, was felt to be too large, expensive and complex for the mass production techniques of the period. Consequently the GMC T36 passed into history.

Attention then passed to the Multiple Gun Motor Carriage T52 (MGMC T52), this time involving the chassis of the Medium Tank M4, widely known as the Sherman. At the beginning of the MGMC T52 project the domed turret was meant to house two M1 Bofors Guns side-by-side but in the event this was changed to a single gun and two 0.50/12.7mm M2 machine guns mounted co-axially. The design of the turret and mounting became the responsibility of the Firestone Tire & Rubber Company of Akron, Ohio, who devised the Combination Gun Mount T62. The internal arrangements of this mounting were rather cramped, the gunner being enclosed deep within the turret, and were so arranged that at high angles of barrel elevation the gun body protruded through an octagonal hole in the turret floor.

When the turret, gun and tank chassis combination was tested at Aberdeen Proving Ground the staff there found little worthy of approval. Not only was the weapon installation regarded as too complicated but the external ballistic trajectories of the 40mm gun and the two 0.50/12.7mm M2 machine guns did not match. As well as the interior being cramped it was considered that the turret traversing rates were too slow for firings against low-flying aircraft and, once again, it was felt there was too much tank for too little gun power. If all this was not enough it was considered that the overall weight of 29,675kg was excessive. On the recommendation of the Aberdeen Proving Ground staff the MGMC T52 project was terminated.

The next episode in the story of the American fully-tracked Bofors Gun carriage came with the 40mm Multiple Gun Motor Carriage T65 (MGMC T65). Development of this vehicle began in October 1942 at the request of the US

The Multiple Gun Motor Carriage T52 involved a M4 medium tank chassis, a single 40mm Bofors Gun and two 0.50/12.7mm M2 heavy machine guns. It did not meet with approval.

Army Antiaircraft Command who wanted a lightly-armoured mobile platform carrying two M1 Bofors Guns for the defence of mobile armoured columns in the field. This time the chassis selected was produced by combining elements of the Light Tank M5A1 and Medium Tank M7 but to allow the chassis to carry two M1 guns it had to be lengthened and the suspension gained another set of twin road wheels each side. That was not the only modification for the twin Cadillac engine installation of the Light Tank M5A1 had to be relocated from the rear to a central compartment to provide space for the two guns to be placed on a mounting ring over the back of the vehicle, although at one early stage only one gun was installed. Known as the Twin 40mm Gun Mount T12 (a slightly modified version, the T21E1, was later type classified as the M4), the powered mounting having a light armoured shield and a ring of ammunition stowage boxes around the periphery. An ammunition and supplies carrier, the Cargo Carrier T23, was developed to accompany the MGMC T65.

Prototypes of the gun and the ammunition carrier were produced by the Cadillac Motor Car Division of the General Motors Corporation starting in February 1943, with the understanding that 1,000 vehicles would be required. Both prototype vehicles were sent to Aberdeen Proving Ground for trials, during

Based on a mixture of the M5A1 and M7 light tank chassis, the Multiple Gun Motor Carriage T65 with two 40mm Bofors Guns was passed over in favour of the T65E1, later to be the Multiple Gun Motor Carriage M19.

which it was found that the gun carrier became unstable during prolonged automatic firings. However, it was considered that this shortcoming could be readily solved by modifications.

Those modifications were destined never to be made to the MGMC T65 for by then the US Army had turned its attention elsewhere. This was not on technological grounds for the MGMC T65 could have met the Army's requirements (once the necessary modifications had been incorporated) but the matter hinged on production. By early 1943 the Light Tank M5A1 chassis was being phased out of production as by then it was no longer considered as a viable combat vehicle and more promising options were in the offing. The US Army was therefore reluctant to retain the M5A1 production lines in being and wanted to procure something better. That something was the Light Tank T24, later to become the Light Tank M24 Chaffee. A T24 chassis was therefore modified to assume the same overall layout as the defunct MGMC T65 and became the 40mm Gun Motor Carriage T65E1, later the Multiple Gun Motor Carriage M19 (MGMC M19). A slightly revised version later became the MGMC M19A1 (originally the T65E2), featuring an auxiliary engine and generator to provide power to keep the gun mounting operational when the main engines had to be switched off. Provision for two spare barrels to be carried on the vehicle became official on the MGMC M19A1.

The MGMC M19 and M19A1 had the same overall layout as the MGMC T65, with the engine installation in the centre of the vehicle and the gun mounting, the Twin 40mm Gun Mount M4, at the rear. The latter had a slightly modified and more angular gun shield outline but was otherwise much the same as that devised for the MGMC T65. As might be expected, the stabilisation modifications derived from testing the MGMC T65 were incorporated into the MGMC M19. The crew was five or six: driver, co-driver, vehicle commander, two loaders and, sometimes, a spare gunner. A total of 352 rounds could be carried on the vehicle plus a further 320 rounds in an optional towed Ammunition Trailer M28. The provision of the latter indicated that the notion of a dedicated ammunition and supplies carrier for the MGMC M19 had been dropped.

It was May 1944 before the MGMC M19 was type classified and production did not start until August of that year, when 904 units were requested. Once again the Cadillac Motor Car Division was involved but the full anticipated production run was again not to be completed. By the time the production line was in full swing the requirements for the MGMC M19 had been re-examined, the outcome being that chassis originally intended for the air defence role were diverted to the production of M24 Chaffee light tanks. Just 285 examples of the MGMC M19 and M19A1 were manufactured before the war ended.

MGMC M19s were mainly deployed to the European theatre where there was little enough for them to do in their intended anti-aircraft role. By the time

The Multiple Gun Carriage M19 was based on the chassis of the M24 light tank.

the first of them arrived in Europe the *Luftwaffe* had been driven from the skies of Western Europe. Instead the M19s were often employed as a form of assault gun in support of infantry operations, a role in which it proved to be very effective. None were assigned for Lend-Lease. The MGMC M19 saw further service during the Korean conflict, again mainly as an infantry fire support weapon.

MGMC M19A1s survive in various museums, perhaps the oddest example being a M19A1 in the collection of the Tank Museum at Kubinka in Russia.

DATA FOR MGMC M19	
Crew	6
Weight	17,463kg
Length	5.46m
Width	2.845m
Height	2.997m
Ground clearance	432mm
Max speed	56.3km/h
Cruising range	241km
Engine	Twin Cadillac Model 42 V-8 220hp petrol
Gun elevation	-5° to +85°
Gun traverse	360°
Ammunition stowage	352 rounds

At the same time as the fully-tracked self-propelled carriage developments for the Bofors Gun were under way, a parallel development programme was in progress based on the Half-Track Personnel Carrier M3. Several different models appeared in a rather confusing sequence of events, but the one thing they all had in common was that none came to anything for the simple reason that the base M2 and M3 half-tracks (although the M3 was meant to be a weapon carrier) were too light to withstand the weight and firing stresses of a Bofors Gun, to say nothing of the weight of the crew, associated equipment and a useful ammunition load. Although it was never borne out in practice, the lack of space on a Bofors Gun self-propelled half-track would have meant that most of the crew (and ammunition) would have had to travel in another half-tracked or wheeled carrier to accompany the gun vehicle, adding considerably to the complexity, cost and logistic load of keeping a single gun in the field.

The first of the Bofors Gun half-track carrier projects began in June 1942 with the initial development of the 40mm Gun Motor Carrier T54 (GMC T54). This involved the chassis of the Half-Track Personnel Carrier M3 and only one pilot model was manufactured. It emerged as a fairly straightforward conversion, typical of the others that were to follow, with a single M1 gun mounted on the flat and open rear area of an M3. There was no protection for the gun crew and stowage capacity was minimal. Early firing tests demonstrated that some form of carriage stabilisation using jacks and outriggers would be needed, so a second pilot model, the T54E1, was devised to test various forms of these stabilising measures. In addition, the T54E1 also introduced a device that cut out the vehicle suspension during firing. However, all these measures proved to be inadequate and the T54E1 was abandoned.

Some of the test and engineering data provided by the T54/T54E1 project was introduced into the next development stage which concerned the 40mm Gun Motor Carriage T59 (GMC T59). This follow-on project again involved a M3 half-track but this time using a new stabilising outrigger system and a revised method of blocking out the vehicle suspension. The outriggers were designed to be installed rapidly and were also employed on a companion vehicle, the Half-Track Instrument Carrier T18 that carried a Director M5 (the Kerrison predictor) and a Generating Unit M5 with all the necessary interconnecting cables, the intention being that the two vehicles would operate together. Unfortunately, tests carried out at Aberdeen Proving Ground proved that the GMC T59 was no more stable when firing than its predecessors. A T59 (Modified) version, later known as the T59E1 and with a slightly revised fire-control system, fared no better so the T59/T59E1 programme also came to an end.

At around the same time the T59 project was in progress yet another half-track project was being tested, this time the Multiple Gun Motor Carriage T60 (MGMC T60). This time the M3 half-track was the carrier for the Combination

The first of the Bofors Gun carriages based on the M3 half-track was the 40mm Gun Motor Carriage T54 – it was not a success.

Outriggers and suspension changes were added to the 40mm Gun Motor Carriage T54E1 but firing stability problems persisted.

The 40mm Gun Motor Carriage T59 fared no better than its predecessors.

Gun Mount T65 that carried a single M1 gun and two 0.50/12.7mm M2 machine guns. Only one pilot model of the T60 was produced, to be followed by the T65E1 with revised stowage and different shields. Neither was developed very far before being dropped in favour of the more promising fully-tracked 40mm MGMC T65 mentioned above. There was also the problem that the external ballistic trajectories of the Bofors Gun and the two machine guns did not match over the operational range of the 40mm weapon so the notion of using tracer from the machine guns to aim the main 40mm gun would not work at longer ranges.

By the time all these half-track projects were even half completed it had been established that the basic vehicle was unsuitable for carrying a Bofors Gun. Even so, this did not prevent the American Ordnance Company, an old-established gun-making concern of Bridgeport, Connecticut, proposing yet another M3 half-track carrier, this time with <u>two</u> M1 guns. This carrier was eventually known as the 40mm Gun Motor Carriage T68 (GMC T68) and featured a very odd gun layout. The guns were placed, linked one above the other, in an 'over-and-under' configuration with a prominent overhead equilibrator cylinder to take the weight of the mounting arrangement which featured each gun mounted on brackets with their axis well to the rear of the guns themselves. Overall the mounting looked high and awkward while protection for the guns and their crew was minimal.

On the Multiple Gun Mount T60 the Bofors Gun was augmented by two co-axial 0.50/12.7mm heavy machine guns. The alliance was not a success as the external ballistics of the two types of weapon did not match.

The odd-looking (and unsuccessful) 40mm Gun Motor Carriage T68.

It was June 1943 before the GMC T68 was submitted for trials. Although the single example of the GMC T68 was tested by the Antiaircraft Artillery Board they simply did not like what they saw and that was the end of that experiment.

Throughout the war years nearly all American attempts to produce a self-propelled Bofors Gun platform came to a fruitless end. Thankfully, the resources of the United States were such that all the time, resources and efforts expended on the self-propelled Bofors Gun projects that brought no useful result, were all commodities that could be relatively easily afforded. It should not be forgotten that there was one successful end result, the MGMC M19, an effective and reliable air defence platform that was destined to remain in US Army service for years after 1945. Half-tracks did feature on the wartime air defence scene carrying multiple 0.50/12.7mm M2 machine guns or the 37mm Antiaircraft Gun M1A2, either by itself (M15) or co-axially with two 0.50/12.7mm M2 machine guns (M15A1). Due to its lower recoil forces the 37mm gun it could just be accommodated on the Half-Track Car M2 which then became the Multiple Gun Motor Carriage M15 or M15A1 (MGMC M15 or M15A1).

From the early 1950s onwards the United States overcame the earlier self-propelled air defence shortcomings by introducing numerous self-propelled air defence platforms that became the mainstay of the Western World's mobile low-level anti-aircraft measures. This change of fortunes commenced in August 1951 when authorisation was given to develop the replacement for the MGMC M19A1, this time involving the Light Tank M41 chassis. Two vehicles mounting twin M1 Bofors Guns were proposed, one being the T141 regarded as an 'interim' vehicle pending the introduction of the T141E1, then considered the preferred 'ultimate' solution. A fire-control vehicle, the T53, was also proposed but, this, along with the T141E1, was cancelled during May 1952 on the grounds that the costs were too high and both would take too long to develop. That left the T141, the prototype of which was ready by late 1951.

The T141 took very little time to progress for it was based on the Light Tank M41, already in series production. All that was necessary was the placement of what was virtually the same turret and mounting as the MGMC M19A1 into the 76mm gun turret ring of the M41. In October 1953 the vehicle and gun combination was type classified as the Gun, Antiaircraft Artillery, Self-propelled: Twin 40mm, M42, often known more simply by its nickname of 'Duster'. By October 1953 the M42 had already been in series production for more than a year at the Cleveland Tank Plant, Ohio. The T141 was designed by the Cadillac Motor Car Division of General Motors, who also manufactured the Light Tank M41.

Production of the M42 continued at Cleveland from the end of 1951 until June 1956. From early 1952 production also commenced at ACF Industries Incorporated at Berwick, Pennsylvania, and lasted until December 1953. In all 3,700 M42s were produced, the only production change being with the M42A1, into which a revised fuel injection system was installed. This change provided

Gun Antiaircraft Artillery, Self-propelled: Twin 40mm, T141. This was the forerunner of the M42 series, still with the usual muzzle flash hiders installed.

A US Army M42 Duster on a training exercise on Okinawa, May 1955.

Cannon 40mm Dual Automatic Gun M2A1 as produced for the M19 and M42 Duster.

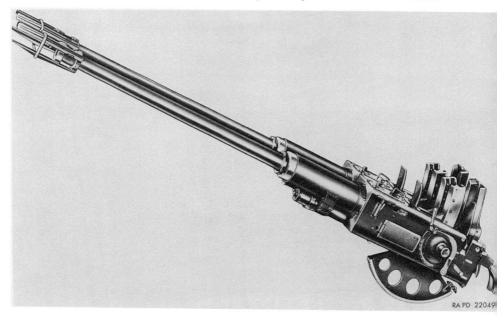

fuel consumption economies of up to 20 per cent, extending the road range to about 190km. Most M42s were eventually brought up to M42A1 standard.

Compared to the earlier MGMC M19 the M42 had the gun compartment in the centre of the vehicle with the engine compartment at the rear. The gun mounting continued to be the Twin 40mm Gun Mount M4, as used with the M19A1, the guns being the Cannon 40mm Dual Automatic Gun M2A1, a type specially produced for the MGMC M19/M19A1 and M42/M42A1. This gun variant differed from the standard M1 gun only in mounting detail, while the two guns and their mounting weighed about 907kg. Most of the ammunition was stowed in lockers along each side of the upper hull, rather than around the mounting as had previously been the case, although some ready-use racks were provided to the rear of the turret. The first guns for the developmental T141 retained their usual conical flash hiders although by the time series production commenced they had been replaced by three-pronged fork-pattern flash suppressors. A local defence 7.62mm M1919A4 or M60 machine gun could be mounted on the left rear of the turret.

The M42 and M42A1 remained in service with the US Army until 1969 when they were withdrawn. Some were passed to the National Guard who, by 1969, already had the type in their inventory, and with them the Duster soldiered on until 1991. The M42/M42A1 served in Vietnam, once again as a ground support weapon. Its eventual replacement was the 20mm Vulcan Air Defense System in either towed or self-propelled form, or some form of missile system,

A West German Bundeswehr *M42A1.*

This illustration depicts an attempt to provide the M42/M42A1 with some form of target-tracking and ranging radar. The idea did not result in any in-service equipments.

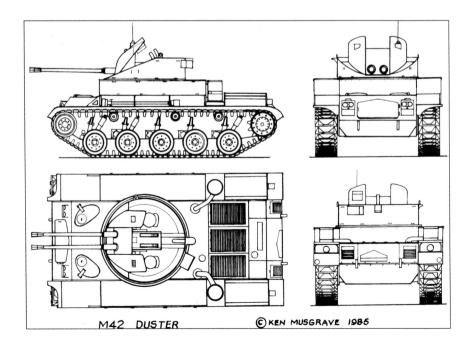

M42 DUSTER   © KEN MUSGRAVE 1985

even though the 20mm Vulcan gun lacked the range and firepower of the Bofors Gun, relying on radar fire-control and a high rate of fire for its effectiveness. Yet by the 1980s the M42/M42A1 was overdue for replacement as it was essentially a fair-weather system, the only fire-control assistance being derived from a M24C reflex sight unit with no recourse to radar or any other sensor, rendering the system increasingly ineffective against high speed targets or during poor visibility conditions. Trials were carried out with forms of on-vehicle target ranging and tracking radars but none were adopted. In addition to these fire-control shortcomings the open-topped turret offered little protection for the crew against overhead fire or any form of NBC warfare.

The M42 and M42A1 were widely distributed among NATO and other forces such as Austria, Israel and Japan. As late as 1998 they were still in service with Greece (95, from Germany), Guatemala (number not known), Jordan (216), Lebanon (10, status uncertain), Taiwan (295, some converted to launch TOW anti-tank missiles), Thailand (16), Turkey (262, from Germany) and Venezuela (6).It is known that Taiwan developed a 32-round box magazine for the Bofors Guns carried on their M42 series vehicles.

DATA FOR **M42** AND **M42A1**	
Crew	6
Weight	22,452kg
Length	6.356m
Width	3.224m
Height	2.848m
Ground clearance	438mm
Track	2.602m
Max road speed	72.4km/h
Fuel capacity	530 litres
Max road range	161km
Engine	Continental or Lycoming 500hp petrol
Gun elevation	-3° to +86°
Gun Traverse	360°
Ammunition stowage	480 rounds

The twin-gun mounting employed on the M42/M42A1 was also involved with an amphibious vehicle intended for the US Marine Corps and known as the LVTAA-X1. Nicknamed the 'Twin Forty', it was derived from the LVT-P5 amphibious personnel carrier series produced in 1954. It was a modification of a standard vehicle carried out by the Ingersoll Products, Kalamazoo Division,

The one and only example of the amphibious LVTAAX1 based on the LVT-P5 and armed with the same twin gun mounting as the M42.

Another amphibious vehicle venture carrying the M42 gun mount was the LVT(P)X2. It did not pass the prototype stage.

to accommodate the Twin 40mm Gun Mount M4 of the M42/M42A1 Duster. The mounting was adopted virtually unchanged although tubes were routed from the mounting to the hull interior deck for spent propellant case disposal. Ready-use ammunition was stowed in eight ammunition compartments each holding seven four-round chargers, making a total of 224 rounds. A further 776 rounds could be stowed inside the hull, making a potential 1,000 rounds in all, although it was recommended that only 800 be carried during amphibious operations to improve buoyancy. Only one LVTAA-X1 was produced.

A similar conversion was made using the LVT(P)X2, an amphibious version of the M59 (T59) armoured personnel carrier produced during the early 1950s by the Food Machinery Corporation of San Jose, California. This Bofors Gun carrier was designated the LVT-(AA)X2 and was intended to be one of a family of vehicles that would replace the LVT-3C series of amphibious carriers. In the event the programme was discontinued so only one example of the LVT-(AA)X2 appeared. Once again, the complete twin gun mounting from the M42/M42A1 was involved.

The same M42/M42A1 pattern mounting was again employed for yet another one-off project which was rather more of an experiment than a serious attempt to develop a production vehicle. Introduced during the late 1960s, again by the Food Machinery Corporation, this project was based on the M548 cargo carrier variant of the M113 armoured personnel carrier family, onto which the M42/M42A1 mounting was added housed in a raised superstructure to produce the Gun Motor Carriage XM166. While the idea might have seemed promising it came to naught for the chassis was too light for the loads involved, while the centre of gravity was too high for comfort.

Throughout the 1960s and 1970s the M42A1 Duster remained the only self-propelled carriage for the Bofors Gun in American service. It was not until late 1970 that the first serious thoughts regarding an air defence weapon system to meet future requirements reached the point of a study phase with the establishment of the Gun Air Defense Effectiveness Study (GADES). This was completed in 1974, concluding that the in-service 20mm Vulcan Air Defense System lacked range, accuracy and lethality and that something better was necessary. At about the same time another study known as the Divisional Air Defense Study, or DIVADS, was in progress and some of the GADES findings were incorporated into that programme. Yet another study in progress at around that same time was the Gun Low Altitude Air Defense System, or GLAADS, which was really a test-bed study to determine what development paths had to be followed to meet future requirements. GLAADS was concluded during Spring 1976.

From all these studies the US Armament and Research and Development Command at Dover, New Jersey, started negotiations with several contractors for the full-scale engineering development of the Divisional Air Defense Gun

System, retaining the acronym DIVADS. From these negotiations emerged two contractors with development contracts. One was General Dynamics and the other Ford Aerospace.

For DIVADS these two companies were to produce prototypes of air defence weapon systems that could be mounted on existing M48A5 medium tank chassis, large numbers of which had been stockpiled after their withdrawal from US Army service in favour of the M60 tank series. The General Dynamics prototype carried two 35mm GAU-8/A (Oerlikon-Contraves KDA) cannon while the Ford Aerospace submission was armed with two L/70 Bofors Guns. During 1980 the two prototypes were subjected to a five-month 'shoot-out' that covered all manner of trials, including firing at various types of target. Any trials that could not be physically conducted for any reason were carried out using forms of computer simulation.

In May 1981 it was announced that a contract was to be awarded to the Ford Aerospace and Communications Corporation to build 276 DIVADS over a three-year period, with a possible final total of 618 units. At the same time it was also announced that the DIVADS would be known as the M247 Sergeant York, the NCO appellant being a 1918 Congressional Medal of Honor recipient.

From that stage onwards the DIVADS programme took on a life all of its own, a life marked by haste, poorly-defined specifications and rushed development. Ford Aerospace and Communications Corporation established its own DIVADS Division headquartered at Newport Beach, California, with three major sub-contractors. They were the AAI Corporation who were responsible

An M247 Sergeant York with its twin Bofors Guns in action.

for the turret, AB Bofors who supplied the L/70 guns and their ammunition, and the Westinghouse Electric Corporation, Defense and Electronics Center, who were responsible for the radar suite. The DIVADS Division retained responsibility for overall systems integration, the fire-control system, an electronic counter-countermeasures (ECCM) suite, the ammunition feed arrangements, a training and troubleshooting system, plus all the various support logistics.

In theory the M247 Sergeant York system was virtually automatic since all the two-man crew inside the NBC-protected steel turret had to do once a potential target was detected was to press a trigger. The fire-control system then took over to determine target priority, conduct an IFF interrogation, compute the range at which fire was to be opened, select the ammunition type and burst length, and compute the barrel off-set angle. A roof-mounted stabilised sight had both day and night channels and an integral laser rangefinder. The only other crew member was the driver in the hull front.

The L/70 guns had muzzle velocities slightly higher than standard. They fired either high explosive point-detonating (HEPD) rounds at a muzzle velocity of 1,030m/s or pre-fragmenting proximity-fuzed (PFPX) rounds at 1,100m/s. Each PFPX projectile contained 640 tungsten pellets and 120 grams of Octol (HDX/TNT) for employment against targets such as missiles and low-flying aircraft, but primarily against attack helicopters, the Soviet Mi-24 Hind being taken as a typical potential target. Each gun had two magazines with PFPX being stored in one and HEPD in the other, selection being by the flick of a switch. All four magazines contained a total of 502 rounds and reloading took approximately 15 minutes.

The Westinghouse radar was derived from the widely-used AN/APG-66 mounted on the F-16 Fighting Falcon jet fighter series and was a Doppler I-band search/track system with an integral IFF function. It had two turret roof-mounted antennae that could be folded down when not in use.

The first M247 Sergeant Yorks were delivered during 1984 and almost at once serious doubts began to arise. In fact the doubts had surfaced earlier when it began to be appreciated that many nations within NATO had come to prefer the 35mm Oerlikon-Contraves KDA gun rather than the slower-firing L/70 Bofors Gun, but by then the 40mm die had been cast. Those arguments were soon submerged into the realisation that it was highly unlikely that the system could ever produce the required results. In fact, it soon became painfully obvious that the M247 Sergeant York system could not even approach the specified levels of performance.

For a start, the system could only remain effective out to a maximum range of 4,000m rather than the called-for 6,000m. The system was not effective against low-flying aircraft travelling at high speed since the rate of turret traverse was too slow, even if the tracking radar functioned as specified, which it often did not. A recurrent problem was system interference from unwanted radar returns from the ground or foliage to the extent that very often the radar could not find or track helicopter targets even when they were hovering. At high barrel elevation angles the barrels could also interfere with radar performance while the ECCM suite proved to be easily defeated by the simplest counter-measures. To add to all these woes there were frequent ammunition feed problems, turret hydraulic system leaks seemed endemic, and the top speed of the M48 tank chassis was too slow to keep up with the M1 Abrams tanks and other vehicles the M247 Sergeant York was supposed to support, one reason being that the turret weight emerged as heavier than intended. Yet the Bofors Guns performed as specified with no apparent problems.

All the time costs were escalating. By the time the first vehicles off the line appeared no less than US$1.8 billion had been expended on the programme. Once the problems became apparent it was estimated that the further development costs needed just to overcome (yet probably not completely rectify) the shortcomings encountered to that date would require at least another US$4.8 billion. If the planned production run of 618 units was to be completed the estimated cost of each individual vehicle would have been over US$6.5 million and that was probably an underestimate.

All this was quite simply too much for the American Treasury to bear and there was no indication that the troubles of the M247 would ever be overcome. In early December 1986 the entire DIVADS/M247 Sergeant York programme was terminated. Just 50 examples were actually completed, only to be junked (although some ended up in museums or private collections).

The M247 Sergeant York did leave one major legacy – it remains a textbook example of how not to approach and conduct a major defence development programme.

DATA FOR M247 SERGEANT YORK	
Crew	3
Weight	54,240kg
Length overall	7.674m
Width	3.632m
Height, antennae up	4.611m
Ground clearance	419mm
Max road speed	48km/h
Engine	Continental 750hp diesel
Gun elevation	-5° to +85°
Turret traverse	360°
Ammunition stowage	502 rounds

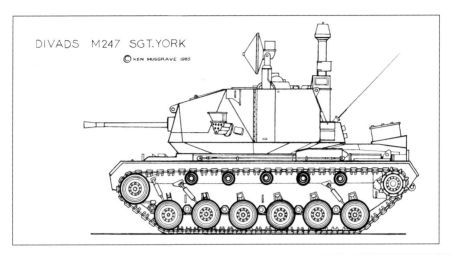

DIVADS M247 SGT.YORK
© KEN MUSGRAVE 1985

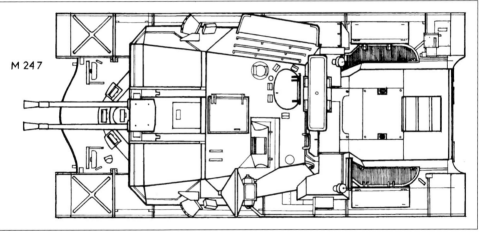

M 247

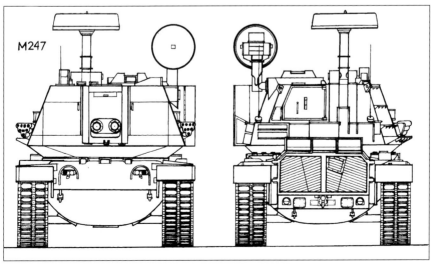

M247

Chapter 11

CV90

By the 1980s the Swedish Army's fleet of armoured personnel carriers was not only getting rather elderly but there were too many different types for logistic and maintenance comfort. To alter this situation and provide the Swedish Army with a state-of-the-art infantry combat vehicle rather than an armoured box that acted as a 'battlefield taxi', a development contract for a fleet of replacement vehicles was issued to a holding company known as HB Utveckling AB. In their turn this 'paper' company issued further contracts to its two major owners, namely AB Bofors (now BAE Systems Bofors AB) and Hägglunds Vehicle AB (now BAE Systems Hägglunds AB) to actually carry out the development work. The new family of vehicles would come under the name of *Stridsfordon 90* (Strf 90) or Combat Vehicle 90, generally known as CV90. Deliveries began in 1995–1996.

As far as the Swedish Army is concerned there are five main models of CV90. In combat and numerical terms the most important is the CV9040, the base *Stridsfordon 90* described below. This vehicle has a single 40/70B Bofors Gun as its main armament. Also armed with a single 40/70B gun is the TriAD air defence vehicle, notable in that it was selected over a proposed air defence guided-missile system. That proposal, codenamed BOSAM, was also intended to be carried on a CV90 chassis, and involved the Saab Bofors Dynamics RBS 90 missile.

Three further Swedish CV90 models are armed with only a 7.62mm machine gun, namely a forward command vehicle, a forward observation vehicle for artillery batteries, and an armoured recovery vehicle. The latter three vehicles are outside the remit of this account which will concentrate on the two models armed with the 40/70B gun.

40/70B

As far as this account is concerned the main distinguishing point of the CV9040 mechanised infantry combat vehicle (MICV) is that it is armed with a variant of the 40mm L/70 Bofors Gun known as the 40/70B (at an early stage referred to as the 40mm L/70 Combat Vehicle Gun). The first of these guns was ready for initial trials during 1985. To all intents and purposes the 40/70B is a modified

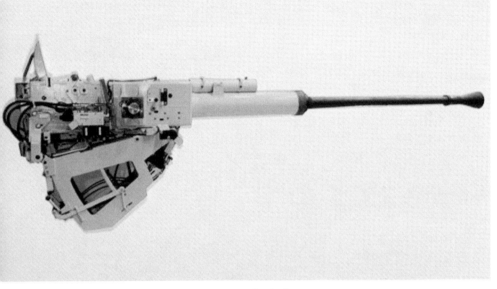

Side view of the Bofors 40mm 40/70B armoured vehicle gun.

L/70 that has been inverted to allow it to be installed within the confines of a two-man turret. Four-round chargers are therefore loaded upwards into the gun, rather than from above, and spent propellant cases are ejected upwards and out through the turret roof. A 24-round magazine is located under the breech area with its interior divided into three eight-round feed compartments. It is possible to load a different nature of ammunition into each compartment, selection then being at the actuation of a switch. Magazine loading and reloading takes about one minute.

There are two sub-variants of this gun. Early production CV9040 models carried a version known as the 40/70Ba. To enhance gun accuracy when firing from the stabilised gun mount a slight modification was introduced to the striker pin release mechanism. Once modified the gun became the 40/70Bc, the type installed in late production turrets. A close variant of the 40/70B is employed with the Bofors Mark 4 naval gun system (see Chapter 9)

The 40/70B has a cyclic fire rate of 300rpm. A fire selector can be set to produce single shots (at up to 60rpm), two-, four- or eight-round bursts or continuous automatic fire. All L/70 ammunition types, as outlined in Chapter 7, can be fired from this gun, including the programmable 3P round. The prime anti-armour projectile is the APFSDS-T developed for firing from the CV9040 and TriAD (see below); it can be fired at the full automatic fire rate. The tactical range against ground targets and helicopters is given as from 500 to 4,000m, the minimum possible tactical range being 200m. When firing against armoured vehicles the maximum upper range bracket is between 1,500 and 2,000m.

It should be repeated here that the 40/70B gun was also tested in the French SAMM TTB 140 turret trialled on the ERC armoured car and the AMX-10P infantry combat vehicle. Details of these are given in Chapter 10.

At one stage it was planned that the 40/70B gun would act as the co-axial secondary armament for Sweden's next generation of main battle tanks that would carry a 140mm main gun. With the end of the Cold War that proposal was no longer seen as necessary so what would have been an expensive development proposition was abandoned in favour of the Swedish Army's acquisition of a fleet of 280 German Stridsvagn 121 or 122 (Leopard 2) tanks armed with 120mm smoothbore main guns and a secondary armament of 7.62mm machine guns.

DATA FOR 40/70B	
Weight	
Gun and magazine	640kg
Gun, magazine and 24 rounds	700kg
Length	
Forward of trunnions	3.315m
Rear of trunnions	710mm
Width overall	450mm
Height above trunnions	170mm
Depth below trunnions	770mm
Magazine capacity	24 rounds
Rate of fire, cyclic	300rpm
Maximum range	
Armoured vehicles	1,500–2,000m
Ground targets	3,500–4,000m

CV4090

On the CV9040 the 40/70B gun is located in a gyro- or fully-stabilised mounting together with a co-axial 7.62mm m/39B machine gun (a modernised version of an air-cooled, belt-fed, Colt/Browning design dating from 1936) located to the left of the main gun. Apart from the twenty-four 40mm rounds carried in the gun magazine beneath the breech area, there are a further forty-eight rounds located in a carousel under the turret floor. A further 166 rounds are stowed around the vehicle interior. Firing can be controlled by either the vehicle commander, seated to the left of the gun, or the gunner, the only two crew members located inside the electrically-controlled, all-steel turret. The only other crew member dedicated to the vehicle is the driver located in the hull on the front left, next to the 550hp Scania V-8 diesel engine compartment.

For fire control the gunner is provide with a Saab Systems Universal Tank and Anti-Aircraft Sight (UTAAS). This stabilised sight can be used by day or night, the latter role involving a thermal imager. The UTAAS incorporates an integral laser rangefinder and a fire-control computer. As its name implies this sight is intended for employment against both ground and air targets, and updates introduced since the first UTAAS installations enable the gun to be aimed and fired while the vehicle is on the move.

Inside the hull rear there is provision for an infantry section of seven or eight soldiers, seated each side and facing inwards. These passengers exit and enter the vehicle through a large door in the hull rear, although roof hatches are provided. Details of the protection provided for the occupants of the turret and hull have not been released but informed estimates rate it as proof against 14.5mm AP projectiles.

Ancillary self-protection measures include twelve French Giat Industries (now Nexter) Gallix discharger tubes launching grenades ranging from screening smoke to infra-red decoy flares. Two 71mm Lyran mortar tubes (another Bofors product) are mounted on the turret rear to fire illuminating projectiles out to a maximum range of 1,500m for target illumination or surveillance.

Production of the CV9040 for the Swedish Army is complete with 509 units delivered. Also delivered were forty turretless chassis for storage until Patria Hägglunds AMOS 120mm twin-barrel mortar turret systems can be installed on at least some of them. The chassis for all CV90 variants were manufactured by BAE Systems Hägglunds who also installed the guns and turrets manufactured by BAE Systems Bofors.

Apart from the base CV9040 there are three sub-variants in service with the Swedish Army. The CV9040A has a gyro-stabilised gun. On the CV9040B the gun is fully stabilised. There is also a CV9040C intended for international rapid response or peacekeeping operations. This variant has extra passive armour and a tropical kit, the latter being something not normally necessary under Swedish climatic conditions.

Trial installations of the CV9040 turret, complete with the 40/70B gun, were made on a Swiss MOWAG 10 × 10 Shark chassis and two Polish tracked chassis. One of the latter was a locally-manufactured and lengthened variant of the Soviet MT-LB tracked carrier and the other the BWP-40, a locally-built copy of the Soviet BMP-1 infantry combat vehicle. None of these installations passed the trials stage.

DATA FOR **CV9040**	
Crew	3 + 8
Weight	22,800kg
Length, hull	6.471m
Width	3.192m
Height, turret roof	2.5m
Ground clearance	450mm
Track width	533mm
Max road speed	70km/h
Road range	300km/h
Engine	Scania DI 14 550hp V-8 diesel
Gun elevation	-8° to +35°
Gun traverse	360°
Ammunition stowage	
40mm	238 rounds
7.62mm	500 rounds

TriAD

TriAD (Autonomous Armoured Air Defence System) is the air defence component of the CV90 family and is deployed only by the Swedish Army. In general, the layout of the hull and turret are similar to that of the CV9040 but the entire vehicle is configured for the air defence role. At one stage this vehicle was known as the *Luftvärnskanonvagn 90*.

On TriAD the 40/70B gun remains the same as on the CV9040 but the maximum barrel elevation angle is raised to +50° compared to +35° on the CV9040. Two hundred and thirty-four rounds of ammunition are carried: twenty-four rounds in the three-compartment magazine, forty-eight rounds in the same carousel as on the CV9040, and the remaining 162 rounds stowed around the vehicle. As with the CV9040 the gun can fire the full family of L/70 ammunition although the usual round involved for the air defence role is the programmable multi-mode 3P. APFSDS-T is also carried for use against armoured targets. The gunner's sight remains the UTAAS, complete with a laser rangefinder and thermal imager for poor visibility or night operations. A co-axial 7.62mm m/39B machine gun as fitted to the CV9040 is also provided.

The main external recognition feature on the TriAD is the drum-shaped radar housing located on the rear of the turret. This housing encloses the antenna for the French Thales Gerfaut target acquisition radar system that incorporates an IFF function. The radar searches for targets out to a selected range of 7,000m or 15,000m. Once a target is detected its range, speed and course are all calculated and displayed while, after selection by the operator, it is automatically tracked. Up to six targets can be processed at the same time. The system can evaluate and display threat levels and slew the gun and turret onto the most threatening target. Once the gunner has located the target the UTAAS is employed from then onwards, the gunner selecting the ammunition and burst duration, a typical burst against an air target being four rounds.

Three crew members using and operating the radar are located inside the hull rear. They are the radar operator, the combat controller and an external co-ordinator who co-ordinates the vehicle activities with other local forces. The driver is located in the same position at the left front as on the CV9040. There are no roof hatches on this model.

It is intended that mid-life upgrades will include the incorporation of a facility that will allow the TriAD to engage aircraft targets while on the move.

DATA FOR TRIAD	
Crew	6
Weight	23,000kg
Length, hull	6.471m
Width	3.192m
Height, turret roof	2.5m
Ground clearance	450mm
Track width	533mm
Max road speed	70km/h
Engine	Scania DI 14 550hp V-8 diesel
Gun elevation	-8° to +50°
Gun traverse	360°
Ammunition stowage	
40mm	234 rounds
7.62mm	500 rounds

Chapter 12

Postscript

As these words were written during 2013 the 40mm Bofors Gun in one form or another was still giving sterling service all around the world. Exactly when it will pass from the scene is difficult to forecast for, as the contents of these pages will have shown, every time that solemn pronouncements are made that the air defence gun no longer has a viable role in modern warfare, something or other crops up to prolong its life or some new use is found, the American AC-130 gunships and the 40/70B armoured vehicle gun being cases in point. The launch of the Bofors 40mm Mark 4 naval gun system during late 2012 demonstrated that a potential market for air defence guns still exists.

Yet there is also a case that the Bofors Gun has been overtaken by other products to the extent that it no longer reigns supreme in its field. The continuing popularity of the Oerlikon-Contraves 35mm KBA guns has grown to the point where their market impact approaches that of their Bofors rivals (especially for land-based applications) but still the Bofors Gun continues to thrive, greatly assisted by the family of advanced 40mm ammunition that has managed to keep pace with changing requirements to the point where some 40mm ammunition natures are still way ahead of their potential markets.

It must not be forgotten that some licence manufacturers are still busy marketing Bofors Gun products such as the OTO Melara Fast Forty, still not so far removed (other than in performance) from that Model 1932 prototype that did so much to alter the future of low level air defence, both on land and sea. The odds remain that 40mm Bofors Guns will still be around in 2032 and after, a service life that will remain unchallenged in terms of longevity and design origins by any other artillery piece.

Bibliography

Manuals and Official Publications

Beskrivning over 40mm Lufvärnsautomatkanon m/36. 1943

Handbook for the Ordnance, Q.F. 40-mm, Marks 1*, 1/2 and C Marks 1 and 1*. 1941

Maintenance Manual for the Ordnance, Q.F. 40mm, Marks 1, 1* and 2/1. 1946

40mm ivakan m/48. 1964

Gun Equipment, 40/70 A.A., L3. 1960

40/70 Ammunition. 1973

Artillery Equipments (Volume 1). Canadian Military Headquarters. London 1945

Artillery Training Volume IV Part I AA Gunnery Pamphlet No 1. Characteristics of Anti-Aircraft Artillery Equipment. 1951

Artillery Training Volume IV Part I AA Gunnery Pamphlet No 1 Part 1. Low Level Air Defence Equipment. 1970

TM 9-252. 40mm Automatic Gun M1 (AA) and 40 mm Antiaircraft Gun Carriage M2 and M2A1. 1944

TM 9-2300. Standard Artillery and Fire Control Materiel. 1944

TM 9-2300. Artillery Matériel and Associated Equipment. 1949

Bofors FAK 40/70B Bofors. 1981

SAK 40/70A. Bofors. 1983

SAK 40/70A3. Bofors. 1983

Published Works

AB Bofors. *Bofors*. Undated

AB Bofors. *A Century of Ordnance*. 1983

Albarda/Kroesen. *Nederlands Geschut sinds 1677*. Van Kolkema & Warendorf, Bussum, 1978

Ballard, Jack S. *Development and Employment of Fixed-Wing Gunships 1962-1972*. Washington DC, Office of US Air Force History, 1982

Barnes, Leslie. *Canada's Guns. An Illustrated History of Artillery*. Ottawa, National Museums of Canada, 1979

Campbell, John. *Naval Weapons of World War Two*. London, Conway Maritime Press, 1985

Chamberlain, Peter and Ellis, Chris. *British and American Tanks of World War II*. London, Arms & Armour Press, 1969

Chamberlain, Peter and Gander, Terry. *WW2 Fact Files. Anti-Aircraft Guns.* London, Macdonald and Janes, 1975

Chamberlain, Peter and Milsom, John. *WW2 Fact Files. Self-propelled Anti-Tank and Anti-Aircraft Guns.* London, Macdonald and Janes, 1975

Chinn, George M. *The Machine Gun,* Vol 3. Washington DC, Bureau of Ordnance, Department of the Navy, 1951

Collier, Basil. *The Defence of the United Kingdom.* London, HMSO, 1957

Crismon, Fred W. *US Military Tracked Vehicles.* Osceola, Motorbooks International, 1992

Dobinson, Colin, *AA Command.* London, Methuen, 2001

Farndale, Gen Sir Martin and Hughes, Major General B.P. *History of the Royal Regiment of Artillery.* Various volumes

Ferrard, Stéphane. *Les Materiels de l'Armee de Terre Française 1940, tome 1.* Paris, Charles-Lavauzelle, 1982

Ferrard, Stéphane. *France 1940, l'Armement Terrestre.* Boulogne, E.T.A.I., 1998

Försvarsstabens Krighistoriska Avdelning. *Boforskanonen I Andra Väraldskriget.* Stockholm, Fröléen & Comp AB, 1961

Foss, Christopher F. *Jane's Armour and Artillery.* London, Jane's Information Group, various editions

Foss, Christopher F., and Cullen, Tony. *Jane's Land-Based Air Defence.* London, Jane's Information Group, various editions

Francotte, A and Gaier, C. *FN 100 Years.* Brussels, Didier Hatier, 1989

Fransson, Stig A. *Bofors 350 år.* Stockholm, Probus, 1996

Frantzen, Ole L., Mortensen, Michael H., Probst, Niels M. and Thiede. Sven E. *Dansk Søartilleri 1400-2000.* Copenhagen, Tøjhusmuset, 1999

Friedman, Norman. *US Naval Weapons.* London, Conway Maritime Press, 1983

Gander, Terry J. *The 40mm Bofors Gun.* Wellingborough, Patrick Stephens, 1986 and 1990

Gander, Terry J. *Jane's Ammunition Handbook.* London, Jane's Information Group, various editions

Gander, Terry J. *Military Vehicles in Detail, US Half-Tracks.* Hersham, Ian Allan, 2004

Gower, S.N. *Guns of the Regiment.* Canberra Australian War Memorial, 1981

Green, Constance, Thomson, Harry and Roots, Peter. *The Ordnance Department: Planning Munitions for War.* Washington DC, Office of the Chief of Military History, 1953

Herlitz, Carl. *Svenska arméns, Luftvärn.* Stockholm, Armémuseum, 1985

Hodges, Peter and Friedman, Norman. *Destroyer Weapons of World War 2.* London, Conway Maritime Press, 1979

Hogg, Ian V. *British & American Artillery of World War 2.* London, Arms & Armour Press, 1978

Kiiskinin, Pekka and Wahlman, Pasi. *Itsenäisen Suomen Laivaston Laivtykit 1918-2004*. Helsinki, Typomic Oy, 2003

King, Doug. *Tools of the Trade – Equipping the Canadian Army*. Ottawa, Service Publications, 2005

Klinkert, W., Otten, R. and Plasmans, J. *75 jaar Luchtdoel-artillerie 1917-1992*. The Hague, Section Militaire Geschiedenis, 1992

Malmassari, Paul. *Les Trains Blindés 1826-1989*. Bayeux, Editions Heimdal. 1989

Postan, M. M., Hay, D. and Scott, J. D. *Design and Development of Weapons*. London, HMSO, 1964

Magnuski, Janusz. *Bron 1939-1972*. Warsaw, undated

Müller, Werner. *Die leichte und mittlere Flak 1906-1945*. Friedberg, Podzun-Pallas, 1990

Pile, Gen Sir Frederick. *Ack-Ack*. London, Harrap, 1949

Riccio, Ralph A. *The Irish Artillery Corps Since 1922*. Petersfield, MMP Books, 2012

Routledge, Brig N. W. *Anti-Aircraft Artillery 1914-55*. Royal Artillery Institution, 1994

Rowland, B., and Boyd, W. H. *US Navy Ordnance in World War II*. Bureau of Ordnance, undated

Rozwadowski, Piotr. *Polskie armaty przeciwlotniceze 75mm wz 36/37 oraz 40mm Bofors*. Warsaw, 1998

Thomson, H. C., and Mayo, L. *The Ordnance Department: Procurement and Supply*. Washington DC, Office of the Chief of Military History, 1960

Touzin, Pierre. *Les véhicules blindés français 1945-1977*. Nancy, Editions EPA, 1978

Urrisk, Rolf. *Die Bewaffnung des österreichischen Bundesheeres 1918-1990*. Graz, H Weishaupt Verlag, 1990

Vehviläinen, R., Lappi, A. and Palokangas, M. *Itsenäisen Suomen Ilmatorjuntatykit 1917-2000*. Helsinki, Sotamuseo, 2005

Zaloga, S. and Madej, V. *The Polish Campaign 1939*. New York, Hippocrene Books Inc, 1991

Index